DisplayWrite 3: *A Practical Approach*

Jane Troop
Instructor, Word Processing
Cypress College
Cypress, California

Donna Woo
Department Chairman, Word/Information Processing
Cypress College
Cypress, California

Published by

SOUTH-WESTERN PUBLISHING CO.

CINCINNATI   WEST CHICAGO, IL   DALLAS   PELHAM MANOR, NY   LIVERMORE, CA

Copyright © 1986

by SOUTH-WESTERN PUBLISHING CO.

Cincinnati, Ohio

ALL RIGHTS RESERVED

The text of this publication, or any part thereof, may not be reproduced or transmitted in any form or by any means, electronic or mechanical, including photocopying, recording, storage in an information retrieval system, or otherwise, without the prior written permission of the publisher.

ISBN: 0-538-23201-3 (W20)
       0-538-23202-1 (W20U)

Library of Congress Catalog Card Number: 85-62513

1 2 3 4 5 M 0 9 8 7 6

Printed in the United States of America

Many of the illustrations in this book were reprinted by permission from DisplayWrite 2 Procedures Guide, Copyright © 1984, and DisplayWrite 3 User's Guide, Volume 1 and Volume 2, Copyright © 1985 by International Business Machines Corporation. For a complete list of the pages on which these illustrations appear, see page 376.

Preface

The office is in a state of flux. The masses of documents that are generated daily are often produced through the use of dedicated word processors and microcomputers.

Because of the integration of technology, the microcomputer is becoming more and more popular. Its power and versatility enable it to run database, communication, spreadsheet, word processing, and other useful programs. It is replacing the dedicated word processor. Additionally, the demand for schools to offer more varied courses around the use of a microcomputer makes purchasing dedicated word processors an expensive extra.

Is it possible to enjoy the advantages of the microcomputer and, at the same time, use an easy-to-learn word processing program that is similar to an IBM* dedicated unit already in use? Yes!

The IBM DisplayWrite 3 word processing program is similar to Textpack 6 for the Displaywriter. The program easily can be learned by those who have little or no experience in computers. Instructors who have taught the Displaywriter can teach DisplayWrite 3 with very little retraining. In view of the rapidly moving software market, this in itself is a real boon.

We have endeavored to present the applications which will enable students to handle the most common business word processing applications first and then move on to the more complicated. Using this line of reasoning, students who attend schools offering intensive training of a short duration can master those skills necessary to produce mailable documents using DisplayWrite 3. Students who enroll in schools offering traditional semester-length courses will learn the more sophisticated applications that may be used on specialized jobs. All students will benefit from the easy transferability of skills to the Displaywriter.

To facilitate learning, <u>DisplayWrite 3: A Practical Approach</u> is organized so that each concept is discussed briefly, and the student works through an example. Application problems are given regularly throughout the text to give practice on each of the major areas introduced. We believe this reinforcement will provide sufficient practice for students to become competent in the use of DisplayWrite 3.

ACKNOWLEDGMENTS

We would like to thank Marilyn Harris of El Camino College and Dr. Nancy Billett of California State University in Los Angeles who reviewed the manuscript for this book.

---

*IBM is a registered trademark of International Business Machines Corporation. Any reference to the IBM Personal Computer refers to this footnote.

We wish to thank the following people at Cypress College: Olga Fusco, Donna Riedel, Lynn Mattingly, Ron Von Soosten, Dick McKnight, Dale Craig, Alan Ransom, Jean Gonzalez, the staff of the Information Processing Center, and the students who used early drafts of this book and for whom it was written. Special thanks go to these friends at Grosse Pointe North High School in Michigan for testing this book: Jack Harrigan, Paul Pierron, Marie Parzych, Carol Reitmyer, Shirley Reile, Jane Leonard, Sharon Schmidt, Brian Killian, Tom Boos, and Gail Migliazzo.

A special thanks goes to Bill Nelson, who was instrumental in the development of this book. We would also like to thank the following individuals: Frank Goodyear of Coastline Community College District; Edgar Troop, for his unfailing support; Selma Barajas and Helen Metzler of IBM; Tina Be of Gateway Computers in Cerritos, California; and Bruce Aronson of Computerland in Newport Beach, California.

We appreciate the cooperation of the people at IBM. We would like to thank IBM for permission to use its drawings from DisplayWrite 3.

                                                            Jane Troop
                                                            Donna Woo

Table of Contents

CHAPTER 1   GETTING STARTED   1

　　　　　　Starting Up the System - Formatting a Disk -
　　　　　　Loading DisplayWrite 3 - Interacting with
　　　　　　DisplayWrite 3 - Naming and Creating a Document -
　　　　　　Procedures for Completing the Exercises in This
　　　　　　Book - DisplayWrite 3 Basics

CHAPTER 2   EDITING 18

　　　　　　Making Revisions - Displaying Codes - Underscoring -
　　　　　　Deleting Text - Using Undo Delete - Adding Text

CHAPTER 3   MAJOR REVISIONS 35

　　　　　　Steps in Moving a Block of Text - Steps for Copying
　　　　　　a Block of Text - Steps for Overstriking a Block of
　　　　　　Text - Using Search/Replace

CHAPTER 4   DOCUMENT FORMAT 54

　　　　　　Document Format - Steps in Changing the Line Format
　　　　　　of a Document - Steps in Changing the Page Format of
　　　　　　a Document - Steps in Changing the Margins and Tabs
　　　　　　Format of a Document

CHAPTER 5   PRINTING 66

　　　　　　Introduction - Managing the Foreground Print Queue -
　　　　　　Steps for DisplayWrite 3 Background Printing -
　　　　　　Managing the Background Print Queue

CHAPTER 6   PAGINATION 76

　　　　　　Introduction - Manual Pagination - Automatic
　　　　　　Pagination - Dictionary Hyphenation - Required Page
　　　　　　End

CHAPTER 7   UTILITIES 100

　　　　　　Introduction - DOS Global Characters - Checking the
　　　　　　Directory - Selecting a Document from the Directory -
　　　　　　Typing with Auto Carrier Return Off - Personalizing
　　　　　　Text and Work Station Defaults by Creating, Revising,
　　　　　　and Activating Profiles - DOS Command Task

| CHAPTER | 8 | FORMATTING . . . . | 116 |

Introduction - Changing Line Format - Changing Page Format - Changing Typestyles - Using Alternate Format - Reformatting a Document

| CHAPTER | 9 | MODIFYING TEXT APPEARANCE . . . . | 138 |

Justifying Text - Adjusting Line Endings - Steps for Inserting Keep Codes - Steps for Inserting a Required Space - Making Text Bold - Indenting Paragraphs

| CHAPTER | 10 | CREATING HEADERS AND FOOTERS . . . . | 156 |

Superscripts and Subscripts - Creating Headers and Footers - Creating Alternating Headers and Footers

| CHAPTER | 11 | CREATING ENVELOPES . . . . | 174 |

Steps for Creating Envelopes - Blocks of Text

| CHAPTER | 12 | SPELLING . . . . | 184 |

Introduction to Spell Checking - Kinds of Spelling Checks - Spell Word and Spell Page - Spell Checking in Prompted Mode and Converting Words in the System Supplement to a Supplement Dictionary Program - Automatic Spell Checking - Begin and End Spelling Check Codes - Working with the Supplement Dictionary Program - Revising a Supplement Dictionary Program

| CHAPTER | 13 | COLUMNS OF TEXT . . . . | 199 |

Setting Up and Typing Text Columns - Creating a Set-Up Document - Aligning Paragraphs - Revising Columns of Text - Changing Text Column Format - Line Adjust - Quick Reference for Creating Columns of Text

| CHAPTER | 14 | NUMERIC TABLES . . . . | 215 |

Numeric Tables - Creating Numeric Tables - Isolating Columns and Adding Numbers in Numeric Columns - Deleting a Number from a Column - Adding an Entire Column to a Numeric Table - Deleting an Entire Column from a Numeric Table - Moving a Column in a Numeric Table - Copying Columns in a Numeric Table - Revising Column Format in Numeric Tables

CHAPTER 15	REFERENCE AREAS 236

Introduction - Setting Up a Table Containing Columns Using Reference Areas - Creating a Table Using a Reference Area - Setting Up a Top Reference Area - Revising with the Reference Areas - Screen Movement Keys - Placing Characters at the Right or Left Edge of the Screen - Moving an Entire Screen Width to the Right or Left - Moving the Length of the Screen

CHAPTER 16	MATH 253

Introduction - Adding Columns and Rows - Steps for Using Math Functions - Steps for Calculating Averages - Constants

CHAPTER 17	FOOTNOTES 265

Introduction - Creating and Revising a Footnoted Document - Modifying the Appearance of Footnotes - Storing Footnotes for Repeated Use

CHAPTER 18	AUTOMATIC OUTLINING AND CURSOR DRAW 283

Introduction to Outlining - Revising an Outline - Resetting Outline Characters - Introduction to Cursor Draw

CHAPTER 19	KEYSTROKE 295

Keystroke Programming - Using Pause - Defining Programmable Function Keys - Saving and Recalling Keystroke Programs

CHAPTER 20	USING GET FOR REPETITIVE DOCUMENTS 308

Introduction - Paragraph Libraries - Using the Paragraph Library to Construct a Document - Stop Codes - Producing a Personalized Document

CHAPTER 21	MERGING WITH NAMED VARIABLES 320

Merging Text with Named Variables - Merging Documents

CHAPTER 22	DOCUMENT ASSEMBLY 329

Document Assembly - Creating and Storing a Paragraph Library Document - Creating the Document Assembly Paragraph Library - Revising Variable Names - Printing a Reference Copy of Your Paragraph Library - Creating the Document Assembly Fill-In - Creating the Document Shell - Merging in Document Assembly

CHAPTER 23   MERGING WITH FILES 344

           Introduction to Merging with Files - Creating a
           Shell Document - Math Format for Numeric Variables -
           Conditional Text - Math Instructions - Skip-to-Line
           Intructions - File Descriptions - Revising File
           Descriptions

APPENDIX 365

INDEX 367

ILLUSTRATION REFERENCES (IBM) 376

Chapter 1
GETTING STARTED

When you complete this chapter, you will be able to:

1. Start up an IBM Personal Computer system.
2. Load in the disk operating system (DOS).
3. Format disks to be used on the IBM Personal Computer.
4. Load the DisplayWrite 3 software.
5. Create a simple document.
6. Type using the auto carrier return feature.
7. Use the tab key for paragraph indentions.
8. Use the center key for centering titles.
9. End a task.
10. Send a document to print.

STARTING UP THE SYSTEM

In order to run a software program such as DisplayWrite 3, you need to load the operating system into the computer first. The operating system you will be using is called DOS or disk operating system. The operating system consists of programs that control the various functions of the computer such as inputting, printing, and storage. Follow the steps given to start up the system.

1. Turn on your monitor.

2. Insert the DOS disk in drive A (left). The label on the disk should be facing up when you are inserting the disk (see Figure 1.1).

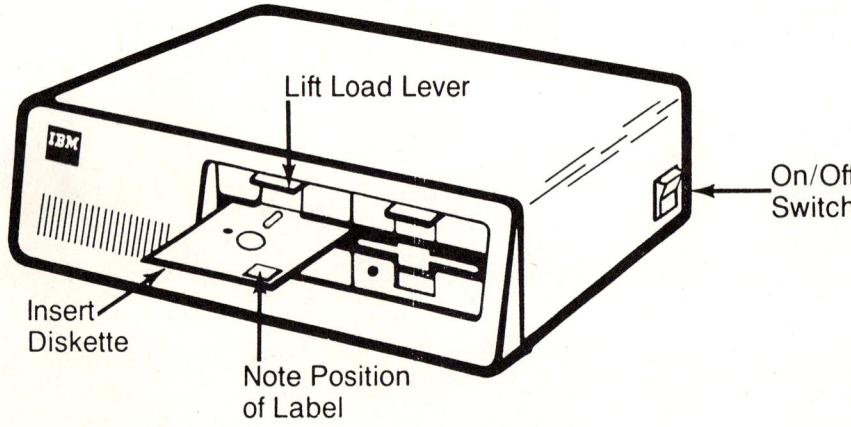

Figure 1.1   Inserting the Disk

3. Push the load lever down.

4. Turn on the IBM Personal Computer by lifting up on the orange on/off switch.

5. The red In-Use Light will come on. The red light and the clicking noise indicate that the disk drive is reading the information from the DOS disk.

    Note: Whenever either of the red In-Use Lights is on, do not press any keys or open the load lever (see Figure 1.2).

6. A prompt will come on the screen asking you to enter the date.

    You can either press the Enter key or type the date and press Enter.

    To type the date, you must use the number keys across the top of the keyboard. Do not use alphabetic letters. Separate the month, day, and year with either /´s or -´s.
    Example: 9-12-86 or 9/12/86

7. A prompt will come on the screen asking you to enter the time.

    You can either press the Enter key or type in the time and press Enter.

To type the time, use the number keys across the top of the keyboard. The format used for entering the time is as follows: hours:minutes: seconds.hundredths of seconds. Notice that a colon must be typed between the hours and minutes and between minutes and seconds. A period is placed between seconds and hundredths of seconds. Example: 1:43:10.20

8. The DOS prompt A> will appear on the screen.

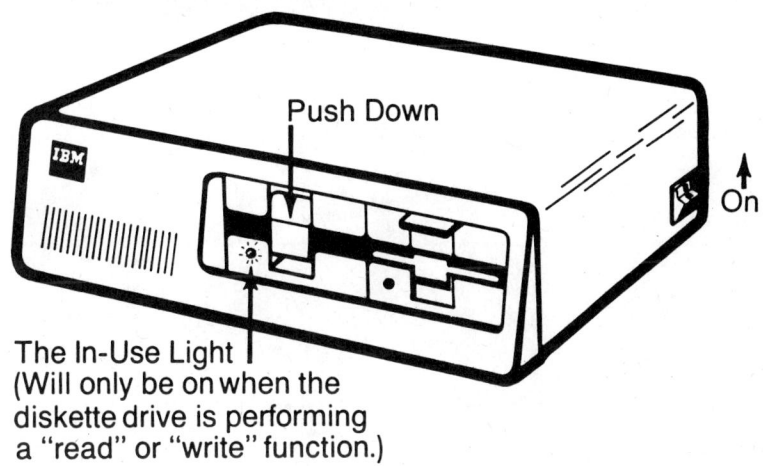

Figure 1.2   In-Use Light

FORMATTING A DISK

You will be creating many documents and storing them on disks. Before the disks can be used for storage, first they must be formatted using the DOS format command. The DOS format command erases anything that is on the disk and checks to see if there are any defective tracks on your disk.

To format a disk you will need the DOS disk and a blank 5 1/4-inch, double-sided, double-density disk. Figures 1.3 - 1.9 illustrate the steps in formatting a disk.

1. Insert the DOS disk in drive A. If you just completed STARTING UP THE SYSTEM, your DOS disk is already in drive A.

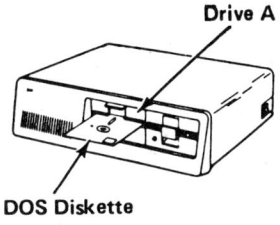

Figure 1.3   DOS Diskette

2. The screen displays the DOS prompt A>.

Chapter 1   Getting Started

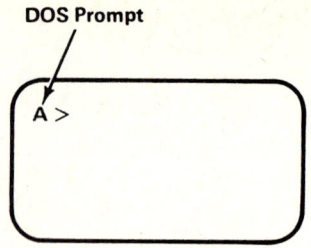

Figure 1.4   DOS Prompt

3. At the DOS prompt, type: format b:

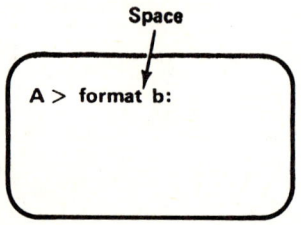

Figure 1.5   Format Command

4. Press Enter.

Figure 1.6   Enter Key

5. A prompt appears on the screen asking you to insert a disk in drive B.

Figure 1.7   Prompt to Insert Diskette

6. Insert your blank disk in drive B and press any key.

7. If the system indicates that you have a defective track on your disk, you will need to format another disk.

8. A prompt "Format another (Y/N)?" appears on the screen. If you do not have a defective disk, type N and press Enter.

9. The DOS prompt A> should appear on the screen.

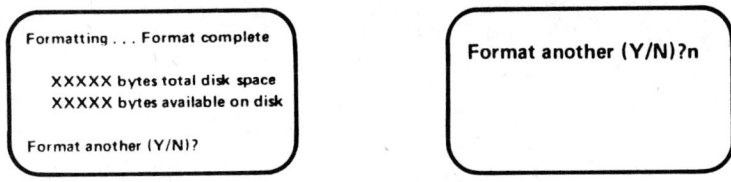

Figure 1.8   Format Prompt

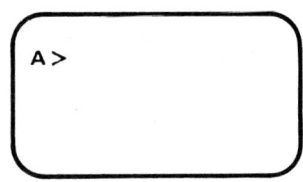

Figure 1.9   DOS Prompt

10. Give this formatted disk to your instructor to copy some prerecorded documents onto your disk.

LOADING DISPLAYWRITE 3

If the system was turned off, you will need to turn on the system after placing the DisplayWrite 3, Vol. 1 disk in drive A. A prompt will appear on the screen asking for the date. Press Enter. A prompt will ask for the time. Press Enter again. Follow the steps and Figures 1.10 - 1.12 to load DisplayWrite 3.

1. The prompt A> displays on the screen.

2. At the A> prompt, type: dw3. If you make a mistake while typing, use the backspace key to erase the error.

3. Press Enter.

4. A prompt will appear on the screen asking for the name of the list device [PRN]. Press Enter. (This assumes that you will use the printer attached to the LPT1 port. See your instructor if you are using a printer attached to another port.)

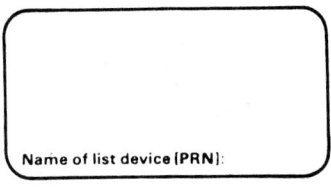

Figure 1.10   List Device Prompt

5. The IBM logo appears on the screen. Press any key to continue.

Chapter 1   Getting Started

Figure 1.11   IBM Logo

6. The Text Task Seletion Menu appears on the screen.

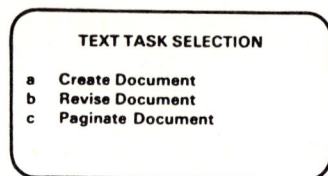

Figure 1.12   Text Task Selection Menu

7. Remove the DisplayWrite 3, Volume 1 disk from drive A.

8. Insert the DisplayWrite 3, Volume 2 disk in drive A.

INTERACTING WITH DISPLAYWRITE 3

The DisplayWrite 3 software will interact with you as you perform various functions. The following is a brief explanation of the items and procedures that make interaction possible.

MENUS

A menu is a display on your screen which presents you with the selection of tasks that can be performed.

Every menu has at least two parts: ID letters and ITEM description. ID letters (a, b, c, and so on) are used to identify the choices. ITEM descriptions describe each item in detail (see Figure 1.13).

PROMPTS

Prompts are statements from the system that are displayed at the bottom of your screen. The prompts are directions from the system telling you the specific action you need to take in order for the task to continue.

MESSAGES

Messages are statements telling you what is happening in the system. They are displayed at the bottom of the screen (see Figure 1.14). You may hear a beep when the system has a message for you. If the message indicator changes from a blinking > to a highlighted message symbol (■), that means that the system has additional messages for you. Press the Msg key to view the next message.

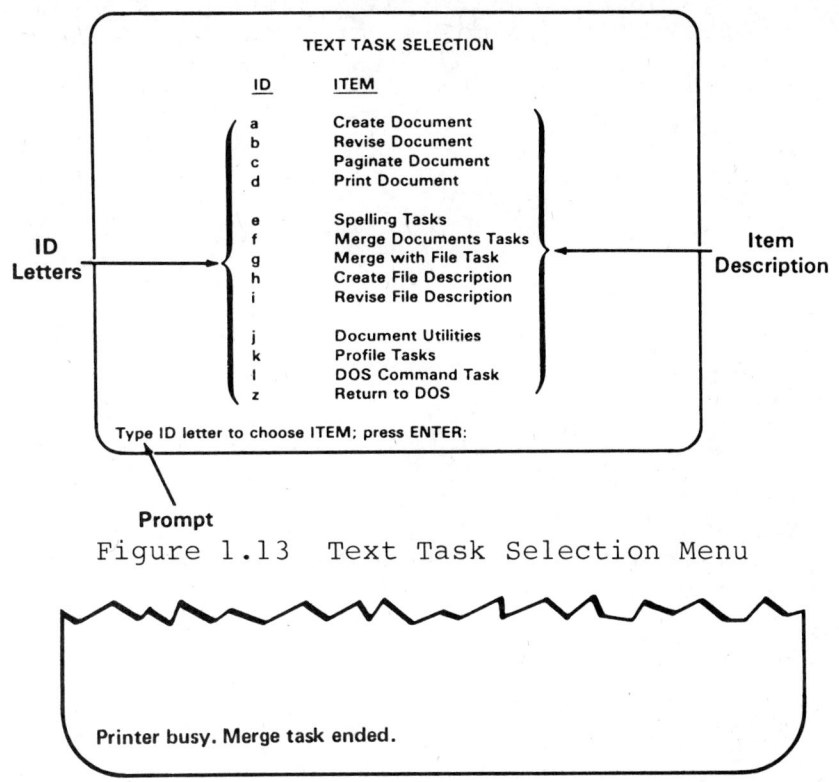

Figure 1.13   Text Task Selection Menu

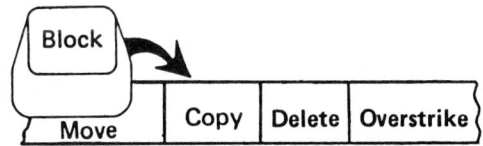

Figure 1.14   Message

PROMPT LINE CHOICES

There are ten function keys located to the left of your keyboard. These function keys are labeled F1 through F10. Function keys do not actually type text on the screen; rather, they help you perform various functions. When you press certain function keys, prompt line choices will appear at the bottom of your screen (see Figure 1.15). Prompt line choices are similar to menus. You choose the appropriate item for the task you wish to perform. To make your choice, you can type the first letter of the item you want or tab to the desired choice and press Enter.

Figure 1.15   Function Key and Prompt Line Choices

KEYBOARD TEMPLATE

As shown in Figure 1.16, a keyboard template is a chart that shows you where the function keys are located. You will notice that the function keys F1-F10 have been relabeled to reflect the function that is performed by each key. To use the function shown on the top half of the key, just press the key. To use the function shown on the bottom

Chapter 1   Getting Started

half of the key, press the Ctrl key and the function key at the same time. If you have selected a function or task in error, press the Esc key to cancel the selection.

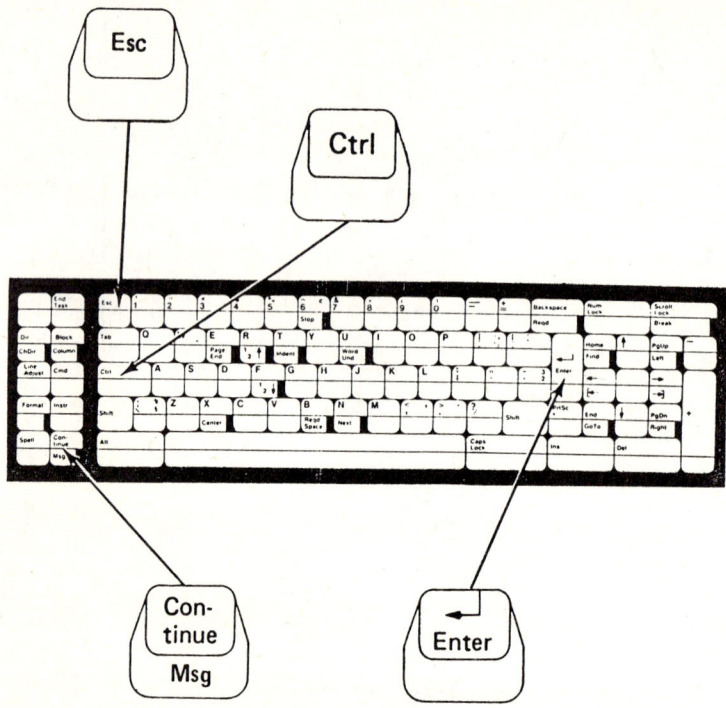

Figure 1.16   Keyboard Template

DEFAULTS

Defaults are preset selections of commonly used choices in menus. The system assumes these choices unless you choose others. Defaults apply to many functional areas of DisplayWrite 3, ranging from the way documents are formatted to the drive which contains your disk.

THE HELP KEY

The DisplayWrite 3 software contains Help panels that provide you with information about the menus, prompt line choices, keys, and functions. The Help panels reside on your Volume 4 disk. If you press the Help key (F1) while a disk other than your Volume 4 disk is loaded into the system, you have instant access to two of the Help topics: "Keys" and "How to use Help."

To Use Help:

1.   Insert the DisplayWrite 3, Volume 4 disk into drive A.

2.   Press Help (F1) (see Figure 1.17).

The Help panel that displays depends on where you are in the system:

Menus   If a menu is displayed on the screen, help
                         for the topic related to that menu is
                         provided.

Prompt line choices	If prompt line choices are displayed on the screen, help for those prompt line choices is provided.
Typing frame	If you are in a typing area, help for keys is provided. This describes the functions of the keys used with DisplayWrite 3.
Other	The Help key will take you directly to the first page of the two-page index. Then you may select which Help panel you would like to view.

3. Use the prompt line choices or the Cursor Movement keys to view the desired Help panel.

4. Select End_help to return to the previous DisplayWrite 3 task.

Figure 1.17   Help Key

NAMING AND CREATING A DOCUMENT

The first step in creating a document is to assign a document name. When naming a document, you should choose a meaningful name that describes the contents of the document.

Also you may add a short suffix, called an extension, to the document name. An extension is used to describe the document further. It consists of a period followed by a maximum of three characters typed at the end of the document name.

If you do not add an extension, the system will add one for you, such as .TXT. If you do not want an extension added, type a period at the end of the document name.

You may want to develop your own procedures for adding meaningful extensions. For example, if your typing involves two departments, Accounting and Marketing, you may use extensions .ACT and .MKT to identify the two departments. If you wish to add an extension of your own, do not use .TMP or .RES. These are extensions that are reserved for system use.

DOCUMENT NAMES:

--May contain one to eight characters.
--May contain numerals or characters.
--May not contain spaces.
--Should be descriptive.

--May contain upper- or lowercase characters. If you type lowercase
  letters, the system will convert them to uppercase.
--May include special characters ($ & # @ ! % ( ) - { } ^ ~).

DOCUMENT EXTENSIONS:

--May contain one to three characters, not including the period.
--If no extension is desired, type a period following the document
  name.
--If you do not type an extension or a period, the system uses the
  default extension, .TXT.

DOCUMENT COMMENTS:

--May contain up to 44 characters.
--Are optional.

STEPS FOR CREATING A DOCUMENT:

This is information for you to read. Do not perform these steps at
this time.

1. The DisplayWrite 3, Volume 2 disk should be in drive A. A formatted disk should be in drive B.

2. From the Text Task Selection Menu, select Create Document. The prompt "Type document name; press ENTER" displays at the bottom of the screen.

3. Type the name of the document and an extension, if desired. If you make an error while typing the document name, just press the backspace key to erase the error.

4. Press Enter. The Create or Revise Document Menu is displayed on the screen.

5. If you wish to add a comment, select Document Comment and press Enter. Continue with Step 6. If you do not wish to add a comment, continue with Step 7.

6. Type a comment that contains up to 44 characters and press Enter.

7. Press Enter to reach the typing area.

Note: If you make a wrong selection from a menu, press Esc to cancel
the selection.

PROCEDURE FOR COMPLETING THE EXERCISES IN THIS BOOK

In this book there are several exercises which you, the student, will
be doing for practice. These exercises will be enclosed in boxes.
Material that is not enclosed in boxes is for you to read only.

As you can see in the following box, the page is divided into two
columns. The left column gives the procedures you will need to follow

to complete the assignment. The right column contains explanatory material that will make understanding the procedures easier.

The following is a sample of how your exercises will be presented. You are not to perform the steps inside this box.

PROCEDURES	COMMENTS
1. Press Ctrl--U.	The word just before the underscore command will be automatically underscored.
2. Press End.	The cursor will go directly to the end of the page.

EXERCISE 1

In Exercise 1, you will be taken step-by-step through all of the procedures from creating a simple document to the printing of a document.

Whenever the computer has been turned off, you must always follow the start-up procedure: Load DisplayWrite 3 Volume 1, and then insert Volume 2 in drive A. The prerecorded document disk should be in drive B.

PROCEDURES	COMMENTS
1. The Volume 2 disk should be in drive A, and the prerecorded document disk should be in drive B.	
2. The Text Task Selection Menu should be displayed on the screen.	
3. Type a.	This is to select Create Document.
4. Press Enter.	A prompt appears asking you for the document name.
5. Type b:Exercis1.	The "b" tells which drive you are using. Remember, the name of the document is limited to eight characters. That is why the final "e" was left off in the word Exercise.
	Continued

Chapter 1 Getting Started

PROCEDURES (Continued)	COMMENTS (Continued)
6. Press Enter.	The Create or Revise Document Menu displays.
7. Type a.	This is to add a document comment.
8. Press Enter.	A prompt asks you for the comment.
9. Type Create Document.	This is the document comment.
10. Press Enter.	The comment appears in the menu.
11. Press Enter.	The typing area displays.

Leave the typing area displayed on the screen and continue reading the rest of the chapter.

DISPLAYWRITE 3 BASICS

The remainder of this chapter will explain the typing area, the cursor, the auto carrier return, and the center key. You will type, end, and print Exercise 1.

THE TYPING AREA

When you reach the typing area, you will see a blank screen with some information across the top. The first two lines are called the status lines. The status lines provide you with valuable information about the task you are performing. The third line is called the scale line. The scale line shows you the margin settings, tab settings, center point, and cursor position. Figure 1.18 identifies the parts and symbols on the status lines and the scale line.

THE CURSOR

The cursor is the blinking light that you see on the screen. It is similar to the printing point indicator on a typewriter. It marks your current horizontal position in the typing area. As you type, the cursor moves to the right to show you where you are typing.

AUTO CARRIER RETURN

With the DisplayWrite 3 software, you do not need to insert a carrier return at the end of each line. You will just continue to type the information, and as the cursor reaches the right margin, the system will automatically return the carrier for you.

The only time that you will be inserting carrier returns will be at the ends of short lines that do not pass the right margin.

Examples include the following:

--The inside address of a letter.
--The last line of a paragraph.
--The need for multiple carrier returns.

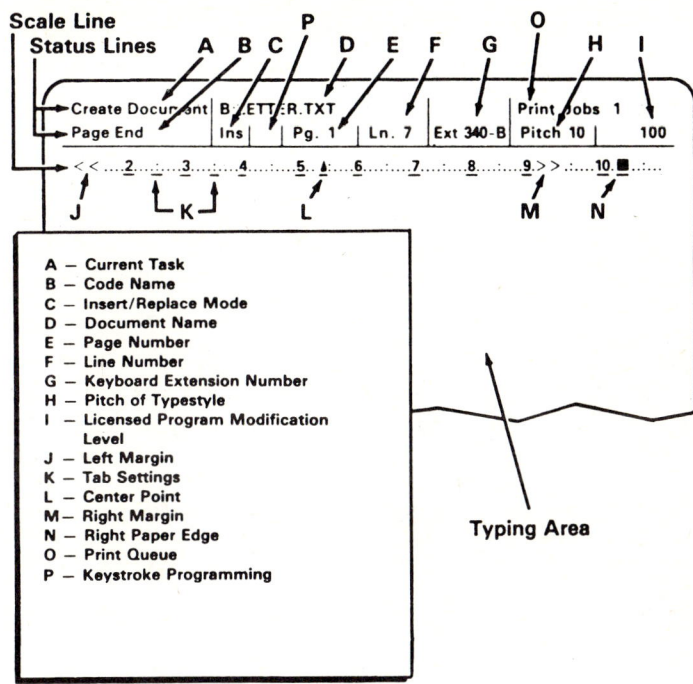

Figure 1.18   Status and Scale Lines

EXERCISE 1 (Continued)

Type the following paragraph. Remember, you do not need to press carrier return; the system will automatically do this for you. If you make a mistake, use the backspace key to remove the incorrect character(s). Then type the correct character(s). If you discover an error in a previous line, do not attempt to correct it; you will learn how to do this in a later lesson.

---

12. Type:

    Auto Carrier Return is a feature of the system that is designed to help you type faster and easier. If the cursor passes the right margin as you type, it automatically returns to the beginning of the next line.

13. Press the carrier return twice.

Leave this exercise on the screen and continue reading; you will be adding on to this exercise.

Chapter 1 Getting Started   13

USING THE TAB KEY

Press the tab key (see Figure 1.19) to reach the tab position you want. Tabs are preset every five spaces on the scale line.

Figure 1.19 Tab Key

You will type the same paragraph again. This time, however, you will insert a tab at the beginning of the first line.

---

14. Type:

   Auto Carrier Return is a feature of the system that is designed to help you type faster and easier. If the cursor passes the right margin as you type, it automatically returns to the beginning of the next line.

15. Press the carrier return four times.

Leave this exercise on the screen and continue reading.

USING THE CENTER KEY

1. In the typing area, space to the center of the page. The center of the page is indicated on your scale line with a pyramid-shaped symbol ⌂. The highlighting on the scale line indicates your cursor position. Press the space bar until the pyramid symbol is highlighted on your scale line.

2. Press Ctrl--Center. (Hold the Ctrl key down, and at the same time press Center, as shown in Figure 1.20.) A center code is inserted. A center code can be inserted at any position on a line by spacing to the position and pressing Ctrl--Center.

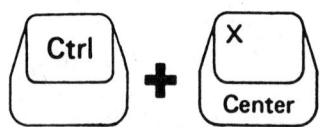

Figure 1.20 Ctrl--Center

3. Type the words you want to have centered. As you type, the words automatically align around the center code.

ENDING A DOCUMENT

Press End Task (F2) when you have completed your task. This saves the text and ends the task.

Chapter 1 Getting Started

PRINTING A DOCUMENT

1. In the Text Task Selection Menu, select Print Document and press Enter.

2. A prompt will appear asking for the document name. The system assumes that the document you want to print is the document you just typed. Therefore, the name of the document you just typed appears on the prompt line automatically.

3. Press Enter.

4. The Print Document Menu displays. Press Enter.

5. The document has been sent to the printer. See your instructor if you do not know how to operate your printer.

EXERCISE 1 (Continued)

PROCEDURES	COMMENTS
16. Press the space bar until the cursor is at the center of the page.	The center of the page is marked with the ⌂ symbol.
17. Press Ctrl--Center.	This will enter a center code.
18. Type AUTO CARRIER RETURN.	This should appear centered as you type it.
19. Press the carrier return three times. Then type the following paragraphs: Auto Carrier Return is a feature of the system that is designed to help you type faster and easier. If the cursor passes the right margin as you type, it automatically returns to the beginning of the next line.	
20. Press F2.	This will end the task. The Text Task Selection Menu is on the screen.
21. Type d and Enter.	This will select Print Document.
22. Press Enter.	The Print Document Menu displays.
23. Press Enter.	The document is sent to the printer.

Continued

Chapter 1 Getting Started

PROCEDURES (Continued)	COMMENTS (Continued)
24. Pick up the document at the printer. It should look like Figure 1.21.	The Text Task Selection Menu is displayed on the screen.

Auto Carrier Return is a feature of the system that is designed to help you type faster and easier. If the cursor passes the right margin as you type, it automatically returns to the beginning of the next line.

    Auto Carrier Return is a feature of the system that is designed to help you type faster and easier. If the cursor passes the right margin as you type, it automatically returns to the beginning of the next line.

AUTO CARRIER RETURN

    Auto Carrier Return is a feature of the system that is designed to help you type faster and easier.

    If the cursor passes the right margin as you type, it automatically returns to the beginning of the next line.

Figure 1.21 Exercise 1 Printout

CHAPTER SUMMARY

A. Starting Up the Computer System

1. Turn on the CRT monitor.
2. Insert the DOS disk in drive A.
3. Close the latch to the disk drive.
4. Turn on the computer (lift up the on/off switch).
5. When the prompt appears on the screen asking for the date, respond by pressing Enter or typing in the date.
6. When the prompt appears on the screen asking for the time, respond by pressing Enter or typing in the time.
7. The DOS prompt A> appears on the screen.

B. Formatting a New Disk

1. At the DOS prompt A>, type **format b:**
2. Press Enter.
3. Follow the prompt to insert a disk in drive B.
4. Strike any key.
5. When the prompt "Format another (Y/N)?" appears on the screen, type **Y** if you want another disk formatted. Type **N** if you do not want any other disk formatted.

C. Loading DisplayWrite 3

   1. The DOS prompt A> should be on the screen.
   2. Remove the DOS disk and insert the DisplayWrite 3, Volume 1 disk.
   3. At the A> prompt, type **dw3**.
   4. A prompt will appear on the screen asking for the name of the list device [PRN]. Press Enter.
   5. When the IBM logo appears on the screen, press any key. The Text Task Selection Menu will display.

D. Creating a Document

   1. In the Text Task Selection Menu, choose Create Document by typing **a** and pressing Enter.
   2. Name the document by typing **b:** followed by a maximum of eight characters.
   3. If you wish to add a document comment:
      a. Type a.
      b. Press Enter.
      c. Type the comment.
      d. Press Enter.
   4. Press Enter to reach the typing area.

E. Using the Auto Carrier Return

   The system will automatically return the carrier for you at the end of each line. You do not need to type carrier returns except at the ends of short lines or when you need multiple carrier returns.

F. Using the Tab Key

   Tabs are preset every five spaces on the scale line. To use any of the existing tabs, press the tab until you reach the desired point.

G. Using the Center Key

   1. Move to the point where you want the material centered.
   2. Press Ctrl--Center (Ctrl--X).
   3. Type the material to be centered.

H. Ending a Document

   Press End Task (F2). This stores the document on your disk and displays the Text Task Selection Menu so you can continue with your next task.

I. Printing a Document

   1. Choose Print Document in the Text Task Selection Menu.
   2. Type the document name if it is not already displayed on the prompt line.
   3. Press Enter.
   4. Press Enter again.

Chapter 2
EDITING

When you complete this chapter, you will be able to:

1. Recall a document to the screen to be revised.

2. Use the cursor movement keys, Home key, End key, Page Up key, and Page Down key to move the cursor to different locations in a document.

3. Use the Find key to search for a specific sequence of characters.

4. Use the Go To key to go directly to a specific page in the document.

5. Turn on and off Display codes in a document.

6. Use the Underscore key to underscore individual words as well as a series of words.

7. Use the Delete function to delete characters, codes, and blocks of text.

8. Use the Undo_delete feature to recover a deleted block of text.

9. Use the Insert mode for adding text.

10. Use the Replace mode for replacing unwanted text with new text.

MAKING REVISIONS

In Chapter 1, you learned how to create and store a document. In this chapter, you will learn to recall a stored document to the screen and learn how to make some revisions in the document.

RECALLING A DOCUMENT TO THE SCREEN

The first step in revising a document is to recall the document to the screen. This is done by selecting Revise Document from the Text Task Selection Menu. The system will prompt you for the document name. You will need to type the document name and the extension. If you used the default extension .TXT, you do not need to type the extension. If you have forgotten the name of the document, use the DIR key to view a list of the documents on your disk. See Chapter 7 for information on "Directories."

GETTING TO THE REVISION POINT

You can use one, all, or a combination of the following keys to get to the revision point in the typing area. These keys will move your cursor around on the screen without altering the text.

Cursor movement keys are located at the right side of your keyboard. They are marked with up, down, left, and right arrows. The cursor movement keys will move your cursor around on your page in the direction that the arrow is pointing.

Screen movement keys move the screen window up, down, left, or right.

Home key takes you directly to the first position on the page.

End key takes you directly to the last position on the page.

Go To key takes you to a specific page in the document.

Find key searches forward from your cursor to a specific sequence of characters.

EXERCISE 2

In Exercise 2 you will be recalling a prerecorded document, b:Stress, to the screen. If the prompt "B:STRESS.TXT not found" appears on the screen when you attempt to revise the document, see your instructor.

PROCEDURES	COMMENTS
1. The Text Task Selection Menu should be displayed on the screen. The pre-recorded document disk should be in drive B.	
	Continued

PROCEDURES (Continued)	COMMENTS (Continued)
2. Type b.	This will select Revise Document.
3. Press Enter.	If you are just completing Exercise 1, you must depress Esc to cancel the file name b:Exercis1.
4. Type b:Stress.	The "b" is the name of the drive. Stress is the name of the document.
5. Press Enter.	The Create or Revise Document Menu displays.
6. Press Enter.	The first page of the document displays.
7. Press the down arrow key several times.	The cursor will move down the page.
8. Press the right arrow key several times.	The cursor will move to the right.
9. Press the left arrow key several times.	The cursor will move to the left.
10. Press the Ctrl and right arrow keys at the same time.	The cursor moves directly to the end of the line.
11. Press the Ctrl and left arrow keys at the same time.	The cursor moves directly to the beginning of the line.
12. Press the up arrow key several times.	The cursor will move up the page.
13. Press the Home key.	The cursor moves directly to the beginning of the page.
14. Press the End key.	The cursor moves directly to the end of the page.
15. Press the Page Down key (PgDn) twice.	Page 2 appears on the screen.
16. Press the Page Up key (PgUp).	The previous 25 lines appear on the screen.
17. Press Ctrl--Go To (Ctrl--End).	The prompt "Type page number; press ENTER" displays.

Continued

PROCEDURES (Continued)	COMMENTS (Continued)
18. Type 1 and press Enter.	Page 1 displays on the screen.
19. Press Ctrl--Find (Ctrl--Home).	The prompt "Find what?" appears on the screen. The Find function searches only in a forward direction; therefore, the cursor must be at the beginning of the document.
20. Type **stress** and press Enter.	The cursor moves to the first "stress" that it finds.
21. Press Ctrl--Find.	You do not need to type the word "stress" again. Pressing Enter tells the system to find the next occurrence of the same word.
22. Press Enter.	
23. End this task by pressing F2.	This stores the document and brings you back to the Text Task Selection Menu.

DISPLAYING CODES

There may be times when you will need to see all of the codes that have been entered in a document. By turning on the Display codes, all of the codes in your document will be displayed, along with the text, on the screen.

When Display codes is off, the code will be displayed only when the cursor is under it. The default for Display codes is off.

When Display codes is turned on, the Display codes may cause the text to be incorrectly positioned in relation to the scale line. The cursor position on the scale line will indicate the correct horizontal location. When working with Display codes on, be sure to watch the cursor on the scale line to determine the true position of the cursor in the text. Display codes stays on until you turn it off.

Steps 1-3 have information for you to read. Do not perform these steps.

1. The typing area of your document should be displayed on the screen. Press Cmd (F6). The prompt line choices appear at the bottom of the screen (see Figure 2.1).

2. Select Display codes by typing **d**, or move the cursor to Display codes and press Enter. All the codes in your text now appear on the screen.

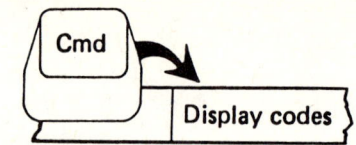

Figure 2.1 Display Codes

3. To turn off the codes, repeat Steps 1 and 2.

In Exercise 3 you will be displaying the codes in the document b:Exercis1.

EXERCISE 3

PROCEDURES	COMMENTS
1. Type b and press Enter.	This selects Revise Document from the Text Task Selection Menu. The prerecorded document disk must be in drive B. If you are just completing Exercise 2, Esc to cancel the file name b:Stress.
2. Type b:Exercis1.	This is the document name.
3. Press Enter.	The Create or Revise Document Menu displays.
4. Press Enter.	The document is displayed.
5. Press Cmd (F6).	The prompt line choices are displayed.
6. Type d.	This selects Display codes. All codes are displayed in the text.
7. Take a few minutes to look at the various symbols on the screen. If you are not sure what the symbol represents, move the cursor under the symbol. The description of the code will appear on the status line.	
8. Repeat Steps 5-6 to turn off Display codes.	The codes are turned off.

Continued

PROCEDURES (Continued)

9. Press End Task (F2).

COMMENTS (Continued)

This ends the task and brings the Text Task Selection Menu to the screen.

UNDERSCORING

The DisplayWrite 3 software allows you to use broken underscores and continuous underscores. Broken underscoring is used when you need to underscore one word at a time. In continuous underscoring, you are underscoring a block of several words or even several sentences. With continuous underscoring, the words, punctuation, and spaces between words are all underscored. Broken underscoring only underscores each word.

The underscoring does not show up on the screen, but the text will be underscored when it is printed. Underscore does, however, appear in a different color on the screen if you are using a color monitor. If you are using a monochrome monitor, the underscored words will appear highlighted. You can also check to see if an underscore code has been inserted by using the cursor movement keys to place the cursor underneath the underscore code.

UNDERSCORING ONE WORD AT A TIME

1. Type the word you want underscored. Do not type the punctuation or the space that follows the word.

2. Press Ctrl--Word Und to insert a word underscore code (see Figure 2.2).

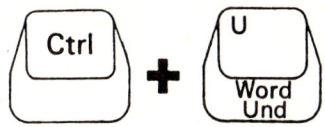

Figure 2.2 Word Underscore Code

3. Type the necessary punctuation and space and continue typing.

UNDERSCORING A SERIES OF WORDS

1. Place the cursor on the first character of the first word you want to underscore.

2. Press Instr (F8). A prompt line will appear at the bottom of your screen (see Figure 2.3).

3. Choose Begin by:
   --Typing b or
   --Move the cursor to Begin and press Enter or
   --Tab to the choice Begin and press Enter.

Chapter 2 Editing

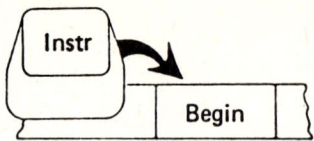

Figure 2.3 Underscoring a Series of Words

4. Choose Underscore by:
   --Typing u <u>or</u>
   --Move the cursor to Underscore and press Enter <u>or</u>
   --Tab to the choice Underscore and press Enter.

5. Type all of the words you want underscored. (If the text had been typed previously and you are now adding the underscore, move the cursor to where the underscore is to end.) Do not space after the last letter of the last word.

6. Press Instr (F8).

7. Choose End.

8. Choose Underscore. An end underscore code is inserted.

9. Type the necessary spaces and continue with your work.

EXERCISE 4

PROCEDURES	COMMENTS
1. From the Text Task Selection Menu, select Create Document.	
2. Type b:**Exercis4**.	This is the document name.
3. Press Enter.	
4. Type **a**.	This is to add a document comment.
5. Press Enter.	
6. Type **underscoring**.	
7. Press Enter.	
8. Press Enter again.	This will bring you to your typing page.

Type Exercise 4 as shown following these procedures. When you reach the symbol ⬡ , stop typing and refer to the corresponding procedures. For example, type until you see the symbol ⬡9 . Stop typing and read Procedure 9 for further directions.

Continued

24   Chapter 2 Editing

PROCEDURES (Continued)

COMMENTS (Continued)

9. Your cursor should be placed where the "O" in Optical will print.

    Press Instr (F8).   A prompt line appears.

    Type b.   This is to choose Begin.

    Type u.   This will select Underscore.

    Continue typing up to ⟨10⟩. Do not type the comma.   The begin underscore code has been inserted; the sentence is being underscored as you type.

10. Press Instr (F8).   A prompt line appears.

    Type e.   This is to choose End.

    Type u.   This is to choose Underscore; an end underscore code has been inserted.

    Continue typing up to ⟨11⟩.

11. Type: **automatically**.

    Press Ctrl--Word Und.   This inserts a word underscore code.

    Continue typing up to ⟨12⟩.

12. The cursor should be where the "O" in OCR will print.

    Press Instr (F8).   A prompt line displays.

    Select Begin.   See Procedure 9 if you have forgotten how to do this.

    Select Underscore.

    Continue typing up to ⟨13⟩. Do not type the period at the end of the sentence.

13. Press Instr (F8).   A prompt line displays.

    Select End.   See Procedure 10 if you have forgotten how to do this.

Continued

Chapter 2 Editing

PROCEDURES (Continued)	COMMENTS (Continued)
Select Underscore.	
Continue typing up to ⑭.	
14. Type: typewriter.	
Press Ctrl--Word Und. Finish typing the remainder of the exercise.	This inserts a word underscore code.
15. Press End Task (F2).	This will end the task.
16. Choose Print Document and Enter.	
17. Press Enter.	The Print Document Menu displays.
18. Press Enter.	The document has been sent to the printer.

EXERCISE 4

OPTICAL CHARACTER READER

With the use of an ⑨ Optical Character Reader (OCR) ⑩, information can be keyboarded on a standard typewriter and then "read" and auto-matically recorded onto a floppy disk or other magnetic media. The disk then can be inserted into a word processing system for text ⑪ editing.

⑫ OCR machines are fast and quite accurate. ⑬ The advantage of using OCR is that it allows the first draft of a document to be prepared on an ordinary typewriter. This means that the more expensive word processors are now ↑ free to do the work they do best--text editing.
⑭

DELETING TEXT

There are two methods of deleting text. One method is Character Delete and the other method is Block Delete. The Del key (Character Delete) is used to delete a character at a time. Block Delete is used to delete sentences, paragraphs, or other blocks of text. Figure 2.4 illustrates an example of using Character Delete and Block Delete.

Once the material has been deleted, the system will automatically rearrange the lines when you move the cursor to a different line.

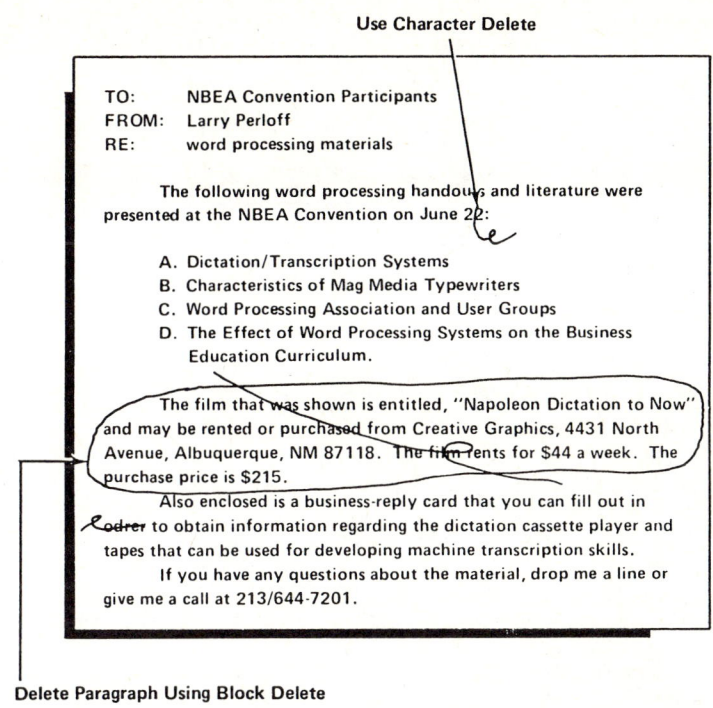

Figure 2.4   Character and Block Delete

TO USE CHARACTER DELETE

1. Use the cursor movement keys to place the cursor on the character you want to delete.

2. Press Del (see Figure 2.5). The character is deleted and the following characters move to the left. The Del key is a repetitive key. If you continue to hold the Del key down, it will continue to delete characters until you release the key.

Figure 2.5   Delete Key

TO DELETE CODES

1. Place the cursor on the code you want to delete.

2. Press Del.

3. Follow the prompt and press Enter.

TO USE BLOCK DELETE

1. Use the cursor movement keys to place the cursor on the first character or code to be deleted.

Chapter 2   Editing

2. Press Block (F4).

3. The prompt line choices appear at the bottom of your screen (see Figure 2.6).

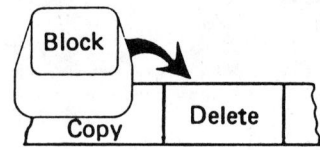

Figure 2.6 Block Delete

4. Select delete by typing d or by moving the cursor to the choice delete and press Enter.

5. The prompt "Move cursor to end of block; press ENTER" appears.

6. Move the cursor to the last character or code to be deleted. The block of text is highlighted. If the highlighted text is not what you want to delete, press Esc to cancel the delete function.

7. Press Enter. The defined text is deleted. The text following the deleted text moves up so that there are no extra blank spaces.

8. Repeat Steps 1-8 until all deletions are completed.

EXERCISE 5

In Exercise 5, you will practice making deletions from the document b:Exercis1. This is a document that you previously created and stored on your disk.

Follow the procedures to make the necessary deletions as shown in the illustration following this exercise.

PROCEDURES	COMMENTS
1. Recall the document b:Exercis1 to the screen.	Select Revise Document.
2. Place the cursor at the beginning of the first paragraph.	The cursor should be under the "A" in Auto (see ⟨2⟩).
3. Press Block (F4).	The prompt line choices display.
4. Type d.	This selects delete; the prompt "Move cursor to end of block; press ENTER" appears.

Continued

PROCEDURES (Continued)

    5. Move cursor to the end of the first paragraph.

    6. Press Enter.

    7. Place cursor under the tab symbol.

    8. Press Del.

    9. Place the cursor on the blank space following the word "faster."

  10. Press the Del key 11 times.

  11. Press End Task (F2).

  12. Select Print Document and Enter.

  13. Press Enter.

  14. Press Enter.

COMMENTS (Continued)

The cursor should be under the second carrier return following "line."

The first paragraph is deleted.

This is the tab symbol (see ⟨7⟩). ⟶

The tab is deleted.

See ⟨9⟩.

The words "and easier" are deleted. The period at the end of the sentence should not be deleted.

This will end the task.

The Print Document Menu displays.

The document is sent to the printer.

EXERCISE 5

delete first paragraph

⟨2⟩ Auto Carrier Return is a feature of the system that is designed to help you type faster and easier. If the cursor passes the right margin as you type, it automatically returns to the beginning of the next line.

⟨7⟩ *delete tab*   ⟨9⟩
Auto Carrier Return is a feature of the system that is designed to help you type faster ~~and easier.~~ If the cursor passes the right margin as you type, it automatically returns to the beginning of the next line.

AUTO CARRIER RETURN

    Auto Carrier Return is a feature of the system that is designed to help you type faster and easier.

Chapter 2 Editing

If the cursor passes the right margin as you type, it automatically returns to the beginning of the next line.

USING UNDO DELETE

A block of text that is accidentally deleted can be recovered with the Undo Delete feature. If you want the system to have the capability of recovering deleted blocks of text, you need to make sure that Retain Deleted Block to Allow Undo_delete is set to "Yes" in the Create or Revise Document Menu.

1. Check to see that Retain Deleted Block to Allow Undo_delete has been set to "Yes" in the Create or Revise Document Menu.

2. Place the cursor under the first character or code you wish the restored block of text to precede.

3. Press Block (F4) and select Undo_delete. The retained block of text is copied into the document at the cursor position.

EXERCISE 6

In Exercise 6, you will be recalling b:Exercis1 to the screen. You will be deleting a block of text, and then using the Undo Delete feature to recover the block of text.

PROCEDURES	COMMENTS
1. Select Revise Document from the Text Task Selection Menu.	
2. Type b:**Exercis1**.	This is the name of the document.
3. Press Enter.	The Create or Revise Document Menu displays.
4. Check to see that item "e" is set to "Yes."	This tells the system to retain the deleted block of text.
5. Press Enter.	The document displays.
6. Use block delete to delete the first paragraph.	If you cannot remember how, review the directions for block delete.
7. Place the cursor at the left margin, on line 7.	This is where you want the recovered text to be placed.

Continued

PROCEDURES (Continued)	COMMENTS (Continued)
8. Press Block (F4).	The prompt line choices display.
9. Select Undo_delete.	The recovered text displays on the screen.
10. Press F2.	This is to store the document.

ADDING TEXT

Adding text in a document is easy to do when using the DisplayWrite 3 software. You place the cursor at the position where you want the inserted text to begin and type the text that is to be added. The existing text moves automatically to the right as you insert new text. This is known as typing in the insert mode. The system is automatically set for typing in the insert mode unless you change it. When you are typing in the insert mode, the characters "Ins" appear on the second status line.

As you are inserting text, you may find that some words move beyond the right margin. When you move the cursor to a different line, the system will automatically rearrange the line for you.

STEPS FOR INSERTING TEXT

1. Place the cursor in the exact position where the additional text is to begin. The cursor must be on the character or space that you want to move over.

2. Type the new text. The line endings may rearrange when you move the cursor to a different line.

There may be times when you will want to replace existing text with new text. Up to this point, if you needed to replace text you would have first deleted the unwanted text and then typed in your new text. There is an easier way to replace text with DisplayWrite 3. You can use the replace mode. When typing in the replace mode, the characters "Repl" will appear on the second status line in place of "Ins."

STEPS FOR REPLACING TEXT

1. Place the cursor under the first character to be replaced.

2. Press the Ins key to turn on the replace mode (see Figure 2.7). The characters "Repl" appear on the second status line.

3. Type the new text. You will see the new text replacing the old text.

4. Press Ins to turn on the insert mode when you have finished replacing characters. The characters "Ins" appear on the status line.

Chapter 2   Editing

Figure 2.7 Ins Key

EXERCISE 7

Exercise 7 will provide you with practice in using the insert mode to add text and the replace mode for replacing unwanted text with new text.

You will need to recall the document b:Exercis4 to the screen. Make insertions and replacements as described in Procedures 1-12 and shown in Exercise 7.

PROCEDURES	COMMENTS
1. Recall the document b:Exercis4 to the screen.	
2. Move the cursor to the c in "can."	
3. Press the Ins key.	"Repl" appears on the status line to let you know you are in the replace mode.
4. Type: may.	The word "may" is replacing "can." Replace every occurrence of the word "can" with the word "may."
5. Press the Ins key.	This takes you out of the replace mode and puts you back in the insert mode.
6. Place the cursor on the blank space following the word "disk."	
7. Type: , magnetic card,	The words have been added, and the rest of the text moves to the right.
8. Press the down arrow key several times.	This moves the cursor down the page; the lines will automatically rearrange.
9. Press F2.	This is to end the task.
10. Select Print Document.	

Continued

PROCEDURES (Continued)	COMMENTS (Continued)
11. Press Enter.	The Print Document Menu displays.
12. Press Enter.	The document is sent to the printer. It should look like Figure 2.8.

EXERCISE 7

OPTICAL CHARACTER READER

With the use of an Optical Character Reader (OCR), information can be keyboarded on a standard typewriter and then "read" and automatically recorded onto a floppy disk or other magnetic media. The disk then can be inserted into a word processing system for text editing.

(2) Replace with the word may
(6) insert , magnetic card,

OCR machines are fast and quite accurate. The advantage of using OCR is that it allows the first draft of a document to be prepared on an ordinary typewriter. This means that the more expensive word processors are now free to do the work they do best--text editing.

OPTICAL CHARACTER READER

With the use of an Optical Character Reader (OCR), information may be keyboarded on a standard typewriter and then "read" and automatically recorded onto a floppy disk, magnetic card, or other magnetic media. The disk then may be inserted into a word processing system for text editing.

OCR machines are fast and quite accurate. The advantage of using OCR is that it allows the first draft of a document to be prepared on an ordinary typewriter. This means that the more expensive word processors are now free to do the work they do best--text editing.

Figure 2.8   Exercise 7 Printout

CHAPTER SUMMARY

A. Using the Cursor Movement Keys

   1. The cursor movement keys move the cursor around in your document without altering the text.
   2. The Home key moves the cursor to the upper left corner of the page.
   3. The End key moves your cursor to the end of your typing on the page.
   4. The Up Page key displays the previous 25 lines on the screen.
   5. The Down Page key displays the next 25 lines on the screen.

B. Displaying Codes

    1. Press Cmd (F6).
    2. Select Display codes.
    3. Repeat the same steps to turn off codes.

C. Underscoring

    1. To underscore one word at a time, type the word and press Ctrl--Word Und (Ctrl--U).
    2. To underscore a series of words:
        a. Place the cursor under the first character to be underscored.
        b. Press Instr (F8).
        c. Choose Begin.
        d. Choose Underscore.
        e. Type all of the words to be underscored.
        f. Press Instr.
        g. Choose End.
        h. Choose Underscore.

D. Deleting Text

    1. To delete a character, place the cursor under the character you want to delete and press Del.
    2. To use Block Delete:
        a. Place the cursor under the first character or code to be deleted.
        b. Press Block (F4).
        c. The prompt line choices display. Select Delete.
        d. Move the cursor to the last character or code to be deleted.
        e. Press Enter.

E. Using Undo Delete

    1. Check to see that Retain Deleted Block to Allow Undo_delete has been set to "Yes" in the Create or Revise Document Menu.
    2. Place the cursor under the first character or code you wish the restored block of text to precede.
    3. Press Block (F4) and select Undo_delete. The retained block of text is copied into the document at the cursor position.

F. Inserting Text

    Place the cursor at the position where additional text is to be inserted. Type the new text.

G. Replacing Text

    1. Place the cursor under the first character to be replaced.
    2. Press Ins.
    3. Type the new text.
    4. Press Ins to return to insert mode.

Chapter 3

MAJOR REVISIONS

When you complete this chapter, you will be able to:

1. Use the Move function to move a block of text to a different location within the document.

2. Use the Copy function to duplicate a block of text within a document.

3. Use the Overstrike function to mark over existing text.

4. Use the Search/Replace function.

STEPS IN MOVING A BLOCK OF TEXT

There may be times when you will want to rearrange your text by moving a sentence, paragraph, or several paragraphs to a different location in your document. This task can be easily accomplished by using the Move function. With the Move function, you first indicate the block of information you want moved by highlighting the text. You then indicate the new location for the text. The system automatically inserts the highlighted text at the new location in your document. Information can be moved so that it appears either before or after its original position in the document.

1. You must be in the typing area of the document being revised.

2. Place the cursor under the first character of the section of text to be moved. Take a look at the codes which come before the first text character and after the last text character to be moved. You will need to decide if any of these codes should be included with the text to be moved. You can look at the status line as you move the cursor to determine whether a code exists either before or after the text.

   If you highlight text you do not want to move, press Esc to cancel the highlighting and try again; or use the left arrow key to move the cursor back to remove the highlighting.

3. Press Block (F4). The prompt line choices will appear at the bottom of your screen (see Figure 3.1).

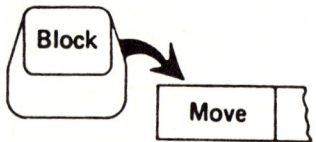

Figure 3.1   Moving a Block of Text

4. Type M to select Move. If Move is already highlighted, just press Enter. The prompt "Move cursor to end of block; press ENTER" displays.

5. Place the cursor under the last character or code of the block of text to be moved and press Enter.

6. The block of text is highlighted and the prompt "To Where? Move cursor, press ENTER" displays.

   If the highlighted text is not what you want moved, press Esc to cancel the highlighting, and start at Step 2 again.

7. Place the cursor at the location where you want the text to be moved. You can move the text before or after the original location in the document.

8. Press Enter. The text is deleted from its current location and moved to the new location.

EXERCISE 8

In Exercise 8 you will recall the document, b:Eating, to the screen and rearrange the text by using the Move function.

PROCEDURES	COMMENTS
1. Recall the document b:Eating to the screen.	Remember how? Choose Revise Document; Enter. Type B:Eating; Enter. Press Enter again.
2. Highlight the tab (→) at the beginning of the second paragraph.	
3. Press Block (F4).	The prompt line choices appear at the bottom of the screen.
4. Type M. If Move is already highlighted, press Enter.	A prompt appears at the bottom of the screen asking you to move the cursor to the end of the block of text to be moved.
5. Press the down arrow key three times.	The first three lines of the paragraph are highlighted.
6. Press the right arrow key until the fourth line of the paragraph is completely highlighted, including the required carrier return (◀) following the word "incorrectly."	The entire second paragraph, including the codes, should be highlighted.
7. Press Enter.	The prompt "To Where? Move cursor; press ENTER" displays.
8. Press Ctrl--Go To (Ctrl--End).	The prompt "Type page number; press ENTER" displays.
9. Type 2 and press Enter.	Page 2 is brought to the screen.
10. Use the down arrow key to move the cursor to the carrier return below the last line of typing.	This indicates to the system where you want the paragraph to be moved.
11. Press Enter.	The paragraph is moved to the new location.
12. Press F2.	This ends the task.

Continued

Chapter 3   Major Revisions

PROCEDURES (Continued)	COMMENTS (Continued)
13. Print a copy of the document. It should look like Figure 3.2.	Remember how? Select Print Document and press Enter. Press Enter again.

SENSIBLE EATING CAN BE DELICIOUS

Its obvious pleasures aside, the family dinner table is filled with all kinds of hidden benefits. The family that eats well is generally healthier and happier, filled with energy and a sense of well-being.

A balanced diet is the key to good eating habits. Unfortunately, to many people the term "diet" brings an immediate image of "reducing diet" or "ulcer diet" or some other punishing regime. This is not true. A balanced diet is the daily selection of a variety of foods that fulfills the body's needs for essential nutrients such as proteins, carbohydrates, fats, vitamins, minerals, and water.

FATS

A word about fats. All fats are not alike. Most Americans eat too much of the "wrong" kind of fat. Saturated fat tends to increase the level of cholesterol in the blood. The "right" kind of fat is polyunsaturated fat which tends to lower the level of blood cholesterol. A diet providing more of the "right" kind of fat is vital for good health.

PROTEINS

Protein is the chief organic part of all muscle, gland and nerve tissue, and of blood. It plays a significant role in the fluid balance of the body. Proteins are indispensable and normal parts of almost every living cell.

The National Research Council's Recommended Daily Dietary Allowance for Protein for Healthy Adults is 0.9 grams per day for each 2.2 pounds of body weight.

The human body is a biological machine. It has to be nourished properly and cared for to work smoothly and efficiently. What you eat can make the difference between feeding your body correctly or incorrectly.

Figure 3.2   Exercise 8 Printout

STEPS FOR COPYING A BLOCK OF TEXT

The Copy function allows you to duplicate a block of text without having to retype it. An example where you might use the copy function would be to copy the inside address of a letter onto an envelope. This saves you from having to retype the address on the envelope. You may also have a multiple-page document where you would want the same paragraph to appear on several pages. With the copy function, you need only to type the paragraph once and then have the system make a copy on each of the additional pages.

The difference between the Copy function and the Move function is that with the Move function, the block of text is deleted from its original location and MOVED to the new location. With the Copy function, the block of text remains in its original location and a COPY of text is also placed at another location.

When specifying the text to be copied, you must highlight any punctuation, spaces, carrier returns, or codes you want copied as part of the text. You can copy the block of text so that the duplicate appears either before or after the original in the document. Follow the steps for copying a block of text.

1. You need to be in the typing area of the document to be revised. Place the cursor under the first character or code to be copied.

2. Press Block (F4). The prompt line choices display (see Figure 3.3).

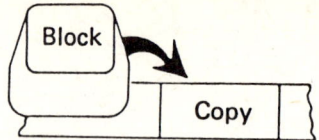

Figure 3.3   Copying a Block of Text

3. Select Copy by typing C or moving the cursor to the choice Copy and press Enter. The prompt "Move cursor to end of block; press ENTER" displays.

4. Place the cursor under the last character or code to be copied and press Enter. The text to be copied is highlighted and the prompt "To Where? Move cursor; press ENTER" displays.

5. Move the cursor to the place where you want the text copied and press Enter. The text is copied in the new location. The original text remains in place.

EXERCISE 9

Exercise 9 will give you practice in moving and copying text. You will need to recall the document b:Eating to the screen. Make the revisions as they are illustrated in Exercise 9 following these procedures.

PROCEDURES	COMMENTS
1. Recall the document b:Eating to the screen.	
2. Place the cursor under the "F" in FATS.	
3. Press Block (F4).	The prompt line choices display.
4. Type C.	The prompt "Move cursor to end of block; press ENTER" displays.
5. Press the down arrow key six times.	The entire section below FATS is now highlighted except for the last line.
6. Press the right arrow key until the last line is highlighted, including the required carrier return (◀).	
7. Press Enter.	The prompt "To where? Move cursor; Press ENTER" displays.
Continued	

PROCEDURES (Continued)	COMMENTS (Continued)
8. Press Ctrl--Go To (Ctrl--End).	The prompt "Type page number; press ENTER" displays.
9. Type 2 and press Enter.	Page 2 is displayed.
10. Move the cursor down the page until the required carrier return following the last line in the last paragraph is highlighted.	Your screen should look like this: feeding your body . . . ◀.
11. Press Enter.	A copy of the highlighted text appears on page 2.
12. Highlight the tab (⟶) at the beginning of the second paragraph on page 2.	Your screen should look like this: ⟶ The National . . .
13. Press Block (F4).	The prompt line choices display.
14. Press Enter.	This selects Move.
15. Press the down arrow key twice.	The first two lines of the paragraph are highlighted.
16. Press the right arrow key until the entire last line of the paragraph, including the required carrier return, is highlighted.	
17. Press Enter.	The prompt "To where? Move cursor; press ENTER" displays.
18. Press Ctrl--Go To.	
19. Type 1 and press Enter.	Page 1 of the document is displayed.
20. Place the cursor under the tab at the beginning of the second paragraph.	This marks the position where the paragraph is to be moved.
21. Press Enter.	The paragraph from page 2 has been moved to page 1.
22. Press F2.	This will end the task.

Continued

Chapter 3 Major Revisions

PROCEDURES (Continued)	COMMENTS (Continued)
23. Print a copy of your revised document. It should look like Figure 3.4.	

EXERCISE 9

SENSIBLE EATING CAN BE DELICIOUS

Its obvious pleasures aside, the family dinner table is filled with all kinds of hidden benefits. The family that eats well is generally healthier and happier, filled with energy and a sense of well-being.

[move paragraph from page 2 to here]

A balanced diet is the key to good eating habits. Unfortunately, to many people the term "diet" brings an immediate image of "reducing diet" or "ulcer diet" or some other punishing regime. This is not true. A balanced diet is the daily selection of a variety of foods that fulfills the body's needs for essential nutrients such as proteins, carbohydrates, fats, vitamins, minerals, and water.

FATS

A word about fats. All fats are not alike. Most Americans eat too much of the "wrong" kind of fat. Saturated fat tends to increase the level of cholesterol in the blood. The "right" kind of fat is polyunsaturated fat which tends to lower the level of blood cholesterol. A diet providing more of the "right" kind of fat is vital for good health.

[make a copy of this section for page 2]

PROTEINS

Protein is the chief organic part of all muscle, gland and nerve tissue, and of blood. It plays a significant role in the fluid balance of the body. Proteins are indispensable and normal parts of almost every living cell.

(The National Research Council's Recommended Daily Dietary Allowance for Protein for Healthy Adults is 0.9 grams per day for each 2.2 pounds of body weight.) *move to page 1*

The human body is a biological machine. It has to be nourished properly and cared for to work smoothly and efficiently. What you eat can make the difference between feeding your body correctly or incorrectly.

Insert the copied section on Fats here.

STEPS FOR OVERSTRIKING A BLOCK OF TEXT

The Overstrike function enables you to mark over existing text with another character.

The Overstrike function is used quite extensively in the legal profession. Many times authors will want to show proposed changes or deletions to be made on a document. The portion of text that the author is proposing to be deleted will be marked with overstruck characters (see Figure 3.5). That way, others who examine the document are still able to read the proposed deletions. The text remains in the document, but the overstriking identifies it as an area that has been or will be revised.

DisplayWrite 3 allows you to choose the character you would like to use for the overstrike. You indicate where the overstriking is to begin and end, and the system will go through and insert the overstriking for you. If you include a tab preceding a paragraph, you may overstrike the blank spaces of the indentation (see Figure 3.6).

To remove overstriking, delete the Begin and End Overstrike codes.

The cursor must be in the area between Begin and End Overstrike codes to make text revisions to overstruck text. Display codes will need to be turned on when making revisions.

1. Make sure you are in the typing area of your document. Place the cursor at the beginning of the text you want to overstrike.

2. Press Block (F4). The prompt line choices display (see Figure 3.7).

3. Choose Overstrike by typing O. The prompt "Move cursor to end of block; press ENTER" displays.

4. Place the cursor at the end of the text you want to overstrike. Press Enter. The text to be overstruck is highlighted as the cursor moves to the end of the block of text.

5. The prompt "Overstrike with what character?" displays. Type the character you would like to use for overstriking. Press Enter.

The overstrike character replaces the text displayed. You can see the original text by moving the cursor through the text or by turning on Display codes.

When the document is printed, both the text and the overstrike characters are printed.

SENSIBLE EATING CAN BE DELICIOUS

Its obvious pleasures aside, the family dinner table is filled with all kinds of hidden benefits. The family that eats well is generally healthier and happier, filled with energy and a sense of well-being.

The National Research Council's Recommended Daily Dietary Allowance for Protein for Healthy Adults is 0.9 grams per day for each 2.2 pounds of body weight.

A balanced diet is the key to good eating habits. Unfortunately, to many people the term "diet" brings an immediate image of "reducing diet" or "ulcer diet" or some other punishing regime. This is not true. A balanced diet is the daily selection of a variety of foods that fulfills the body's needs for essential nutrients such as proteins, carbohydrates, fats, vitamins, minerals, and water.

FATS

A word about fats. All fats are not alike. Most Americans eat too much of the "wrong" kind of fat. Saturated fat tends to increase the level of cholesterol in the blood. The "right" kind of fat is polyunsaturated fat which tends to lower the level of blood cholesterol. A diet providing more of the "right" kind of fat is vital for good health.

PROTEINS

Protein is the chief organic part of all muscle, gland and nerve tissue, and of blood. It plays a significant role in the fluid balance of the body. Proteins are indispensable and normal parts of almost every living cell.

The human body is a biological machine. It has to be nourished properly and cared for to work smoothly and efficiently. What you eat can make the difference between feeding your body correctly or incorrectly.

FATS

A word about fats. All fats are not alike. Most Americans eat too much of the "wrong" kind of fat. Saturated fat tends to increase the level of cholesterol in the blood. The "right" kind of fat is polyunsaturated fat which tends to lower the level of blood cholesterol. A diet providing more of the "right" kind of fat is vital for good health.

Figure 3.4   Exercise 9 Printout

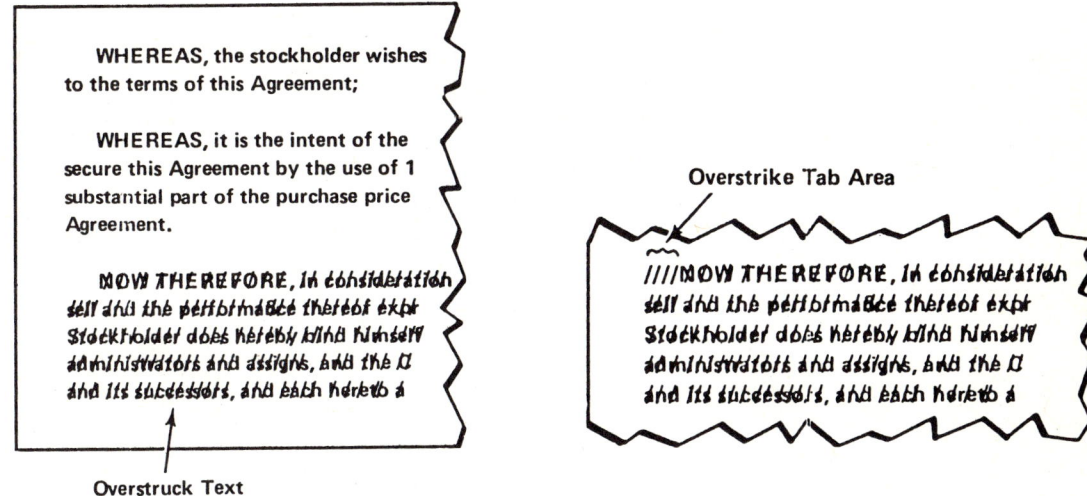

Figure 3.5   Overstruck Text   Figure 3.6   Overstrike Tab Area

Chapter 3   Major Revisions   45

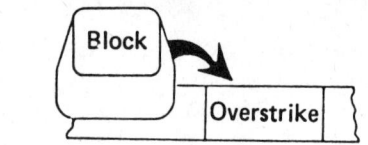

Figure 3.7 Block Overstrike

EXERCISE 10

In Exercise 10 you will be creating the legal document as shown following these procedures. You will print a copy of the document, recall it back to the screen, and add overstriking to part of the text.

PROCEDURES	COMMENTS
1. Create a new document and name it b:Exerci10.	
2. Add the document comment **overstriking text**.	Remember how? Type a and press Enter. Type overstriking text and Enter. Press Enter again.
3. Type the document as shown following these procedures.	
4. Press F2.	This ends the task.
5. Print a copy of the document.	
6. Recall b:Exerci10 to the screen.	
7. Press PgDn.	The next 26 lines display on the screen.
8. Place the cursor under the tab for Enumeration 3.	Your screen should look like this: 3. The said Susan . . .
9. Press Block (F4).	The prompt line choices display.
10. Type O.	The prompt "Move cursor to end of block; press ENTER" displays.
11. Move the cursor to highlight the entire Enumeration 3.	The entire Enumeration 3, including the period at the end, needs to be highlighted.

Continued

PROCEDURES (Continued)	COMMENTS (Continued)
12. Press Enter.	The prompt "Overstrike with what character?" displays.
13. Type / and press Enter.	The overstrike character replaces the text displayed.
14. Press F2.	This ends the task.
15. Print a copy of the document. It should look like Figure 3.8.	

AGREEMENT AND COVENANT NOT TO SUE

WHEREAS, John Doe, party of the first part, and Susan Smith of the second part, entered into a building agreement concerning the construction of a home on 12 Main Street, Cypress, California, and

WHEREAS several disputes have occurred throughout the construction of said house, and

WHEREAS the parties hereto have agreed to terminate said agreement upon the payment of Fifteen Thousand Dollars ($15,000) to Susan Smith. It is further agreed as follows: That the said John Doe will pay unto Kistner and Associates the sum of Ten Thousand Dollars ($10,000), from which the remaining bills of all subcontractors who supplied materials and/or labor to the construction of said house will be paid. Upon such payment to said Susan Smith, the parties herein further agree as follows:

1. The parties hereto release each other from any and all further obligations and liabilities from the term of said Agreement.

2. The said parties covenant not to sue each other for any violations or disputes arising from the terms of said Agreement.

3. The said Susan Smith further agrees to indemnify and save harmless the said John Doe from any and all liabilities in connection with any moneys owed by the said Susan Smith to any subcontractors who performed labor and/or supplied materials in the construction of said house.

IN WITNESS WHEREOF the parties hereto set their hands and seals this 31st day of December, 19--.

_____   _____

AGREEMENT AND COVENANT NOT TO SUE

WHEREAS, John Doe, party of the first part, and Susan Smith of the second part, entered into a building agreement concerning the construction of a home on 12 Main Street, Cypress, California, and

WHEREAS several disputes have occurred throughout the construction of said house, and

WHEREAS the parties hereto have agreed to terminate said agreement upon the payment of Fifteen Thousand Dollars ($15,000) to Susan Smith. It is further agreed as follows: That the said John Doe will pay unto Kistner and Associates the sum of Ten Thousand Dollars ($10,000), from which the remaining bills of all subcontractors who supplied materials and/or labor to the construction of said house will be paid. Upon such payment to said Susan Smith, the parties herein further agree as follows:

1. The parties hereto release each other from any and all further obligations and liabilities from the terms of said Agreement.

2. The said parties covenant not to sue each other for any violations or disputes arising from the terms of said Agreement.

/////3.//The/said/Susan/Smith/further/agrees/to/indemnify/and/save/harmless/the/said/John/Doe/from/any/and/all/liabilities/in/connection/with/any/moneys/owed/by/the/said/Susan/Smith/to/any/subcontractors/who/performed/labor/and/or/supplied/materials/in/the/construction/of/said/house./

IN WITNESS WHEREOF the parties hereto set their hands and seals this 31st day of December, 19--.

Figure 3.8 Exercise 10 Printout

USING SEARCH/REPLACE

There may be instances in which you have used a word that appears frequently throughout a multiple-page document. Perhaps the word needs to be changed or spelled differently. For example, you typed "Inc." and you wish to change the word to "Incorporated." Using the Search/Replace function, you need to type the word change only once. The system will automatically go through your entire document, search for the existing word, and replace it with the revised word.

Using the Search/Replace function, you can make up to three changes at once throughout your document. For instance, you can ask the system to make your change from Inc. to Incorporated, from Aug. to August, and from recieve to receive, all in one search.

Both the searched-for characters and the replaced-with characters are referred to as character strings. The character strings can consist of alphabetic or numeric characters, and they can be either uppercase or lowercase. You can also search for and replace some codes. NOTE: To search for or replace a required carrier return, the character string you type must be Ctrl--L.

It is recommended that you place your cursor at the beginning of your document before starting the Search/Replace function. The system only searches forward; it does not search in reverse. If your cursor is on line 26 and the first word you wanted replaced was on line 7 of the same page, that word would not be changed because the system begins its search on line 26.

Figure 3.9 illustrates the Search/Replace Menu. This will appear on your screen after you choose the Search/Replace function. Examine the parts of the menu.

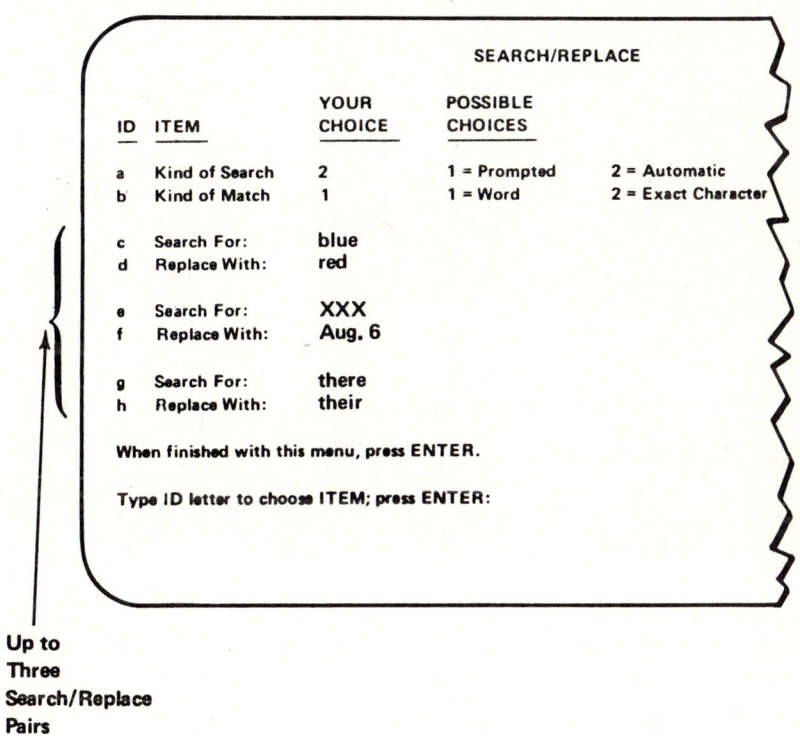

Figure 3.9 Search/Replace Menu

Item a: Kind of Search

You can select either a prompted search or an automatic search. With the prompted mode, the system stops at each occurrence of the search-for character strings to let you check each change before the search-for characters are replaced. Automatic mode makes all the changes without stopping.

Item b: Kind of Match

You will need to select either Word or Exact Character. With the word match, the system searches for characters that match and that do not

Chapter 3 Major Revisions   49 appear within another word. Exact Character also searches within other words. For example, you may ask the system to search for "his." In the Word search, it will search for all occurrences of the word "his." With Exact Character search, it may also find "history."

Items c, e, and g: Search For

Use Item c to type in the first character string for which you want to search. If you are only searching and replacing one character string, then items e, f, g, and h will remain blank.

Items d, f, and h: Replace With

Type the character string that you want the searched-for characters replaced with. Each change can be up to 60 characters long.

STEPS IN USING SEARCH/REPLACE

1. Place the cursor at the beginning of the document (see Figure 3.10).

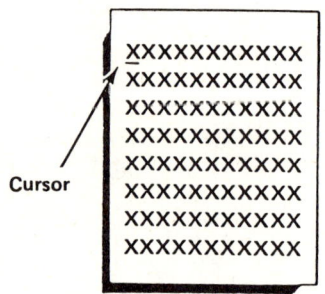

Figure 3.10 Cursor at Beginning

2. Press Cmd (F6). The prompt line choices display (see Figure 3.11).

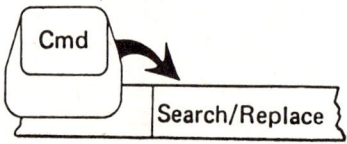

Figure 3.11 Search/Replace Command

3. Select Search/Replace by typing S or moving the cursor to Search/Replace and pressing Enter.

4. The Search/Replace Menu is displayed on the screen. Choose Kind of Search by typing a and pressing Enter. Then select the prompted or automatic mode. (The system has already been set for an automatic search. If this is what you want to use, you can skip Step 4.)

5. Choose Kind of Match and press Enter. Select either Word or Exact Character and press Enter. (The system default is set for Word match. If this is what you want to use, you can skip Step 5.)

50   Chapter 3 Major Revisions

6. Choose the first Search For Menu item and press Enter. Type the first character string you want to search for and press Enter.

7. Choose the first Replace With Menu item and press Enter. Type the character string you want the searched-for characters replaced with and press Enter.

8. If you wish to use a Search/Delete function (that is, search for a word and delete it from the text), you would just leave the Replace With option blank. You are telling the system to search for a word and replace it with nothing.

9. Specify additional character strings to be searched for and replaced, if necessary.

10. Press Enter.

11. If you chose automatic mode, go to Step 12. If you chose prompted mode, the system searches for the first occurrence of the searched-for characters. The prompt "Press Continue to replace or delete, or press Esc" displays. To replace or delete the characters, press Continue (F10). To leave the characters unchanged, press Esc. The prompt "Press Continue to resume search" displays. Press Continue.

12. When all of the searched-for characters have been found, the prompt "Search/Replace completed. ___ (number) phrases changed" displays. Press End Task.

EXERCISE 11

In Exercise 11, you will need to recall the document b:VisitLA to the screen. First you will use this document to perform an Automatic Search/Replace and print a copy of the document. You then will recall the same document to the screen and perform a Prompted Search/Replace.

PROCEDURES	COMMENTS
1. Recall the document b:VisitLA to the screen.	
2. Place the cursor at the beginning of the document.	
3. Press Cmd (F6).	The prompt line choices display.
4. Type S.	This selects Search/Replace. The Search/Replace Menu displays.
Continued	

Chapter 3 Major Revisions
51

PROCEDURES (Continued)	COMMENTS (Continued)
5. Type c and press Enter.	We can skip to c because a and b are already set up as we want them.
6. Type L.A. and press Enter.	This is the searched-for character string.
7. Type d and press Enter.	This selects the Replace With mode.
8. Type Los Angeles and press Enter.	This is the replace-with character string.
9. Press Enter.	The prompt "Search/Replace completed. Sixteen phrases changed" is displayed.
10. Press F2.	
11. Print a copy of the document.	It will not be paginated. You will learn about pagination in Chapter 6.
12. Repeat Steps 1-4.	Recall the same document to the screen. This time we will perform a prompted search.
13. Type a and press Enter.	This is to change the kind of search.
14. Type 1 and press Enter.	This selects the prompted mode.
15. Type c and press Enter.	
16. Type Los Angeles and press Enter.	
17. Type d and press Enter.	
18. Type L.A. and press Enter.	
19. Press Enter.	The document is brought to the screen and the prompt "Press Continue to replace or delete, or press Esc" displays.
20. Press Continue (F10).	The prompt "Press Continue to resume search" displays.
21. Press Continue (F10).	

Continued

PROCEDURES (Continued)	COMMENTS (Continued)
22. Repeat Steps 20 & 21 until all replacements have been made.	The prompt "Search/Replace completed. Sixteen phrases changed" displays.
23. Press F2.	
24. Print a copy.	

CHAPTER SUMMARY

A. Moving Text

   1. Place the cursor under the first character of the section of text to be moved.
   2. Press Block (F4).
   3. Select Move.
   4. Place the cursor under the last character or code to be moved and press Enter.
   5. Place the cursor at the location where you want the text to be moved and press Enter.

B. Copying Text

   1. Place the cursor under the first character of the section of text to be copied.
   2. Press Block (F4).
   3. Select Copy.
   4. Place the cursor under the last character or code to be copied and press Enter.
   5. Move the cursor to the location where you want the copied text to be placed.
   6. Press Enter.

C. Overstriking Text

   1. Place the cursor at the beginning of the text you want to overstrike.
   2. Press Block (F4).
   3. Select Overstrike.
   4. Place the cursor at the end of the text you want to overstrike and press Enter.
   5. Type the character you would like to use for overstriking and press Enter.

D. Using Search/Replace

   1. Place the cursor at the beginning of the document.
   2. Press Cmd (F6).
   3. Select Search/Replace.
   4. Make your choices for Kind of Search and Kind of Match.
   5. Type in the character strings for "Search For" and "Replace With."
   6. Press Enter.

Chapter 4

DOCUMENT FORMAT

When you complete this chapter, you will be able to:

1. Use the Format Selection Menu to select the option of changing the line format, the page format, and the margins and tabs.

2. Use the Line Format Menu to make changes in the arrangement of lines for a document.

3. Use the Page Format Menu to make changes in page layout.

4. Use the Margins and Tabs Menu to change margins and tabs for a document.

DOCUMENT FORMAT

In Chapter 4, you will be learning about document format. The format is the way text is laid out on the page. Some of the decisions that you need to make when setting up a document include margins, tabs, line spacing, and pitch. Up to this point, all the documents that you have created have used the system defaults. That is, the system has preset margins, tabs, line spacing, and so on. Documents created on the system will automatically use the system defaults unless you change them. Figure 4.1 is an illustration of the System's Default Document Format:

System's Default Document Format Characteristics

- 60-character horizontal typing line
- Flush left tab settings every 5 spaces
- Single line spacing
- Lines align at the left
- 10 pitch typestyle
- 2.36 lines/cm or 6 lines/in. vertically
- Line endings are adjusted when a long word would cause a line to exceed the right margin. The entire word is moved to the next line.
- 6 space zone width supplies an area before the right margin where hyphenation can occur if you want a more even right margin than the automatic adjusted line endings provide.
- 215.9 x 279.4mm (8.5 x 11 in.) paper size.
- Printing leaves six blank lines at the top.
- Printing leaves six blank lines at the bottom.
- On the IBM 5218 Printer with sheet feed the paper will be fed from the top drawer.

Figure 4.1   Defaults

DisplayWrite 3 is a menu-driven software system. Each time you want to perform a task, the system presents you with a menu indicating the possible choices that are available to you. After the DisplayWrite 3 software is loaded into the system, the Text Task Selection Menu appears on the screen. You choose from the menu the task you would like to perform. Let us say, for example, that we would like to revise a document by changing the document format. We would select Revise Document from the Text Task Selection Menu. After we have indicated the name of the document to be revised, the Revise Document Menu will appear on the screen. You can see that option "b" on the menu is "Change Document Format." Once you have chosen "Change Document Format," the Document or Alternate Format Menu will appear. Through the Document or Alternate Format Menu, you can choose to change either the line format, page format, or margins and tabs (see Figure 4.2). In this chapter we will examine each of these format changes.

Chapter 4   Document Format

Note: The format changes that you make using the Line Format Menu, Page Format Menu, and Margins and Tabs Menu apply only to the document that you are working on. When you create a new document, the system document format defaults are again in effect.

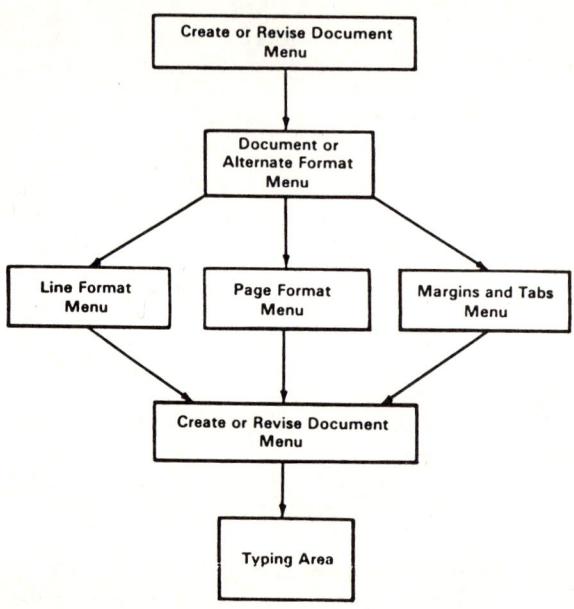

Figure 4.2 Format Choices

STEPS IN CHANGING THE LINE FORMAT OF A DOCUMENT

Any time you wish to change the arrangement of the lines in your document, you will need to go to the Line Format Menu. You can reach this menu by selecting "Change Line Format" in the Document or Alternate Format Menu. Figure 4.3 is the Line Format Menu and an explanation of each of the items in the menu.

a   **Line Spacing** allows you to choose single-, double-, or triple-spacing.

b   **Line Alignment** determines whether lines are even at the left and ragged on the right, even at the left and 1/2 justified, or even at the left and fully justified at the right.

c   **Typestyle Number** determines the size (pitch), style, and design of characters on printed lines.

d   **Lines/cm. or in.** determines how many printed lines occupy a vertical centimeter or inch.

e   **Adjust Line Endings** indicates whether or not line endings are adjusted to fit within the margins chosen.

f   **Zone Width** determines the number of blank spaces from where the system ends a line to the right margin.

```
                        LINE FORMAT

                     YOUR      POSSIBLE
         ID  ITEM    CHOICE    CHOICES
         a   Line Spacing    1    1 = Single   2 = Double    3 = Triple
                                  4 = Half     5 = 1 and 1/2
         b   Line Alignment  1    1 = Left     2 = Justify
                                  3 = 1/2 Justify
         c   Typestyle Number  26   1 - 39 (10 Pitch)    80 -111 (12 Pitch)
                                  154-175 (Proportional)
                                  215-230 (15 Pitch)  240-249 (5 Pitch)
                                  250-259 (16.5 Pitch) 260-269 (8.25 Pitch)

         d   Lines/cm or in.   2    1 = 2.09/cm or 5.3/in.
                                    2 = 2.36/cm or 6/in.
                                    3 = 3.15/cm or 8/in.
                                    4 = 9.45/cm or 24/in.

         e   Adjust Line Endings  1   1 = Yes      2 = No
         f   Zone Width           6   1 = 30
         When finished with this menu, press ENTER.
         Type ID letter to choose ITEM; press ENTER:
```

Figure 4.3   Line Format Menu

Read Steps 1-9. Figures 4.4 - 4.7 illustrate the steps in changing line format.

1. Choose Create or Revise Document in the Text Task Selection Menu.

2. Type the name of the document to be created or revised and press Enter.

3. The Create or Revise Document Menu is displayed on the screen. Choose Change Document Format by typing b and pressing Enter.

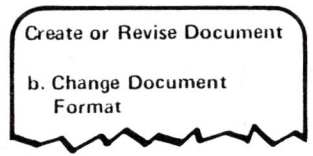

Figure 4.4   Create or Revise Document

4. The Document or Alternate Format Menu is displayed on the screen. Choose Change Line Format by typing a and pressing Enter.

5. Follow the prompt to type the ID letter of the item you want to change.

6. Then, follow the prompt to type the number from the Possible Choices column to make this change.

```
DOCUMENT OR ALTERNATE
          FORMAT
a  Change Line Format
b  Change Margins and Tabs
c  Change Page Format
```

Figure 4.5   Document or Alternate Format Menu

Figure 4.6   Prompt to Type ID Letter

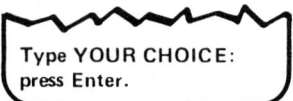

Figure 4.7   Prompt for Possible Choices

7. If you have other items in this menu you want to change, repeat Steps 5 and 6. Otherwise, continue with Step 8.

8. The prompt tells you to press Enter when you are finished making all your changes with this menu. After you press Enter, the Document or Alternate Format Menu will return to the screen.

9. Pressing Enter again will bring you to the typing area of your document.

EXERCISE 12

In Exercise 12, you will be recalling the document b:Exercis4 to the screen and making a line format change.

PROCEDURES	COMMENTS
1. Select Revise Document in the Text Task Selection Menu and press Enter.	
2. Type b:Exercis4 and press Enter.	The Create or Revise Document Menu displays.
3. Type b and press Enter.	The Document or Alternate Format Menu displays.
Continued	

PROCEDURES (Continued)	COMMENTS (Continued)
4. Type a and press Enter.	The Line Format Menu displays.
5. Type a and press Enter.	This indicates to the system that you would like to change the line spacing.
6. Type 2 and press Enter.	This changes it to double-spacing.
7. Press Enter.	This returns you to the Document or Alternate Format Menu.
8. Press Enter.	This returns you to the Create or Revise Document Menu.
9. Press Enter.	Your document is displayed on the screen. The document does not appear double-spaced on the screen.
10. Place the cursor on the first line of the first paragraph and use the down arrow key to move the cursor down the page.	Notice that the line number in the status line increases by two each time you move down.
11. Press F2.	
12. Print a copy of the revised document.	

STEPS IN CHANGING THE PAGE FORMAT OF A DOCUMENT

The Page Format Menu contains items that all relate to the way in which the pages of your document are arranged (see Figure 4.8).

a   **First Typing Line, First Page** identifies the line where printing begins on the first page.

b   **First Typing Line, Following Pages** identifies the line where printing begins on all pages after the first page.

c   **Last Typing Line** identifies the line where printing ends on all pages.

d   **Paper or Envelope Size** specifies the measurements of the page or envelope to be used.

e   **Printing Paper Source** specifies whether the page or envelope will be manually inserted or fed from the top, bottom, or envelope tray. If your printer uses continuous form paper, the default choices of "Top" should be used.

```
                        PAGE FORMAT

                         YOUR     POSSIBLE
   ID   ITEM             CHOICE   CHOICES
   a    First Typing Line,   7    1 – 999
        First Page
   b    First Typing Line,   7    1 – 999
        Following Pages
   c    Last Typing Line    60    2 – 999
   d    Paper or Envelope Size  3  1 = 210x297 mm or 8.27x11.69 in. (A4)
                                   2 = 297x210 mm or 11.69x8.27 in. (A4L)
                                   3 = 215.9x279.4 mm or 8.5x11 in. (P4)
                                   4 = 279.4x215.9 mm or 11x8.5 in. (P4L)
                                   5 = 215.9x355.6 mm or 8.5x14 in. (Legal)
                                   6 = 355.6x215.9 mm or 14x8.5 in. (Legal L)
                                   7 = 241.3x104.8 mm or 9.5x4.13 in. (Env.)
                                   8 = 220x110 mm or 8.66x4.33 in. (DL Env.)
                                   9 = Other in mm
   e    Printing Paper Source  1   1 = Top           2 = Bottom
                                   3 = Bottom, This Page Only
                                   4 = Manual Feed   5 = Envelope
   When finished with this menu, press ENTER.
   Type ID letter to CHOOSE ITEM, press ENTER:
```

Figure 4.8   Page Format Menu

Read Steps 1-10. These are the steps in changing the page format of a document.

1. Choose Create or Revise Document in the Text Task Selection Menu.

2. Type the name of the document you wish to create or revise and press Enter.

3. The Create or Revise Document Menu is displayed on the screen. Choose Change Document Format.

4. The Document or Alternate Format Menu is displayed on the screen. Choose Change Page Format.

5. The Change Page Format Menu is displayed on the screen. Type the ID letter of the item you want to change.

6. Follow the prompt to type the number from the Possible Choices column to make this change.

7. If you have other items in this menu you want to change, repeat Steps 5 and 6. Otherwise, continue with Step 8.

8. Press Enter to return to the Document or Alternate Format Menu. If you have additional document format changes to make, follow the prompt to type the ID letter of your choice from the Document

or Alternate Format Menu. Make the format changes in the menu you have chosen.

9. Press Enter when all document format changes are complete to return to the Create or Revise Document Menu.

10. Press Enter to go to the typing area.

EXERCISE 13

In Exercise 13, you will again recall the document b:Exercis4 and make additional revisions by changing the page format.

PROCEDURES	COMMENTS
1. Select Revise Document in the Text Task Selection Menu and press Enter.	
2. Type b:Exercis4 and press Enter.	The Create or Revise Document Menu displays.
3. Type b and press Enter.	The Document or Alternate Format Menu displays.
4. Type c and press Enter.	The Page Format Menu displays.
5. Type a and press Enter.	This indicates to the system that you need to change the First Typing Line, First Page.
6. Type 13 and press Enter.	The first line of typing will now begin on line 13.
7. Press Enter.	This returns you to the Document or Alternate Format Menu.
8. Press Enter.	This returns you to the Create or Revise Document Menu.
9. Press Enter.	Your document displays on the screen.
10. Place the cursor on the same line as the title.	Notice in the status line that this is line 13.
11. Press F2.	
12. Print a copy of this revised document.	

Chapter 4   Document Format

STEPS IN CHANGING THE MARGINS AND TABS FORMAT OF A DOCUMENT

Anytime you need to change the margins and tabs in a document, you will need to go to the Margins and Tabs Menu. Figure 4.9 is an illustration of the Margins and Tabs Menu. We will discuss each of the items listed in the menu.

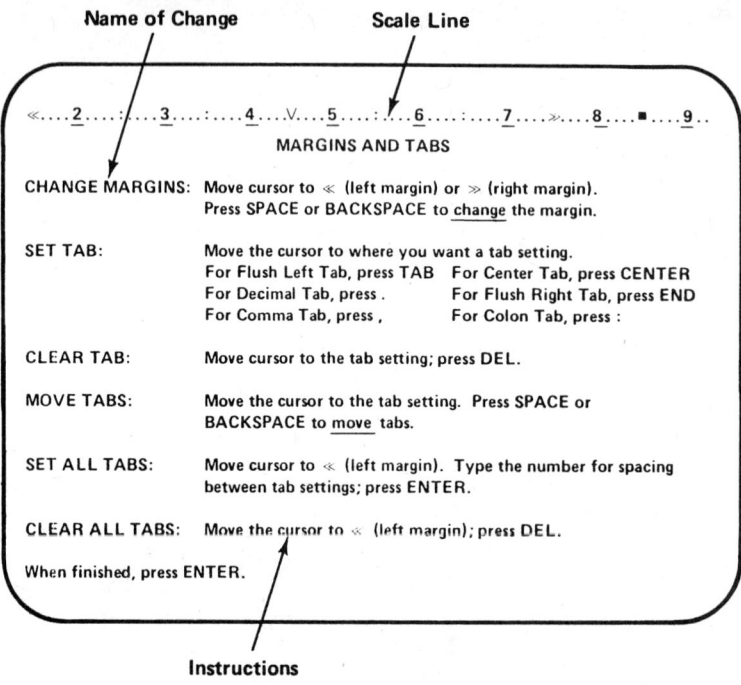

Figure 4.9 Margins and Tabs Menu

CHANGE MARGINS allows you to change the current left or right margin on the scale line. The numbers on the scale line represent increments of 10. For example, the number 1 represents 10, the number 2 represents 20, and so on.

SET TAB allows you to set different kinds of tabs on the scale line. The default tab settings are flush left tabs represented by an underscore every five spaces on the scale line. Most of the tabs you will be setting will be flush left tabs. You will learn to use some of the other tab settings in future lessons.

CLEAR TAB deletes a specific tab setting from the scale line.

MOVE TABS allows you to move current tab settings to new locations on the scale line.

SET ALL TABS allows you to designate a specified number of spaces between tab settings on the scale line.

CLEAR ALL TABS deletes all tab settings from the scale line.

Read Steps 1-10. These are the steps in changing the margins and tabs format.

1. Choose Create or Revise Document in the Text Task Selection Menu.

2. Type the name of the document and press Enter.

3. The Create or Revise Document Menu is displayed on the screen. Choose Change Document Format and press Enter.

4. The Document or Alternate Format Menu is displayed. Choose Change Margins and Tabs.

5. The Margins and Tabs Menu is displayed. The changes that can be made are listed on the left, and the instructions on how to make the changes are on the right.

6. Follow the instructions to make the desired changes. Use the cursor movement keys (the left and right arrow keys) to move to the specified location on the scale line. Follow the instructions to make each change you want.

7. When you have made all changes, follow the prompt to press Enter.

8. This returns you to the Document or Alternate Format Menu. If you have additional document format changes to make, follow the prompt to type the ID letter of your choice from the Document or Alternate Format Menu. Make the format changes in the menu you have chosen.

9. Press Enter when all document format changes are complete to return to the Create or Revise Document Menu.

10. Press Enter and your document or the typing area will be displayed on the screen.

EXERCISE 14

Exercise 14 will give you practice in changing line format, page format, margins, and tabs.

PROCEDURES	COMMENTS
1. Choose Create Document from the Text Task Selection Menu.	
2. Name the document b:Exerci14.	
3. Press Enter.	The Create or Revise Document Menu displays.
4. Type b and press Enter.	The Document or Alternate Format Menu displays.
5. Type a and press Enter.	The Line Format Menu displays.

Continued

PROCEDURES (Continued)	COMMENTS (Continued)
6. Type a and press Enter.	This is to change Line Spacing.
7. Type 2 and press Enter.	This is to choose double-spacing.
8. Press Enter.	The Document or Alternate Format Menu displays.
9. Type c and press Enter.	The Page Format Menu displays.
10. Type a and press Enter.	This is to change the First Typing Line, First Page.
11. Type 10 and press Enter.	This indicates that the first typing line will print on line 10.
12. Press Enter.	The Document or Alternate Format Menu displays.
13. Type b and press Enter.	The Margins and Tabs Menu displays.
14. Press the space bar until the left margin << is set at 20.	
15. Press the right arrow key until the cursor is highlighting the right margin >>.	
16. Press the backspace key to move the right margin to 65.	
17. To clear all tabs, make sure the cursor is at the left margin, and press Del. (Use the left arrow key to move the cursor to the left margin.)	All tab settings are cleared from the scale line.
18. Place the cursor at 25.	Use the cursor movement keys.
19. Press Tab.	This sets a flush left tab at 25.
20. Press Enter.	The Document or Alternate Format Menu displays.

Continued

PROCEDURES (Continued)	COMMENTS (Continued)
21. Press Enter.	This returns you to the Create or Revise Document Menu.
22. Press Enter.	This takes you to the typing area.
23. Type the document that follows these procedures.	Center and type the title. Return three times. Do not indent and type the first paragraph single-spaced. Return two times. Type the last three paragraphs single-spaced, using the tab to indent each paragraph.
24. Press F2 when you are finished with the document.	
25. Print a copy of the document.	

SELECTING PAPER FOR THE COMPUTER

The following tips for better paper selection are especially helpful to minicomputer users:

On printouts, if the e's look like c's, the b's become f's, or 8's are seen as 3's, the cause may be the use of multipart carbon interleaved forms. <u>Carbonless forms</u> cut the bulk of a multipart form nearly in half, making it easier for the printer head to make sharp impressions on duplicate copies.

When possible, use <u>continuous forms</u> rather than single-sheet paper.

<u>Buy quality for economy</u>. High-quality paper forms reduce downtime due to jams and tearing, will not yellow or fade, accept ink without bleeding, and minimize paper dust in a printer.

CHAPTER SUMMARY

To Change a Document Format:

1. Select Change Document Format in the Create or Revise Document Menu.
2. The Document or Alternate Format Menu will appear. From the Document or Alternate Format Menu you can access the:
   a. Line Format Menu.
   b. Page Format Menu.
   c. Margins and Tabs Menu.
3. When you are finished making your changes, press Enter three times to return to the typing area.

Chapter 4   Document Format

Chapter 5
PRINTING

When you complete this chapter, you will be able to:

1. Make any necessary changes in the Print Document Menu in order to print a document as desired.

2. Make any necessary changes in the Printer Description Menu in order to print a document as desired.

3. Use DisplayWrite 3 Foreground Printing.

4. Use DisplayWrite 3 Background Printing.

5. Display the print queue.

6. Cancel a print job.

7. Add jobs to the print queue.

8. Change the print job order in the print queue.

INTRODUCTION

Printing is a two-step process with DisplayWrite 3:

1. The first step is taking the document you select for printing and converting it into a form that allows it to be printed. This form corresponds to the class of printer you wish to use.

   There may be times when you will want to perform the conversion step only of the printing process. This allows you to convert a document and save it on a diskette to be printed at a later time.

2. The second step is when the actual printing takes place.

The DisplayWrite 3 software allows you to print a document using either Foreground Print, DisplayWrite 3 Background Print, or DOS Background Print. We will be discussing only Foreground Print and DisplayWrite 3 Background Print in this chapter. For more information regarding DOS Background Print, consult your IBM DisplayWrite 3 Reference Manual.

Foreground Printing allows you to perform other print tasks while a document prints, such as requesting another document to be printed before the first document finishes. However, you cannot select another task from the Text Task Selection Menu while Foreground Printing is being performed. If you select another print task, converting and printing of the current document are temporarily suspended until you finish the print request. When you finish, the printing will resume.

DisplayWrite 3 Background Print allows you to make another selection from the Text Task Selection Menu while a document is printing. This function will help save time since you do not have to wait for the printing to stop before creating or revising another document.

When you select Print Document from the Text Task Selection Menu, the Print Document Menu displays. Up to this point, each time the Print Document Menu has displayed, you have pressed Enter to accept the system defaults. There will be times when you will need to change some of the options. For example, you may need to print more copies, only print selected pages, or make changes to the printer description.

The choices that are made in the Print Document Menu and the Printer Description Menu determine how the document will print. The Printer Description Menu is accessed by selecting Change Printer Description in the Print Document Menu.

Read Steps 1-7. Figures 5.1 and 5.2 illustrate the steps for Foreground Printing.

1. Make sure that your printer is on and the paper has been loaded.

2. In the Text Task Selection Menu, select Print Document.

3. Type the name of the document.

4. Press Enter. The Print Document Menu will display.

5. Make the necessary changes to the menu.

6. After you have completed making all of the changes to the Print Document Menu, follow the prompt to press Enter. A message informs you that the document has been placed in the DisplayWrite 3 print queue.

    The Foreground Processing for Print screen displays. It will remain on the screen until the document has been printed.

Figure 5.1   Foreground Processing for Print Screen

7. When the document finishes printing, a message displays to confirm that processing is complete.

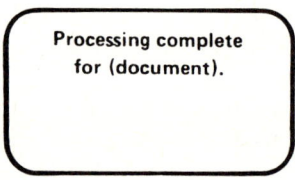

Figure 5.2   Processing Complete Message

The Text Task Selection Menu will display.

EXERCISE 15

Exercise 15 will give you some practice with changing some options in the Print Document Menu. You will request that two copies of page 2 of the document, b:Stress, be printed.

PROCEDURES	COMMENTS
1. Select Print Document in the Text Task Selection Menu.	
2. The document name is b:Stress.	
3. Press Enter.	The Print Document Menu displays.
4. Type a and press Enter.	This will change the From Page.

Continued

PROCEDURES (Continued)	COMMENTS (Continued)
5. Type 2 and press Enter.	This tells the system to print beginning with page 2.
6. Type b and press Enter.	This will change the Through Page.
7. Type 2 and press Enter.	This tells the system to print through page 2.
8. Type c and press Enter.	This will change the Print Quantity.
9. Type 2 and press Enter.	This tells the system to print two copies.
10. Press Enter.	The Foreground Processing for Print screen displays.
11. Pick up the document at the printer.	

MANAGING THE FOREGROUND PRINT QUEUE

Other print tasks can be performed while a document is in the process of being converted and printed. The following tasks can be performed by managing the foreground print queue:

1. Displaying the print queue. The print queue is a list of jobs that have been sent to be printed. You can take a look at the print queue and see the names of jobs queued for processing and the order in which the jobs will be processed.

2. Canceling a print job. If you have sent a document to print and you decide not to print it, you can cancel the document from the queue. You can also cancel a document which is already printing.

3. Changing the order of the print jobs in the queue. You can change the order in which the documents are queued to print. For example, the document that is last on the print queue may be the one you want to print next. You can change the priority of the documents by managing the print queue.

The Foreground Processing for Print screen displays when a document is being printed or converted. This is the only time that you can display a queue, cancel a print job from the queue, or change the order of print jobs in the queue.

DISPLAYING QUEUE OR CANCELING PRINT JOBS

Read Steps 1-5. The steps to display queue or cancel print jobs are illustrated in Figures 5.3 - 5.5.

1. Press Ctrl--Break. This temporarily suspends print processing.
   The Print Tasks Menu will display.

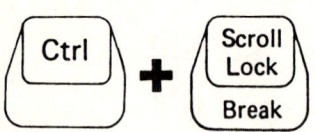 

    Figure 5.3   Ctrl--Break   Figure 5.4   Print Tasks

2. Select Display Queue or Cancel Print Job. The Display Queue or
   Cancel Print Job Menu will display.

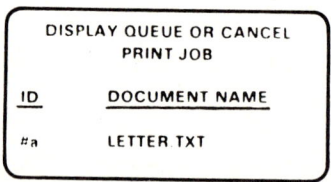

    Figure 5.5   Display Queue or Cancel Print Job Menu

The characters #a appear on the left of the document currently being processed. If you are displaying this menu to confirm that a document is in the queue, and it is, press Enter to resume processing.

3. If you wish to cancel a job, follow the prompt to type the ID letter of the job you wish to cancel.

4. Press Enter. The job you selected is canceled and removed from the queue. Repeat Steps 3 and 4 if there are additional jobs in the queue that you wish to cancel.

5. When you have canceled all of the jobs you want, press Enter.

   The Foreground Processing for Print screen displays. It will remain on the screen until all documents in the queue have been converted or printed. Then the Text Task Selection Menu will display.

ADDING JOBS TO THE QUEUE

1. Press Ctrl--Break. This temporarily suspends printing. The Print Tasks Menu will display.

2. Select Print Document.

3. Continue with the printing process. If you have forgotten how, refer back to Chapter 1. You can have up to ten jobs in the print queue at one time.

CHANGING THE PRINT JOB ORDER

1. Press Ctrl--Break. The Print Tasks Menu will display.

2. Select Change Print Job Order. The Change Print Job Order Menu will display. The characters #a appear to the left of the document currently being processed.

3. Follow the prompt to type the ID letter of the document you want to be processed next.

4. Press Enter. The document you chose will be processed after the document currently being processed is completed.

EXERCISE 16

Exercise 16 will give you practice in adding documents to the print queue and canceling print jobs in the print queue. You will be sending the document b:VisitLA to the printer. You will interrupt the printing process to add another document to the print queue. Once printing resumes, you will again interrupt the printing process. This time you will cancel a print job.

PROCEDURES	COMMENTS
1. Select Print Document from the Text Task Selection Menu.	
2. The document name is b:VisitLA.	
3. Press Enter.	The Print Document Menu displays.
4. Press Enter. As soon as the document begins printing, perform Step 5.	The Foreground Processing for Print screen displays.
5. Press Ctrl--Break.	The Print Tasks Menu displays.
6. Choose Print Document.	
7. The document name is b:Stress.	
8. Press Enter.	The Print Document Menu displays.
9. Press Enter.	The Foreground Processing for Print screen displays.
	Continued

Chapter 5 Printing

PROCEDURES (Continued)	COMMENTS (Continued)
10. Press Ctrl--Break.	The Print Tasks Menu displays.
11. Choose Display Queue or Cancel Print Job.	The Display Queue or Cancel Print Job Menu displays.
12. Type b.	This is to cancel b:Stress.
13. Press Enter.	The document b:Stress is removed from the print queue.
14. Press Enter.	The printing resumes.
15. Pick up the document at the printer.	

STEPS FOR DISPLAYWRITE 3 BACKGROUND PRINTING

Note: You must have at least 320K memory to perform DisplayWrite 3 Background Printing.

1. In the Text Task Selection Menu, select Print Document.

2. Press Enter.

3. Type the name of the document.

4. Press Enter. The Print Document Menu will display.

5. To change to DisplayWrite 3 Background Print, type f to choose Change Print Options.

6. The Print Options Menu will appear on the screen.

7. Type d to choose Processing Mode.

8. Press Enter.

9. Type 3 to choose Background Print.

10. Press Enter.

11. Follow the prompt to press Enter.

12. The document will begin printing, and the Text Task Selection Menu will appear on the screen so that you may continue with another task.

    Note: The printer may slow or stop while you make your selection.

MANAGING THE BACKGROUND PRINT QUEUE

ADDING JOBS TO THE PRINT QUEUE

1. When the Text Task Selection Menu displays on your screen, select Print Document.

2. The Print Tasks Menu will display on your screen. Type a to choose Print Document. Type the document name and press Enter.

3. Follow the prompts to press Enter.

DISPLAYING THE PRINT QUEUE OR CANCELING PRINT JOBS

1. From the Text Task Selection Menu, choose Print Document. The Print Tasks Menu will display.

2. Select Display Queue or Cancel Print Job and press Enter.

3. The Display Queue or Cancel Print Job Menu displays on the screen. The characters #a appear on the left of the document currently being processed. If you are displaying this menu to confirm that a document is in the queue, and it is, press Enter to resume processing.

CHANGING THE PRINT JOB ORDER

1. In the Text Task Selection Menu, select Print Document. The Print Tasks Menu will display.

2. Select Change Print Job Order and press Enter. The Change Print Job Order Menu displays. The characters #a appear to the left of the document currently being processed.

3. Follow the prompt to type the ID letter of the document you want to be processed next.

4. Press Enter. The document you chose will be processed after the document currently being processed is completed.

EXERCISE 17

Note: You must have at least 320K memory to perform this exercise.

PROCEDURES	COMMENTS
1. Select Print Document in the Text Task Selection Menu.	
2. Enter the document name, b:Stress.txt, and press Enter.	The Print Document Menu will display on the screen.

Continued

Chapter 5 Printing

PROCEDURES (Continued)	COMMENTS (Continued)
3. Type **f** to select the Change Print Options Menu.	This will take you to the Change Print Options Menu.
4. Type **d** to select Processing Mode. Type **3** for Background Print, and press Enter.	
5. Follow the prompt to press Enter.	The Text Task Selection Menu will appear on the screen as the document begins printing.
6. Select Create Document in the Text Task Selection Menu.	The printer may slow or stop as you make your selection.
7. Type the document name, b:Backgrnd.txt. Press Enter twice to bring the typing page to the screen.	
8. Type the following text: **With DisplayWrite 3 Background Print, I can create or revise a document while another is at the printer.**	
9. Press F2 to end the document.	
10. Print the document.	

CHAPTER SUMMARY

A. Changes can be made to the Print Document Menu and the Printer Description Menu to change the way a document will print.

B. Displaying the Print Queue or Canceling a Print Job

　　1. Press Ctrl--Break.
　　2. Select Display Queue or Cancel Print Job.
　　3. If you wish to cancel a job, follow the prompt to type the ID letter of the job you wish to cancel and press Enter.
　　4. Press Enter again.

C. Adding Jobs to the Queue

　　1. Press Ctrl--Break.
　　2. Select Print Document.
　　3. Type the name of the document.
　　4. Press Enter.

      5. Make any necessary changes to the Print Document Menu.
      6. Press Enter.

D. Changing the Print Job Order

      1. Press Ctrl--Break.
      2. Select Change Print Job Order.
      3. Type the ID letter of the document you want processed next.
      4. Press Enter.

E. Steps for DisplayWrite 3 Background Printing

      1. In the Text Task Selection Menu, select Print Document.
      2. Press Enter.
      3. Type the name of the document.
      4. Press Enter. The Print Document Menu will display.
      5. To change to DisplayWrite 3 Background Print, type f to choose Change Print Options.
      6. The Print Options Menu will appear on the screen.
      7. Type d to choose Processing Mode.
      8. Press Enter.
      9. Type 3 to choose Background Print.
    10. Press Enter.
    11. Follow the prompt to press Enter.
    12. The document will begin printing, and the Text Task Selection Menu will appear on the screen so that you may continue with another task.

Chapter 6

PAGINATION

When you complete this chapter, you will be able to:

1. Insert a Page End code manually.

2. Explain a decimal system page number.

3. Instruct the system to perform Automatic Pagination.

4. Use Prompted and Automatic Dictionary Hyphenation in conjunction with Automatic Pagination.

5. Insert a Required Page End code in a document.

INTRODUCTION

When you are typing documents that are longer than one page, you need to take into consideration pagination. Pagination is deciding where to end the pages. In most cases, you will want to divide a document into even-sized pages.

The system uses the menu choices you made for page format, line format, and margins and tabs in your Document Format to define page size. Figure 6.1 shows an example of an even-sized page using the system defaults.

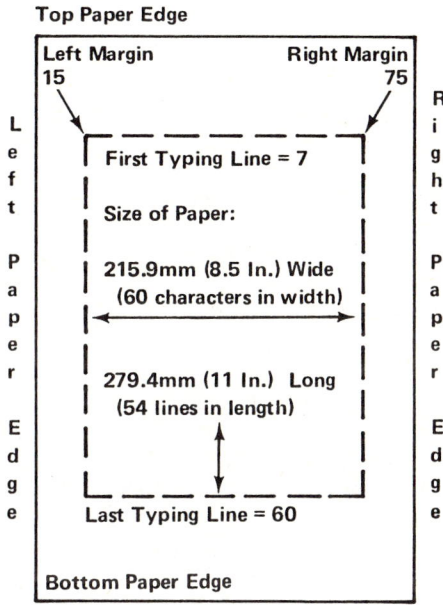

Figure 6.1   System Defaults

There are two methods which can be used for pagination:

1. Manual Pagination is when you insert Page End codes manually while you are creating a document.

2. Automatic Pagination is when the system automatically paginates a document for you after you request that this be done in the Paginate Document Menu.

MANUAL PAGINATION

As you create a document in the typing area, the Page End code always appears at the right of the word you are typing. This Page End code ▲ is provided by the system and will always end the last page of your document. If you have a multiple-page document, you will need a Page End code at the bottom of each page. With Manual Pagination, you will need to insert the Page End code where you want the page to end.

To insert a Page End code manually, press the Ctrl key and the Page End key (the Page End key is the "E" key) simultaneously.

Chapter 6   Pagination

Pressing Ctrl--Page End does the following:

--Inserts a Page End code.
--Stores that page.
--Displays a blank screen for typing the next page.
--Increases the page number on the status line.

Note: These page endings are temporary and can be rearranged by Automatic Pagination. This will be discussed later in the chapter.

STEPS FOR MANUALLY INSERTING PAGE END CODES

When you are creating a document and you are approaching the end of your page, you will hear a "beep" noise. The beep indicates that you are on the last typing line on the page. Once you hear the beep, you should look at your status line. The status line will display Ln. 60 if you are using the system defaults.

Occasionally, you may see Ln. 61 displayed on the status line as the last typing line. You might see this if your document is triple-spaced and line 60 happens to be one of the blank lines between your lines of typing. Follow the steps for manually inserting Page End codes.

1. The system beeps and your status line indicates Ln. 60.

2. Press Ctrl--Page End. This inserts a Page End code to end the page on the screen and takes you to the top of a new page on the screen (see Figures 6.2 and 6.3).

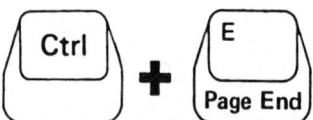

Figure 6.2 Ctrl--Page End

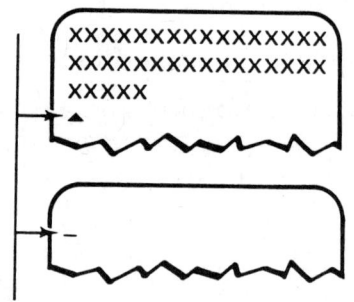

Figure 6.3 Page End Code

3. Type the next page of the document.

4. Repeat Steps 2 and 3 for each page (except for the last page).

5. Press End Task to store the last page and end the document. The Text Task Selection Menu displays so that you can choose another task.

MANUAL PAGINATION AND SYSTEM PAGE NUMBERS

When you create or revise a document, the system assigns page numbers which display on the status line in the typing area of a document.

System page numbers are usually whole numbers (for example: 1, 2, and 3). Occasionally, you may see a decimal system page number (for example, Pg. 1.1) on the status line. This happens if, during revision, you insert an additional page between page 1 and page 2. The system sees the additional text as a new page and assigns 1.1 as its system page number. The system assigns decimal system page numbers between previously defined page numbers to ensure that no subsequent page numbers are affected. Automatic Pagination renumbers pages to whole numbers. This will be discussed later in this chapter.

Let us take a look at an example where you might encounter a decimal system page number. You recall an existing two-page document to the screen and make revisions to it. Your revisions require that you add two more paragraphs to page 1. Page 1 is now longer than 60 lines, so you move your cursor down the page until you reach line 60 and then press Ctrl--Page End.

As Figure 6.4 illustrates, by pressing Ctrl--Page End at this point, the Page End code does the following:

--Ends the page at that
  point on the screen.
--Displays the rest of the
  original page at the top
  of the screen.
--Shows a decimal system
  page number (Pg. 1.1) on
  the status line.

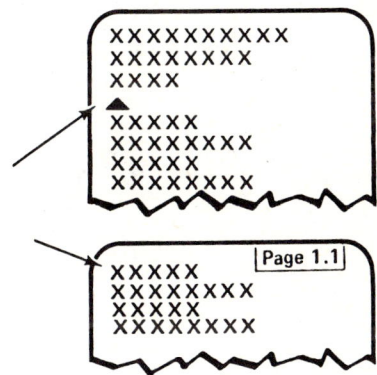

Figure 6.4   Decimal System Page Number

EXERCISE 18

Exercise 18 will give you practice in revising a two-page document by changing the document format and manually inserting a Page End code.

PROCEDURES	COMMENTS
1. Choose Revise Document from the Text Task Selection Menu.	
2. Type b:Exercil4.	This is to revise the document b:Exercil4.
3. Press Enter.	The Create or Revise Document Menu displays.
4. Type b and press Enter.	The Document or Alternate Format Menu displays.

Continued

Chapter 6   Pagination

PROCEDURES (Continued)	COMMENTS (Continued)
5. Type a and press Enter.	The Line Format Menu displays.
6. Type a and press Enter.	This is to change Line Spacing.
7. Type 3 and press Enter.	This is to choose triple-spacing.
8. Press Enter.	The Format Selection Menu displays.
9. Press Enter.	This returns you to the Create or Revise Document Menu.
10. Press Enter.	Your document is displayed on the screen.
11. Press the down arrow key to move the cursor down the screen until you hear a "beep" noise.	The "beep" lets you know that you have reached your last typing line. Your status line should indicate that you are on line 61.
12. Press Ctrl--Page End (Ctrl--E).	Page 2 is brought to the screen with the last three lines of the exercise on it.
13. Press F2.	This will end the task.
14. Print a copy of this document.	

EXERCISE 19

You will be recalling Exerci14 to the screen and adding some text to page 1. You will find that after adding the text, page 1 will be longer than 60 lines as established in the system format default. This will require that you again manually paginate page 1. After doing this, you will find that the system will place the remainder of page 1 on a new page with a decimal system page number. In Exercise 20, you will use Automatic Pagination to convert the document page numbers to whole numbers.

PROCEDURES	COMMENTS
1. Recall Exerci14 to the screen.	
2. Place the cursor under the first letter of the first paragraph.	Your screen should look like this: The following tips ...

Continued

Chapter 6 Pagination

PROCEDURES (Continued)	COMMENTS (Continued)
3. You will be adding the following text to the beginning of the first paragraph. Type: **Selecting paper for the computer can be a very cumbersome task. If you were to browse through the aisles of a computer supply store, you would notice reams of continuous feed paper, individual sheet paper, paper of various weights and colors, and even some with carbons.**	
4. Move the cursor to the left edge of the screen.	Use the left arrow key to do this.
5. Use the down arrow key to move the cursor down the screen. Stop when you hear the beep.	Your status line should show that you are on Ln. 61.
6. Press Ctrl--Page End (Ctrl--E).	The remainder of page 1 now appears at the top of Pg. 1.1.
7. Press Ctrl--End.	The prompt "Type page number; press ENTER:" appears.
8. Type 2 and press Enter.	Page 2 appears on the screen in its original form as was created in Exercise 18.
9. Press F2.	This will end the task.

AUTOMATIC PAGINATION

When creating or revising a document, you can ask the system to paginate the document for you automatically. You may even use Automatic Pagination in addition to Manual Pagination in a document. An example of when this would need to be done is illustrated in Figure 6.5.

Text was added to page 1, making the page longer than is desired according to the document format. The revisions made to page 2 involved deleting some text, which resulted in the Page End code now being halfway up the page. This document needs to be paginated automatically by the system. During Automatic Pagination, the system will rearrange the page endings to fit within the specified document format. The previous Page End codes that were inserted with Manual Pagination will be rearranged to even out the pages. Figure 6.6 shows how the same document will look after Automatic Pagination.

Automatic Pagination takes place after you are finished creating or revising the document. You then will request Paginate Document from the Text Task Selection Menu. Once you request Paginate Document, the Paginate Document Menu will display on your screen as shown in Figure 6.7. Let us take a look at the menu.

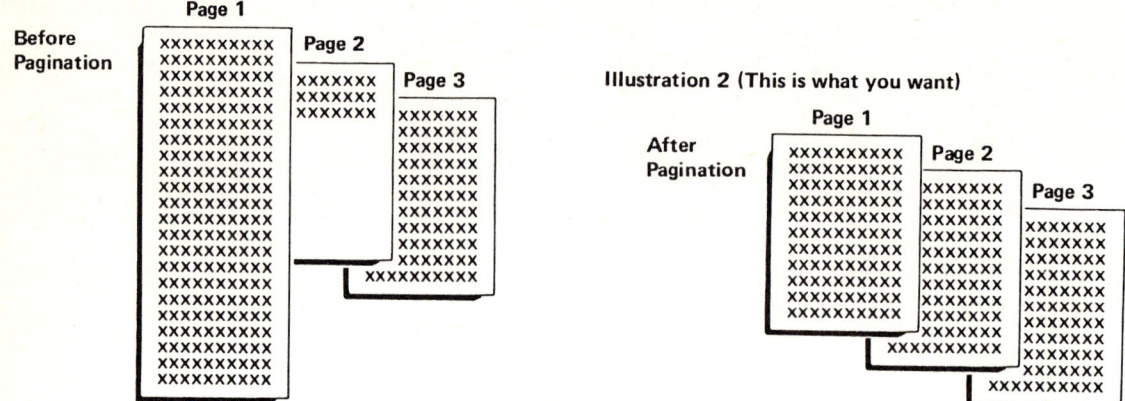

Figure 6.5   Before Pagination   Figure 6.6   After Pagination

```
                    PAGINATE DOCUMENT

                             YOUR      POSSIBLE
     ID   ITEM               CHOICE    CHOICES

     a    Paginate From Page    1      1 – 5

     b    Paginate on Exact Line  2    1 = Yes    2 = No
          Count

     c    Adjust Line Endings   1      1 = Yes    2 = No

     d    Adjust Page Endings   1      1 = Yes    2 = No

     e    Dictionary Hyphenation  3    1 = Prompted  2 = Automatic
                                       3 = None

     When finished with this menu, press ENTER.

     Type ID letter to choose ITEM; press ENTER: ¤
```

Figure 6.7   Paginate Document Menu

Paginate From Page indicates the system page number where pagination begins. Pagination begins with this number that you choose and continues to the end of the document. The choices range from the first to the last page of the document. The default is set to start pagination at the first page. If you want to start pagination at another page, make your choice to reflect the page number on which you want pagination to begin.

Paginate on Exact Line Count requires that you choose "Yes" if you must have exactly the same number of lines on each page. There is a typing rule which states that if you need to divide a paragraph between two pages, you must leave at least two lines on the first page and carry at least two lines to the second page. If you tell the system to paginate on exact line count, it may leave one line of a paragraph at the end of a page; this is called a widow line. The default choice of "No" tells the system to avoid widow lines.

Adjust Line Endings indicates whether line endings are rearranged during pagination. If you choose "Yes," pagination automatically adjusts line endings to fit evenly within the margins. Choose "No" for a document in which pages must end exactly as you typed them.

Dictionary Hyphenation determines whether or not hyphenation decisions are made at the right margin. The default is "None." If you use the default, no words will be hyphenated at the right margin. If you choose "Automatic," the system will insert a syllable hyphen automatically at the correct dictionary hyphenation point to break a long word at the right margin. If you wish to make your own decisions for each case, choose "Prompted." Both Automatic and Prompted Dictionary Hyphenation give you a more even right margin. We will discuss Prompted Dictionary Hyphenation later in this chapter.

Read Steps 1-6. The steps to paginate a document automatically are illustrated in Figures 6.8 - 6.12.

1. After you have finished revising or creating a document, press F2 to store the document.

2. Choose Paginate Document in the Text Task Selection Menu.

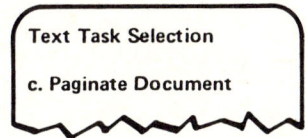

Figure 6.8   Text Task Selection Menu

3. Type the letter of the drive which contains the document you want to paginate, followed by a colon and the document name.

Figure 6.9   Type Document Name Prompt

4. Press Enter. The Paginate Document Menu is displayed on the screen.

5. Make any changes necessary in the Paginate Document Menu. You can use all of the default choices or make other choices in the menu.

6. Press Enter to begin pagination.

   "Paginating Document" appears on the status line. As the system paginates through a multi-page document, the page number on the status line changes.

Figure 6.10
Paginating Document

Chapter 6   Pagination

A message displays when the document has been paginated. The system then returns to the Text Task Selection Menu so you can choose another task.

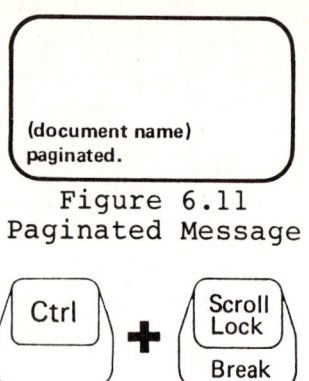

Figure 6.11 Paginated Message

Note: If you have started paginating a document and do not wish to finish, press Ctrl--Break. This stops pagination. The Text Task Selection Menu displays so you can choose another task.

Figure 6.12 Ctrl--Break

EXERCISE 20

In Exercise 19 you recalled the document entitled Exercil4 to the screen, added some text to page 1, and manually paginated page 1 again. This placed the extra lines from page 1 onto page 1.1. We will now use Automatic Pagination to even out the pages and convert all page numbers to whole numbers (as shown in Figure 6.13).

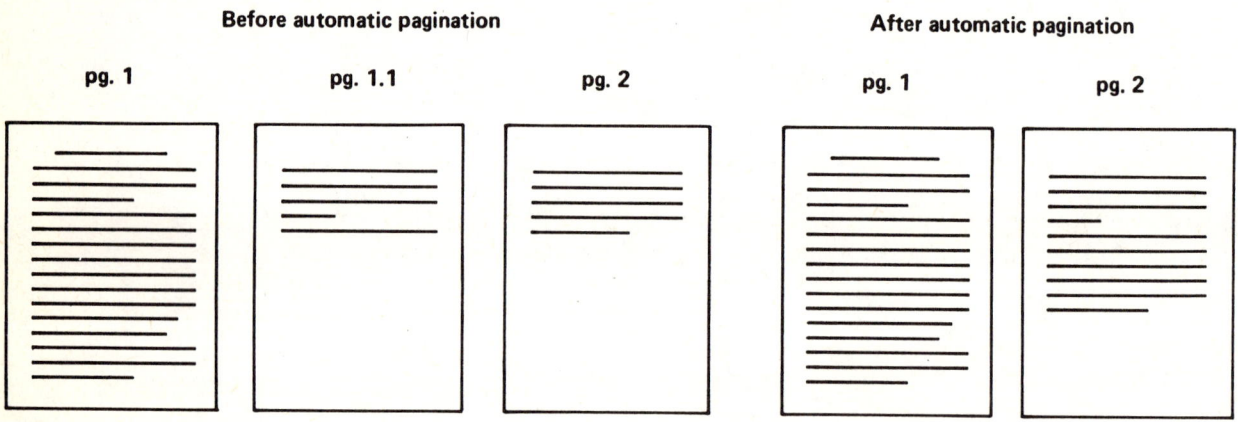

Figure 6.13 Before and After Automatic Pagination

PROCEDURES	COMMENTS
1. The Text Task Selection Menu should be displayed on the screen.	
2. Type c and press Enter.	This is to choose Paginate Document.

Continued

PROCEDURES (Continued)

3. When the prompt "Type document name; press ENTER:" displays, type b:Exerci14 and press Enter.

4. Press Enter.

5. Print the document. It should look like Figure 6.14.

COMMENTS (Continued)

The Paginate Document Menu displays.

This is to accept all of the defaults. The Text Task Selection Menu appears on the screen with the prompt "(B:EXERCI14.TXT) paginated." appearing at the bottom.

DICTIONARY HYPHENATION

The default for Dictionary Hyphenation in the Paginate Document Menu is "None." If you do not want words hyphenated at the right margin, use the default. Automatic or Prompted Dictionary Hyphenation will divide long words at the end of the line, giving you a more even right margin.

With Automatic Dictionary Hyphenation, the system inserts a syllable hyphen at the correct dictionary hyphenation point. The system makes all hyphenation decisions for you.

However, you may want to have the more even right margin that is provided by Dictionary Hyphenation, and make your own decisions about where the words are hyphenated. In this case, you would choose Prompted hyphenation. With Prompted Dictionary Hyphenation, the system shows you the point of hyphenation according to the DisplayWrite 3 dictionary. You can either accept or change this hyphenation point.

Note: The Dictionary Program is on a separate dictionary diskette. Your copy of the dictionary diskette (Vol. 4) must be in disk drive A when you choose Automatic or Prompted Dictionary Hyphenation.

Read Steps 1-6. Steps in using Prompted Dictionary Hyphenation are illustrated in Figures 6.15 and 6.16.

1. Choose Paginate Document in the Text Task Selection Menu.

2. Type the letter of the drive which contains the document you want to paginate, followed by a colon and the document name.

3. Press Enter to display the Paginate Document Menu.

4. Choose Prompted Dictionary Hyphenation. You must insert the dictionary program disk in drive A.

Chapter 6 Pagination

SELECTING PAPER FOR THE COMPUTER

Selecting paper for the computer can be a very cumbersome task. If you were to browse through the aisles of a computer supply store, you would notice reams of continuous feed paper, individual sheet paper, paper of various weights and colors, and even some with carbons. The following tips for better paper selection are especially helpful to minicomputer users:

On printouts, if the e's look like c's, the b's become f's, or 8's are seen as 3's, the cause may be the use of multipart carbon interleaved forms. <u>Carbonless forms</u> cut the bulk of a multipart form nearly in half,

making it easier for the printer head to make

sharp impressions on duplicate copies.

When possible, use continuous forms

rather than single-sheet paper.

Buy quality for economy. High-quality

paper forms reduce downtime due to jams and

tearing, will not yellow or fade, accept ink

without bleeding, and minimize paper dust in

a printer.

Figure 6.14   Exercise 20 Printout

5. Press Enter to begin pagination.

6. The prompt "Hyphenate where?" will appear on the screen each time there is a word to be hyphenated.

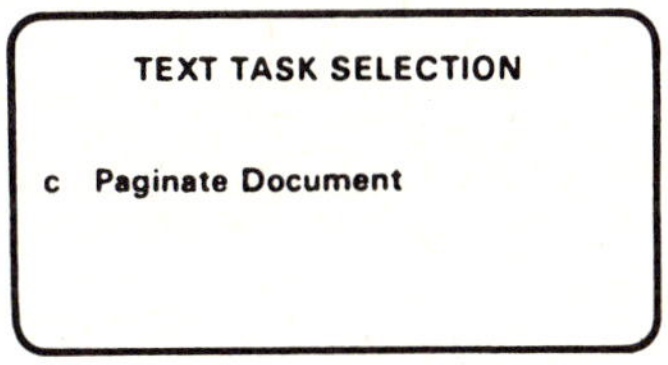

```
TEXT TASK SELECTION

c  Paginate Document
```

Figure 6.15   Text Task Selection Menu

You then make a hyphenation decision using *one* of the following procedures:

- To accept the system's point of hyphenation, press Enter.

- To change the system's point of hyphenation, place the cursor where you want the hyphen to be and press Enter.

- To move the entire word to the next line, place the cursor under the first character of the word, and press Enter.

- To keep the entire word on the *same* line, place the cursor one space *past* the last character of the word, and press Enter.

When the document has been paginated, you receive a message.

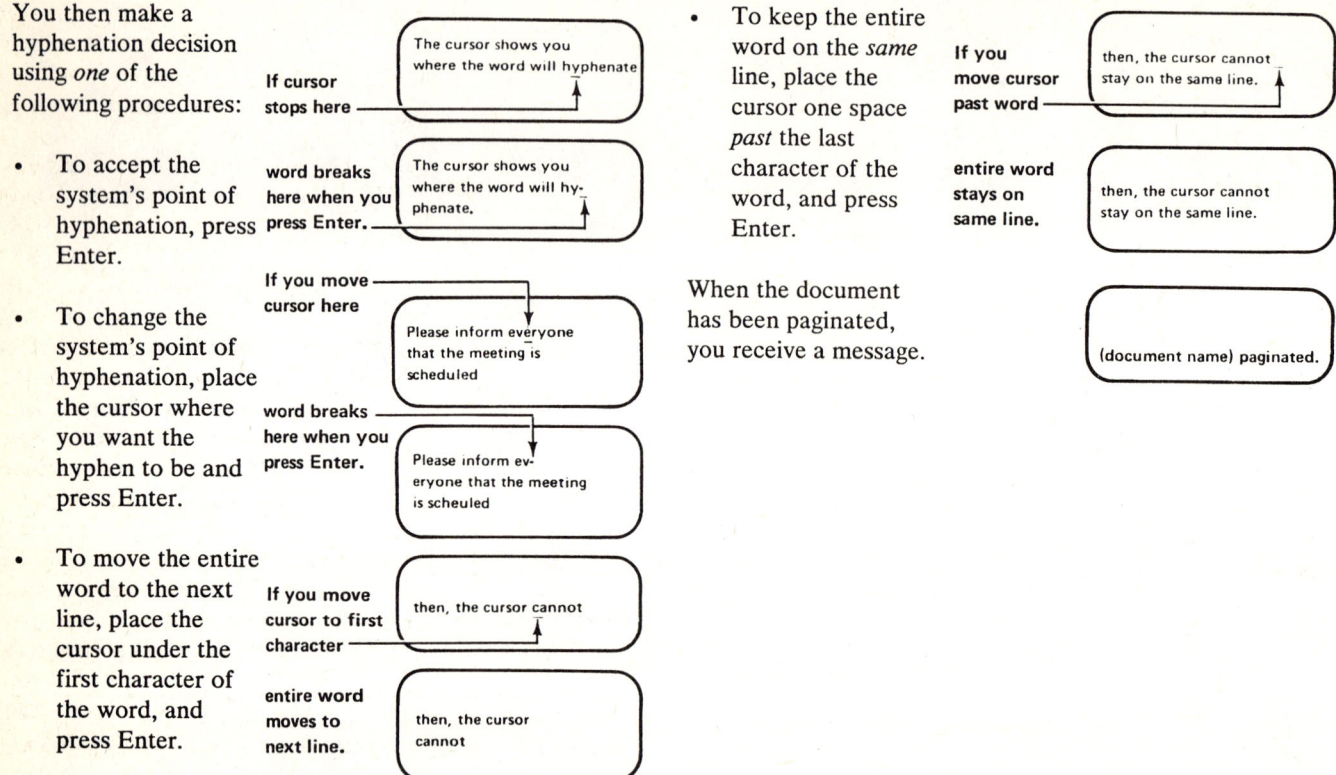

Figure 6.16   Hyphenation Decision Procedures

EXERCISE 21

Exercise 21 will require that you recall the exercise entitled b:Eating to the screen and make some format changes to this document. After the format changes have been made, you will need to paginate the document and request prompted hyphenation.

PROCEDURES	COMMENTS
1. Select Revise Document from the Text Task Selection Menu.	
2. When the prompt asks for the document name, type b:Eating and press Enter.	The Create or Revise Document Menu is displayed.
3. Type b and press Enter.	The Document or Alternate Format Menu is displayed.
4. Type b and press Enter.	The Margins and Tabs Menu is displayed.

Continued

PROCEDURES (Continued)	COMMENTS (Continued)
5. Change the left margin to 20.	Press the space bar until << is on 2.
6. Change the right margin to 70.	Place the cursor on >> and backspace to 7.
7. Press Enter.	The Document or Alternate Format Menu is displayed.
8. Press Enter.	The Create or Revise Document Menu is displayed.
9. Press Enter.	The document is displayed. The new center point would be 45 due to the new margins. Delete seven spaces from the left of the main heading to make it centered.
10. Press F2.	This is to store the document.
11. Select Paginate Document from the Text Task Selection Menu.	
12. A prompt asks for the document name. "B:EATING.TXT" already should be on the screen.	The system assumes that you want to paginate the document you just revised.
13. Press Enter.	The Paginate Document Menu is displayed.
14. Type e and press Enter.	This is to change Dictionary Hyphenation.
15. Type 1.	This is to choose prompted hyphenation.
16. Press Enter.	
17. Insert the dictionary disk (Vol. 4) in drive A and press Enter.	
18. Make hyphenation decisions as they are presented to you on the screen.	When the document has been paginated, you will receive a message.
19. Print the document. It should look like Figure 6.17.	Remember to remove the dictionary disk and put in the Vol. 2 disk.

Chapter 6 Pagination   89

SENSIBLE EATING CAN BE DELICIOUS

Its obvious pleasures aside, the family dinner table is filled with all kinds of hidden benefits. The family that eats well is generally healthier and happier, filled with energy and a sense of well-being.

The National Research Council's Recommended Daily Dietary Allowance for Protein for Healthy Adults is 0.9 grams per day for each 2.2 pounds of body weight.

A balanced diet is the key to good eating habits. Unfortunately, to many people the term "diet" brings an immediate image of "reducing diet" or "ulcer diet" or some other punishing regime. This is not true. A balanced diet is the daily selection of a variety of foods that fulfills the body's needs for essential nutrients such as proteins, carbohydrates, fats, vitamins, minerals, and water.

FATS

A word about fats. All fats are not alike. Most Americans eat too much of the "wrong" kind of fat. Saturated fat tends to increase the level of cholesterol in the blood. The "right" kind of fat is polyunsaturated fat which tends to lower the level of blood cholesterol. A diet providing more of the "right" kind of fat is vital for good health.

PROTEINS

Protein is the chief organic part of all muscle, gland and nerve tissue, and of blood. It plays a significant role in the fluid balance of the body. Proteins are indispensable and normal parts of almost every living cell.

The human body is a biological machine. It has to be nourished properly and cared for to work smoothly and efficiently. What you eat can make the difference between feeding your body correctly or incorrectly.

FATS

A word about fats. All fats are not alike. Most Americans eat too much of the "wrong" kind of fat. Saturated fat tends to increase the level of cholesterol in the blood. The "right" kind of fat is polyunsaturated fat which tends to lower the level of blood cholesterol. A diet providing more of the "right" kind of fat is vital for good health.

Figure 6.17   Exercise 21 Printout

REQUIRED PAGE END

The section on Manual Pagination described how to insert Page End codes in a document by pressing Ctrl--Page End. These Page End codes can be rearranged during Automatic Pagination.

Sometimes, though, you will want a page to end at a particular place, regardless of the length of the page. Some examples would be:

--Title pages
--Last page of a section or chapter
--Table of Contents
--Bibliography
--Reference pages

You can instruct the system to always end a page where you want by entering a Required Page End code. They are called required because the system will not move them during Automatic Pagination.

STEPS FOR INSERTING REQUIRED PAGE END CODES WHILE CREATING A DOCUMENT

Read Steps 1-4. The steps for inserting Required Page End codes are illustrated in Figures 6.18 - 6.20.

1. After you have finished typing the last line on the page, return the carriage once.

2. Press Instr (F8).

3. Choose Req_page_end. This forces a permanent page ending during Automatic Pagination. The Required Page End code does not display a new screen for typing the next page; it only moves you down one line on the screen. If you want to display a new screen for typing the next page, go on to Step 4.

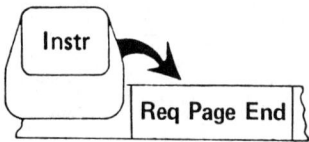

Figure 6.18   Required Page End

4. Press Ctrl--Page End.

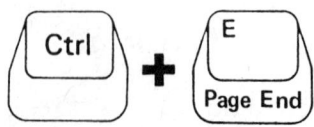

Figure 6.19   Ctrl--Page End

During Automatic Pagination, the system ends pages at the last typing line or at a Required Page End code--whichever occurs first.

A page ending created with the combination of a Required Page End code and a Page End code will end a page with or without Automatic Pagination.

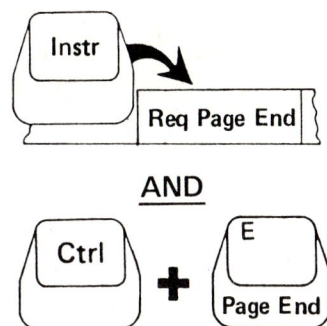

Figure 6.20 Required Page End and Page End Codes

STEPS FOR INSERTING REQUIRED PAGE END CODES DURING REVISION OF A DOCUMENT

1. Place the cursor where you want the permanent page ending to occur during Automatic Pagination and printing.

2. Press Instr (F8).

3. Choose Req_page_end. Remember, this only moves you down one line on the screen. It does not display a blank screen.

   Note: You must use Automatic Pagination to ensure that these Required Page End codes are honored.

STEPS FOR DELETING REQUIRED PAGE END CODES DURING REVISION OF A DOCUMENT

1. Place the cursor under the Required Page End code you want to delete.

2. Press Del to delete the Required Page End code.

   There is no need to delete Page End codes. These will be rearranged during Automatic Pagination to conform to the document format.

EXERCISE 22

In Exercise 22, you will recall the document b:VisitLA to the screen. First you will ask the system to make a search and replace in the document. Then you will add a Reference Page and use a Required Page End code to instruct the system that this page should always be by itself. Then you will paginate the document to see how the system honors a Required Page End code.

PROCEDURES	COMMENTS
1. Recall the document b:VisitLA to the screen.	
2. Press F6.	The prompt line choices display.
3. Type S.	This is to choose Search/Replace. The Search/Replace Menu displays.
4. Type c and press Enter.	
5. Type L.A. and press Enter.	This tells the system to search for L.A.
6. Type d and press Enter.	
7. Type Los Angeles.	This tells the system to replace with Los Angeles.
8. Press Enter.	The Search/Replace is performed by the system.
9. Press Ctrl--Go To (Ctrl--End).	The prompt "Type page number; press ENTER:" displays
10. Type 3 and press Enter.	Page 3 is displayed.
11. Press the End key.	This moves your cursor to the end of the page.
12. Press Instr (F8).	The prompt line choices display.
13. Type R.	This is to select Req_page_end.
14. Press Ctrl--Page End (Ctrl--E).	A new typing page, Pg. 4, is displayed.
15. Type the following:	

   Appreciation is expressed for the help of American Tours Corporation in the preparation of the report, portions of which are drawn from its publication <u>Tours of U.S.A.</u>, Tenth Edition, June, 1984.

16. Press F2.	This is to store the document; the Text Task Selection Menu displays.
17. Select Paginate Document.	

Continued

PROCEDURES (Continued)	COMMENTS (Continued)
18. When the prompt asks for the document name, press Enter since the name of the document already displays.	The Paginate Document Menu displays.
19. Press Enter.	This will accept all defaults in the Paginate Document Menu.
20. Print a copy of the document. Your printout should look like Figure 6.21.	This should be a four-page document, with the Reference Page being page 4.

VISITING LOS ANGELES

Today's TV image of Los Angeles is set by the westside--the broad shady streets of Beverly Hills, the Rolls-lined sidewalks of Rodeo Drive, and the pool-studded homes in the hills above Sunset Boulevard. For much of the world, the "good life" in America has become synonymous with the elegance of places like Beverly Hills, Brentwood, and Westwood. This is where the stars live--and most of the affluent in Los Angeles county.

POINTS OF INTEREST

Star-gazing is very popular in Los Angeles, and there are a number of tours that will guide you past the homes of the stars.

Westwood is the home of the University of California at Los Angeles and the spot where most of Hollywood's new films open. Westwood is a spirited college town with a gala of theaters, bookshops, clothing stores, and restaurants.

WINING AND DINING

The influx of young, ambitious, and creative chefs and restaurateurs have found in Los Angeles an eager clientele to challenge their talents. Because dining in Los Angeles is an important part of the social life, restaurants tend to be exciting and imaginative as well as intensely competitive in the quality of their cooking.

La Cienega's Restaurant Row still illustrates some of the diversity of Los Angeles eating. From Lawry's Prime Rib and Gitanjali's award-winning Indian fare to Benihana's chef floor show, every nationality and taste sensation is represented within a few blocks between Wilshire and San Vicente.

NIGHTLIFE

When people speak of the nightlife in Los Angeles, it is usually the westside's haunts that do the attracting. In Beverly Hills, you can spend a wonderful evening just window-shopping along the streets. This is one of the few neighborhoods in Los Angeles besides Westwood where walking is the main form of transportation.

The scene in Century City is also for walkers but is more sedate. All the restaurants have lovely saloons for the after-theater crowd. In Los Angeles, theaters, movie houses, and the famous Shubert Theatre are all found here on the west side.

THE CITIES OF THE HARBOR

The big, bustling, side-by-side harbors of Los Angeles and Long Beach were, like much of Los Angeles, the product of much sweat and hard work rather than gifts of nature. Today, two harbors constitute the shipping hub of the Pacific Coast, moving more than 125,000 tons of cargo daily along miles of dock that can berth 100 ships. San Pedro, annexed by Los Angeles to gain a seaport, lies at the gateway to the Los Angeles Harbor and forms the western tip of the harbor area crescent. The entire harbor area is married to the sea, and the tourists who come to make use of the harbors' recreation are as critical to the region's economy as fishing and shipping.

Long Beach is the home of the world's largest passenger ship, the Queen Mary, and the world's largest passenger wooden airplane, the Spruce Goose. Long Beach has undergone a dramatic, multimillion-dollar redevelopment program, revitalizing its downtown area and marina to brighten the drab-faced oil and shipping industries.

DISNEYLAND AND KNOTT'S BERRY FARM

For those who are young at heart and possessed with boundless energy, Orange County is an amusement-park paradise. Disneyland is, of course, the crowning jewel. Founded in almost the exact center of Southern California, Disneyland lies 25 miles south of downtown Los Angeles and 15 miles inland from Newport Beach. In the Magic Kingdom, everyone is a child.

Located in Buena Park is Knott's Berry Farm. Knott's Berry Farm carries the Old West motif and is noted for its chicken dinners. One would certainly not leave Los Angeles without visiting Disneyland and Knott's Berry Farm.

Appreciation is expressed for the help of American Tours Corporation in the preparation of the report, portions of which are drawn from its publication <u>Tours of U.S.A.</u>, Tenth Edition, June, 1984.

Figure 6.21   Exercise 22 Printout

CHAPTER SUMMARY

A. Inserting a Page End Code Manually

   1. Type to the position where you want the page to end.
   2. Press Ctrl--Page End.
   3. A new page is brought to the screen.

B. Using Pagination Features

   1. The system assigns a page number to each page of the document you create.
   2. The system assigns decimal system page numbers between previously defined page numbers.

C. Paginating a Document Automatically

   1. Choose Paginate Document in the Text Task Selection Menu.
   2. Type the name of the document and press Enter.
   3. Make the necessary changes in the Paginate Document Menu.
   4. Press Enter.

D. Using Prompted Dictionary Hyphenation

   1. Choose Paginate Document in the Text Task Selection Menu.
   2. Type the document name and press Enter.
   3. Choose Prompted Dictionary Hyphenation (Insert Dictionary Disk).
   4. Press Enter.
   5. Respond to prompts to hyphenate words.

E. Inserting a Required Page End Code

   1. After you have finished typing the last line on the page, return the carriage once. If you are revising a document, place the cursor where you want the permanent page ending to occur.
   2. Press Instr (F8).
   3. Choose Req_page_end.
   4. Press Ctrl--Page End.

Chapter 7
UTILITIES

When you complete this chapter, you will be able to:

1. Use the ? and * DOS global characters.

2. Check the directory and select a document from it.

3. Copy a document on the same diskette.

4. Copy a document to a different diskette.

5. Delete documents.

6. Rename a document.

7. Compress documents.

8. Recover documents.

9. Type with the Auto Carrier Return off.

10. Personalize text and work station defaults by creating, revising, and activating profiles.

11. Work with the DOS Command Task.

INTRODUCTION

You may have occasion to copy, delete, recover, or compress one or more documents. You may also wish to rename a document. These operations are called document utilities, and you will learn how to work with them in this chapter. You may also wish to change the defaults to personalize them. For example, the tabs and margins you use in your work may not be the same as the defaults. You can permanently change the defaults to meet your document needs. You will also learn how to check your work diskette to see the names and sizes of all of the documents contained on it.

You may think of most of these operations as maintaining a file drawer of documents (see Figure 7.1). Since your documents are kept on a diskette instead of in a file drawer, you need to do some "housekeeping" occasionally. For instance, you can weed out those documents that do not need to be saved anymore. Documents which have changed significantly in content can be renamed to reflect their subject matter more accurately. If you want to edit a document while keeping the original intact, the document can be copied electronically.

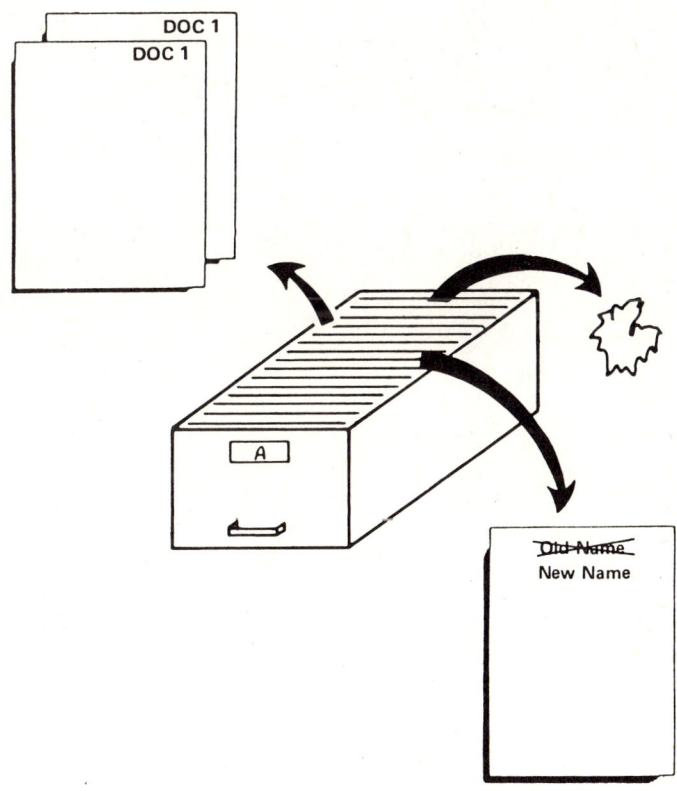

Figure 7.1   Document Utilities

Chapter 7   Utilities   101

DOS GLOBAL CHARACTERS

Time can be saved by using the DOS global characters * and ? when copying, deleting, and recovering documents. The global characters are basically substitutes for other characters that occur on either the right or left of the period which separates the extension from the rest of the document name. For example, if you wished to delete all documents with the extension of 84 (sales.84, acct.84, manufact.84), you could simply type *.84. The * stands for any characters, in this case, which occur before the period. If you wanted to copy documents from the accounting department but could not remember if the abbreviation was "act" or "atg," the system could be told to copy *.ac?.

CHECKING THE DIRECTORY

The directory can list all of the documents on your work diskette and give information about them, such as the name, extension, size, date, and time of creation. To view the "root," or main, directory from the Text Task Selection Menu, press F3. A prompt line will appear which offers you the choice of viewing the directory with or without document comments if you are searching for a specific document. It is recommended that you choose "with comments" so that you can see more information about your documents. To make this choice, press the right arrow to move the highlighting. At the prompt, "Type Document Specification; Press ENTER," type b:\ and Enter. You will be able to see your document names, the document comments (if you selected "with comments" from the prompt line choices), as well as the creation dates and times. A very important piece of information you will also see is the percentage of space left on the diskette. This will enable you to be sure that there is enough space available on your work diskette if you are going to copy a document. A quick glance at the directory will tell you if the disk is close to being full. The directory screen (with different document names) will look like Figure 7.2.

```
Displaying Directory

Drive: B              Available: 9 %         |Ext 340-B|
Directory:
ID   NAME        EXT    SIZE     DATE       TIME
a    OUTLINES    TXT    19456    01-01-80   00:18:16
b    OUTLINE     TXT    5120     01-01-80   00:02:28
c    CHNGLEVL    TXT    3072     01-01-80   10:20:08
d    SCHEDULE    TXT    7680     01-01-80   00:30:52
e    STATS       TXT    4096     01-01-80   00:24:24
f    DOCUMENT    SAC    3584     01-01-80   02:09:12
g    RAE         TXT    16904    01-01-80   04:12:18
h    POINTS      TXT    4096     01-01-80   00:36:16
i    REFUNDS     DIF    759      01-01-80   00:35:12
j    DOCASSEM    LEC    10240    01-01-80   01:53:48
k    DOCUMENT    TXT    3072     01-01-80   00:06:28
l    ORDER       WKS    1408     01-01-80   00:13:52
```

Figure 7.2 Directory

If you want to view the directory without comments, you will see a different screen. If you wish to limit your search, only certain documents may be listed on the screen. If you would like all of the documents with the extension of .TXT, type ***.TXT** and DisplayWrite 3 will list all of the documents with that extension regardless of the first eight characters. The ? will cause the system to ignore a single character in the name of the document. If you wanted to see documents starting with sales, typing **SALES?.TXT** would cause the system to list documents such as sales1.txt, sales2.txt, sales3.txt, and so on. If you are working with a hard disk, you should refer to the manual you received with your DisplayWrite 3 program to learn more about directories.

SELECTING A DOCUMENT FROM THE DIRECTORY

When the directory is on the screen, you can indicate to the system that you want to select a document from it. For instance, if you were about to revise a document and could not remember the name, viewing the directory would be a logical next step. While you are looking at the directory, you can type the ID letter of the document you want. The system will exit the directory and use the name of your chosen document. You will not have to type the name yourself. You can press F3 and take the steps to bring up the directory when you are in the Text Task Selection Menu or whenever you are prompted for a document name.

COPYING A DOCUMENT

When you want to revise a document and still leave an unaltered version on the disk, you can copy the document. Copying a document also compresses it. DisplayWrite 3 can copy DOS as well as DisplayWrite files. If you use the DOS global characters ? and * instead of letters, you can copy multiple documents or an entire directory. The most common use of multi-document copying is transferring documents onto a second disk. In a case where you have started copying more than one document and you must interrupt the copying process, just press Ctrl--Break.

EXERCISE 23

PROCEDURES	COMMENTS
1. Remove Volume 2 from drive A and insert Volume 1. From the Text Task Selection Menu, type j and Enter.	This will put you into the Utilities Menu.
2. From the Document Utilities Menu, select Copy Document and Enter.	This tells the system that you wish to copy.

Continued

Chapter 7 Utilities

PROCEDURES (Continued)	COMMENTS (Continued)
3. Type a and Enter. To copy a document that you have already created, type b:copy???.txt and Enter.	Always use the extension when dealing with utilities. The system does not assign them. You are using ??? because you may not remember the last three letters of the first part of the document name.
4. Select New Document Name and Enter.	You must select a new name so that the duplicate can be distinguished from the original document.
5. Type b:memo.cpy and Enter.	
6. Press Enter again.	

COPYING A DOCUMENT TO A DIFFERENT DISK

If you need to make a copy of your document on another diskette, possibly for someone else to revise, take your program diskette out. Replace it with a work diskette after naming the new document just before you press Enter. When you give the new name, be sure to indicate the correct drive. For example: a:newdoc2.txt.

Figure 7.3 is an illustration of the placement of the diskette onto which you will copy a document from your own diskette.

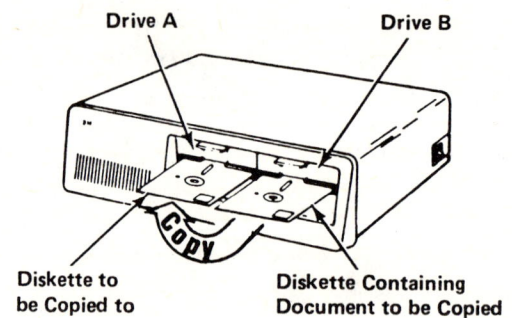

Figure 7.3 Copying a Document

DELETING A DOCUMENT

When your diskette is filling up, you can give yourself more room by deleting documents you no longer need. Before deleting any document, you should ask yourself if you will ever need the document again. If the answer is no, proceed with the deletion. You can delete all of the documents in a directory if you wish by using the global DOS characters * like this *.* If you are deleting more than one document and wish to stop the process, this can be accomplished by pressing control and break at the same time. The DOS character ? may also be used. You are not able to delete system files or DOS hidden files.

To practice deleting a document, you will delete the exercise b:Vacation.txt from your work diskette.

EXERCISE 24

PROCEDURES	COMMENTS
1. In the Text Task Selection Menu, select Document Utilities and Enter.	This will cause the Document Utilities Menu to display.
2. From the Document Utilities Menu, select Delete Document and Enter.	You will see the Delete Document Menu.
3. Select Document Name and Enter.	You are telling the system which document you want to delete.
4. At the prompt, type b:Vacation.txt and Enter.	The document is deleted, and the Document Utilities Menu again appears.
5. Press Enter again.	

RENAMING A DOCUMENT

If the content of a document has been revised to the point that it would be more easily identifiable with another name, a name change can be done in the Document Utilities Menu. Renaming documents can only be done one document at a time. You also have the ability to rename DOS files if you wish. You will rename the document **vacatio2.txt**; the new name will be **notice.txt**. Follow the steps to rename the document:

EXERCISE 25

PROCEDURES	COMMENTS
1. In the Text Task Selection Menu, press "j" and Enter.	This will cause the Document Utilities Menu to appear.
2. In the Document Utilities Menu, select Rename Document and Enter.	
	Continued

Chapter 7 Utilities

PROCEDURES (Continued)

   3.   Select Document Name.

   4.   At the prompt, type b:vacatio2.txt and Enter.

   5.   Select New Document Name and Enter.

   6.   At the prompt, type b:notice.txt and Enter.

   7.   Enter again.

COMMENTS (Continued)

This tells the system the name of the document you want to name again. You must give the extension.

This indicates that you are now ready to give the document a new name.

The system will rename the document, and the Document Utilities Menu will appear again.

COMPRESSING DOCUMENTS

After making revisions in documents, they should be compressed to eliminate empty record space. This allows you to place more documents on the diskette. You may compress one document, the entire directory, or certain selected documents. When you compress documents, a temporary document with the extension .$$t is created. It is deleted when the compression is completed. You must, however, make sure that your disk has enough space on it to hold both this temporary document and the one(s) you are compressing. You can use DOS global characters * and ? to compress more than one document at a time or all DisplayWrite 3 documents in the directory. To practice compressing documents and using the DOS global character *, follow the steps outlined in the next exercise.

EXERCISE 26

PROCEDURES

   1.   Select j in the Text Task Selection Menu.

   2.   Press F3.

   3.   Enter to select directory.

   4.   Type b:\ and Enter.

   5.   Press Enter again.

COMMENTS

This will bring you to the Document Utilities Menu.

You are first going to check the directory to see how much space you have left on the disk.

Continued

PROCEDURES (Continued)	COMMENTS (Continued)
6. Select Compress Documents in the Document Utilities Menu and Enter.	
7. Type a and Enter.	
8. Type b:*.txt and Enter.	
9. Press Enter again.	When the documents have been compressed, the Document Utilities Menu will appear on the screen.
10. Press F3 and Enter.	
11. Type b:\ and Enter to check the directory again.	The directory will show that you have more space on the disk than before condensing. All of the documents with the extension of .TXT have been compressed.

RECOVERING DOCUMENTS

Occasionally the system will display a message that you need to recover a document. This can be caused by circumstances such as a power failure or removing a diskette without pressing End Task. If you should see the "Document Needs Recovery" message on the screen, you will need to recover.

Another message you may see is "Document in Use." If you are prevented from printing or revising a document because of this message, you can gain access to the document by recovering it.

To recover multiple documents, or an entire directory, you may use the * and ? DOS global characters. Use control and break to stop the recovery process.

So that you will have an opportunity to use the recovery utility, follow the procedures in Exercise 27 to see the "Document in Use" message when you attempt to revise b:calendar.txt. This procedure is to produce a situation requiring recovery to access your document again. Do not follow it at any other time.

EXERCISE 27

PROCEDURES	COMMENTS
1. In the Text Task Selection Menu, select Revise Document and Enter.	Vol. 2 should be in drive A.

Continued

Chapter 7 Utilities

PROCEDURES (Continued)	COMMENTS (Continued)
2. Type **b:calendar.txt** and Enter.	
3. Go to the typing area.	
4. When you are in the typing area, turn off the power to the computer and wait ten seconds.	
5. Turn the power back on and follow the steps to get back to the Text Task Selection Menu.	These steps are outlined in the first chapters of this manual.
6. Select Revise Document and Enter.	
7. Type **b:calendar.txt** and Enter.	You will see a message that the document is in use.
8. Press Esc.	This clears the Revise Document Selection.
9. Select Document Utilities and Enter.	Vol. 1 should be in drive A.
10. Type **d** and Enter.	
11. Type **a** and Enter.	
12. Type **b:calendar.txt** and Enter.	
13. Enter again.	You will see two messages in the upper left corner of the screen. The first will say "Recovering Index." The second will say "Recovering Documents." At the end of the recovery operation, the prompt line will carry the message "(B:CALENDAR.TXT) recovered. Check for lost data."
14. Press Enter.	The screen will return to the Document Utilities Menu. At the bottom of the screen, the prompt will read "Recover Documents Complete."

TYPING WITH AUTO CARRIER RETURN OFF

Although it is generally advisable to let the system make the line ending decisions, this can be done with the DisplayWrite 3 program if you wish to make these decisions yourself.

When Auto Carrier Return is turned off, you will have to return at the end of each line (see Figure 7.4). Carrier returns are not required unless you type them while holding down the control key.

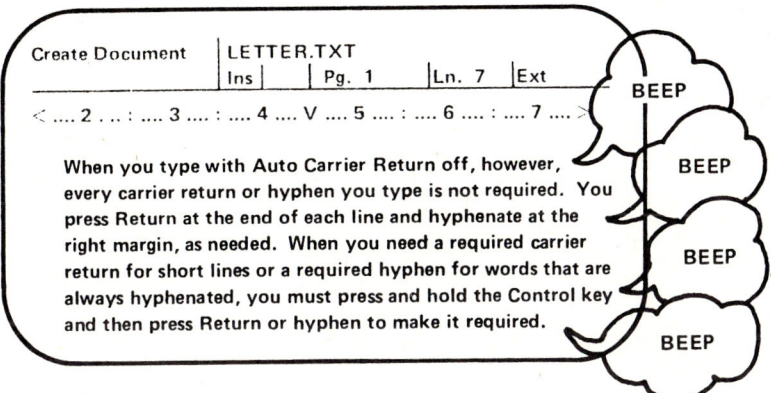

Figure 7.4 Auto Carrier Return Off

Hyphens typed at the right margin are not required. They are sometimes called "syllable hyphens" because they are used to divide words that are too long to fit on a typed line. When typing required hyphens, as in mother-in-law, they must be typed while holding down the control key (see Figure 7.5).

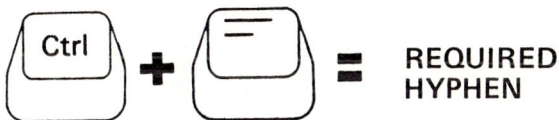

Figure 7.5 Required Hyphen

Some other guidelines to follow when typing with the Auto Carrier Return off are as follows:

--Hold down the control key when striking return for short lines (see Figure 7.6).

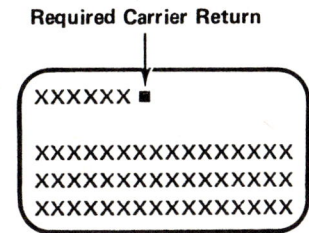

Figure 7.6 Required Carrier Return

Chapter 7 Utilities

--When hyphenating at the right margin, use a syllable hyphen.
--Words that will always be hyphenated should have required hyphens in them (see Figure 7.7).

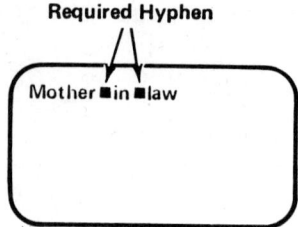

Figure 7.7 Required Hyphens

--Use the Line Adjust key to adjust the line endings.

--Words that should be on the same line will be typed with required spaces between them (as in New York).

--Space two times after all terminal punctuation even if it is at the end of a paragraph. Examples are periods, question marks, and exclamation marks at the ends of sentences.

Follow the procedures outlined in Exercise 28 to turn the Auto Carrier Return off.

EXERCISE 28

PROCEDURES	COMMENTS
1. Insert Volume 1 of DisplayWrite 3 in drive A.	The program used to change the defaults for Auto Carrier Return is on Volume 1. The changes you make here will remain for everything you type until you change them back. You will do that later in this lesson.
2. Select Profile Tasks and Enter.	
3. In the Profile Tasks Menu, select Create Profile and Enter. At the prompt, type b:Profile1 and Enter. In the Create or Revise Profile Menu, choose Change Work Station Defaults and Enter.	

Continued

110   Chapter 7 Utilities

PROCEDURES (Continued)	COMMENTS (Continued)
4. In the Change Work Station Defaults Menu, choose Change Keyboard Description and Enter.	
5. In the Keyboard Description Menu, select Auto Carrier Return and Enter. Type 2 to turn the setting off. Enter.	The system will no longer automatically "wrap" for you. You will now have to adjust every line ending using the Line Adjust key if you want the line endings adjusted. You must now use the control with carrier returns to make them required. You must now use the control with hyphens to make them required.
6. Press Enter enough times to return to the Profile Tasks Menu, and then press "z" to return to the Text Task Selection Menu.	If you have put a write protect tab on your diskette, you will see the message "Diskette in drive A is write protected." You will be returned to the Text Task Selection Menu.

If your Volume 1 program disk was write protected, the user profile was not stored. You can skip Exercise 29.

If your Volume 1 program disk was not protected, you must complete Exercise 29 to change your program defaults back to the original choices.

You have just personalized some of the defaults of the system by making changes on the previous page. You will now have to change those settings back so that the remaining exercises will not be affected by them.

EXERCISE 29

PROCEDURES	COMMENTS
1. While in the Text Task Selection Menu, remove Volume 2 and insert Volume 1. Select Profile Tasks and Enter.	
Continued	

Chapter 7   Utilities

PROCEDURES (Continued)	COMMENTS (Continued)
2. In the Profile Tasks Menu, select Revise Profile and Enter. At the prompt, type b:Profile1 and Enter.	You are revising the profile back to the original settings.
3. In the Create or Revise Menu, choose Change Work Station Defaults and Enter.	Ask your instructor to check the settings before you continue.
4. In the Change Work Station Defaults Menu, choose Change Keyboard Description and Enter.	
5. In the Keyboard Description Menu, select Auto Carrier Return and Enter. Type 1 to turn on the setting. Enter.	
6. Press Esc enough times to return to the Text Task Selection Menu.	

PERSONALIZING TEXT AND WORK STATION DEFAULTS BY CREATING, REVISING, AND ACTIVATING PROFILES

Text and work station defaults are those choices that are the most commonly used and will not have to be changed. They reside in the system profile and cannot be changed. However, it is possible for you to personalize these defaults to suit your individual needs through the USER.UPR profile or creation of your own profiles. The USER.UPR is a copy of the system defaults which you can modify. You may also create, store, and revise these profiles. When you load DisplayWrite 3, though, the system defaults are in effect until you activate another profile. This profile is essentially a collection of default settings that are in effect when the profile is activated. The defaults that can be personalized by you are document format, alternate format, math format, paginate document, check document (spelling), merge tasks, merge with file instruction, block save/recall default path, and document revisions.

Because text defaults usually are changed only once, and due to the number of students using the equipment in most word processing programs, it is practical only to discuss personalizing these defaults. The menus used to personalize defaults are the same as those used when making choices which pertain only to a current document. A student who starts a job using this program, or uses the program on his or her own personal computer, will not have difficulty personalizing the defaults.

DOCUMENT FORMAT

You can personalize the line format, which includes line spacing, line alignment, typestyle, lines per inch, line ending adjustment, and zone width. Margins and tabs can also be customized. Page format can be personalized by changing the choices for first typing lines for the first and following pages, last typing line, paper or envelope size, and printing paper source. Header and footer choices may be changed to affect the first footer and header lines and the print placement of the headers and footers. You may personalize the alternate header and footer choices also.

ALTERNATE FORMAT

The same changes that can be made in document format can be made for the alternate format. Refer to document format for more information.

MATH FORMAT

All four of the math formats may be personalized. The math formats are explained in Chapter 23.

PAGINATE FORMAT

Pagination may be changed relative to exact line count and line ending adjustments. Page ending adjustments and dictionary hyphenation defaults can be changed also.

CHECK DOCUMENT

The kind of spell check may be personalized. Pagination during spell checking and the dictionary program name may also be changed.

OTHER DEFAULTS

Other defaults that can be changed include merge document, document revision, merge with file instruction, and the block save/recall default path. Defaults that can be changed relative to the work station are as follows: print options and LPT printer descriptions, keyboard description, keystroke save/recall default path, as well as the color display description (for those work stations equipped with color monitors).

DOS COMMAND TASK

The DOS command task allows you to leave DisplayWrite 3 temporarily and use DOS commands and return to DisplayWrite 3 without having to reload it. You can return to the Text Task Selection Menu by typing exit when you are in DOS. When you are in DOS, DisplayWrite 3 background print will not work. It starts again upon your return to DisplayWrite 3. If you change the default drive from B when you are in DOS, the change will remain in effect when you return to DisplayWrite 3. If you load another program when you are in DOS, be sure that you exit that program before returning to DisplayWrite 3 so that you will have enough memory to run DisplayWrite 3.

In the next exercise you will delete a document in DOS and then return to DisplayWrite 3.

                              EXERCISE 30

PROCEDURES	COMMENTS
1. In the Text Task Selection Menu, choose DOS Command Task and Enter.	
2. At the prompt, type del b:notice.txt and Enter.	This will delete the document named b:notice.txt from your work disk.
3. Type exit to return to DisplayWrite 3.	You have left DOS and gone back into DisplayWrite 3 without having to boot the program again.

You may wonder why deleting did not just take place in DisplayWrite 3 in the first place. Deleting is, of course, just an example of the many housekeeping chores you can perform in DOS. The true advantage of being able to switch back and forth between DisplayWrite 3 and DOS is that some tasks are just faster in DOS. One such task is deleting many documents, all of which have dissimilar names and extensions, in a short amount of time. You can readily see that the DOS global characters are not the answer here. It is much faster for you to type del and the name of the document to be deleted as many times as there are documents, than for you to use the menu structure. The same concept holds true for renaming, copying, and like operations.

                            CHAPTER SUMMARY

A. You can check the contents of your disk by looking at the directory. Not only are the names of the document listed but also the percentage of remaining disk space.
B. You may also copy documents to another disk or on the same disk.

C. If you no longer need a document and want to utilize the space it occupies on your disk for something else, you may delete that document.

D. When a document is revised to the point that a new name would describe it better, you can rename the document through the rename utility.

E. The compress document utility makes it possible to eliminate empty record space when revisions are made in a document. This is somewhat like "squeezing" a document to the minimum amount of space needed to store it.

F. Document recovery allows you to get back into a document when you have received a "Document in Use" or "Document Needs Recovery" message.

G. At the times when you do not want or need the automatic wraparound feature, you can type without it by using Auto Carrier Return Off.

H. If you daily use margins, tabs, or other formatting parameters that are not system defaults, you may appreciate the ability to personalize the text and work station defaults. You are allowed to change the defaults to suit your needs by the use of user profiles.

Chapter 8
FORMATTING

When you complete this chapter, you will able to:

1. Make page format changes within a document.
2. Make line format changes within a document.
3. Make typestyle changes within a document.
4. Create and use an alternate format.
5. Revise Format Change codes.

INTRODUCTION

In Chapter 4, you learned to change the format for an entire document through the Document or Alternate Format Menu. All these changes were made before going to the typing area. In this chapter, you will learn to change the format for a smaller part of a document after you are in the typing area (see Figure 8.1).

We can think of formats as falling into three categories:

1. A format that affects the entire document. For example, you need to know what printer setup is used when the document is printed (discussed in Chapter 4).

2. A format that affects certain pages of a document. For example, some pages might need different margins or need to be printed on different size paper.

3. A format that affects certain lines within a page. For example, your document may be double-spaced, but you are inserting a long quotation in this document that needs to be single-spaced.

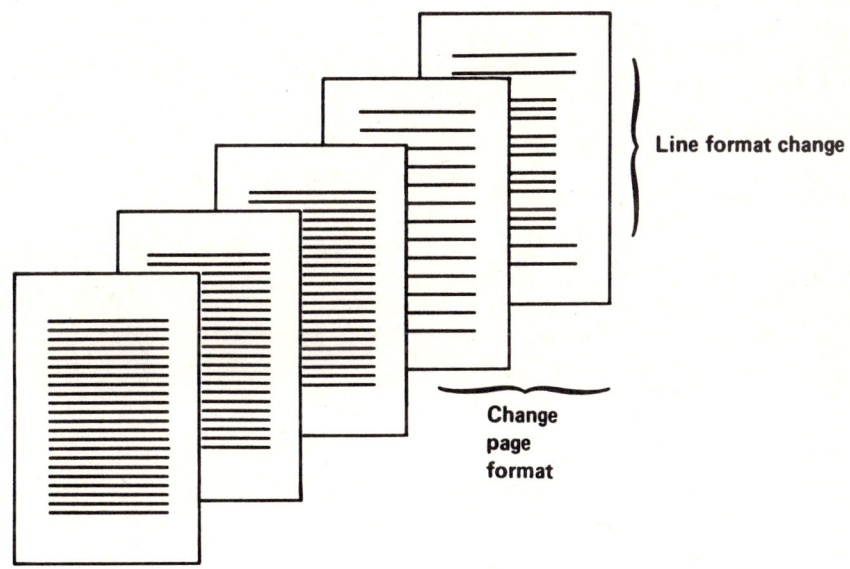

Figure 8.1 Document Format

Note: After making any format changes, you must paginate your document before printing.

CHANGING LINE FORMAT

You may be typing a document and find that you need to change the format for a line or more in the document. An example of this is incorporating a long quote in the body of a report. The report would be double-spaced and the long quote would need to be single-spaced. Change Line Format allows you to change the text that needs a format

Chapter 8 Formatting

different from the one you established through the Document or Alternate Format Menu.

To make a line format change, you need to make sure that your cursor is at the left margin and at the beginning of the line in which the format change is to take place. You then will press the Format key and the Format Change Menu will appear, as shown in Figure 8.2.

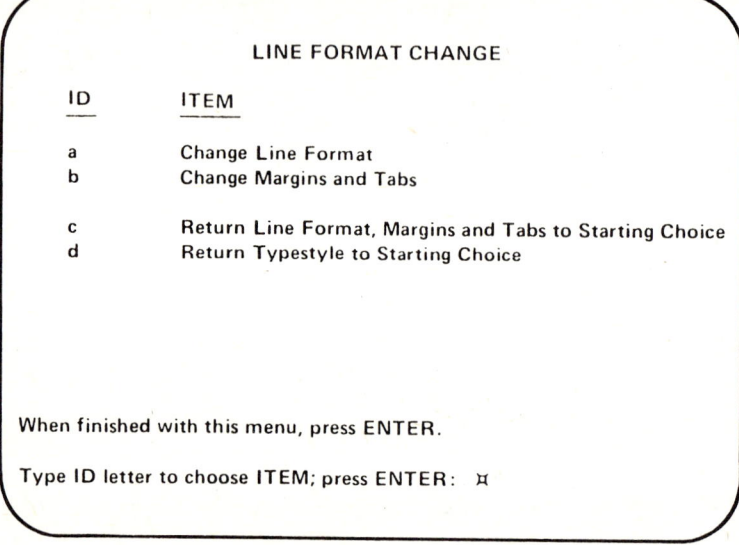

Figure 8.2   Format Change Menu

After you have made your line changes, you can make other format changes or return to the original format. You have two choices for returning to the original format:

1. Return Line Format, Margins and Tabs to Starting Choice. If you choose this option, it will return these items to the original choices you make in the Document or Alternate Format Menu.

2. Return Typestyle to Starting Choice. This option returns only the typestyle to the original choice made in the Document or Alternate Format Menu.

STEPS FOR CHANGING LINE FORMAT

1. The document you are typing should be displayed on the screen. Type to the line where the new format is to begin. <u>Make sure your cursor is at the beginning of the line at the left margin</u> (see Figure 8.3).

2. Press Format (F7). The Format Change Menu displays.

3. Select Change Line Format. The Line Format Menu will display. Make any necessary changes in the Line Format Menu.

4. When you are finished making all of your changes, follow the prompt to press Enter to return to the typing area. A Line Format Change code (see Figure 8.4) is placed in the text. It marks the

beginning of the format change and stays in effect until you change it.

Figure 8.3 Begin New Format   Figure 8.4 Line Format Change Code

5. Type the lines in the new format.

STEPS FOR RETURNING TO THE STARTING LINE FORMAT

1. Place your cursor at the beginning of the line where the original document format will begin again.

2. Press Format (F7). The Format Change Menu displays.

3. Select Return Line Format, Margins and Tabs to Starting Choice. Then press Enter to return to the typing area. A Line Format Return code (see Figure 8.5) is placed in the text. It marks the end of a Line Format Change.

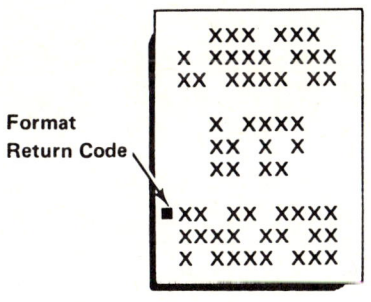

Figure 8.5 Format Return Code

4. Type the remainder of the text in the original format.

5. Press End Task.

6. Use Automatic Pagination to paginate the document.

EXERCISE 31

You will be typing the letter that appears at the end of this exercise. In the middle of the letter you will need to make a line format

Chapter 8 Formatting

change to type the tabulation. Then you will return to the original format again.

PROCEDURES	COMMENTS
1. Select Create Document from the Text Task Selection Menu.	Type **a** and press Enter.
2. Name the document b:Exerci31.	
3. Press Enter.	The Create or Revise Document Menu displays.
4. Type b and press Enter.	This is to select Change Document Format.
5. Type b and press Enter.	This is to select Change Margins and Tabs.
6. Set the left margin at 20.	
7. Set the right margin at 70.	
8. Press Enter.	
9. Type c and press Enter.	This is to select Change Page Format.
10. Type a and press Enter.	This is to change First Line of Typing, First Page.
11. Type 15 and press Enter.	
12. Press Enter.	The Document or Alternate Format Menu displays.
13. Press Enter.	The Create or Revise Document Menu displays.
14. Press Enter.	The typing area displays.
15. Type up to ⟨16⟩.	
16. Type two carrier returns.	
17. Press Format (F7).	The Format Change Menu displays.
18. Type a and press Enter.	This is to select Change Line Format.

Continued

PROCEDURES (Continued)	COMMENTS (Continued)
19. Type a and press Enter.	This is to change Line Spacing.
20. Type 2 and press Enter.	This is to change to double-spacing.
21. Press Enter.	The Format Change Menu displays.
22. Type b and press Enter.	This is to change Margins and Tabs.
23. Set left margin at 25.	
24. Set right margin at 65.	
25. Press Enter.	The Format Change Menu displays.
26. Press Enter.	The typing area displays.
27. Type the names in the left column and tab to 45 to type the titles. Type up to ⬡28.	
28. Return the carriage once after you type the word "Treasurer."	
29. Press Format (F7).	The Format Change Menu displays.
30. Type c and press Enter.	This is to return to starting format.
31. Type the rest of the document.	
32. Press F2.	This will end the task.
33. Paginate the document.	
34. Print the document.	

Exercise 31

January 15, 19--

Mr. Richard McKnight
222 Oak Lane
Grosse Pointe, MI 48236-0630

Dear Mr. McKnight:

Thank you for taking the time to send in your ballot for the election of corporate officers.

We are proud to announce the following 19-- Officers for Tri-County Incorporated: ⬡16

    Jack Harrigan   President

    Paul Pierron   Vice President

    Henry Long   Secretary

    Jane Leonard   Treasurer ⬡28

Attached is a list of the newly elected Regional Vice Presidents.

Thank you again for your participation.

Cordially,

William Nelson
Chairman of the Board

CHANGING PAGE FORMAT

Let us assume that you are creating the document that is illustrated in Figure 8.6. Pages 1 through 3 and 5 through 10 use the same document format. Page 4 is a table which needs to be printed horizontally on the paper.

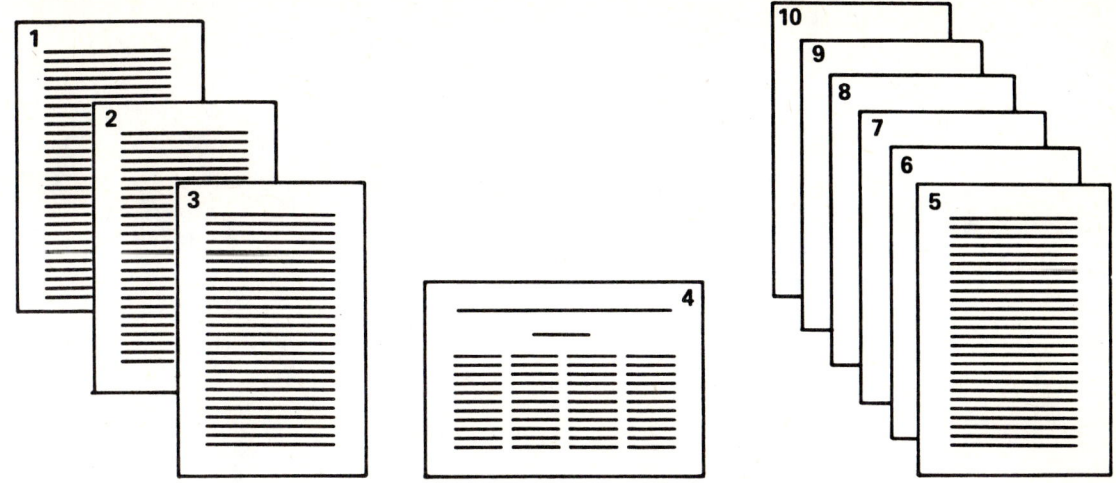

Figure 8.6 Changing Page Format

The best thing to do would be to set your document format for the specifications needed for pages 1 through 3 and 5 through 10. At the beginning of page 4, you will request the Format Change Menu to make the necessary changes for page 4. Then at the top of page 5, you will request that the system return all formats to starting choice (the formats originally set for the document in the Document or Alternate Format Menu). The items illustrated in Figure 8.7 will appear in the Format Change Menu to allow you to make a change in page format.

```
                    PAGE FORMAT CHANGE

           ID        ITEM

           a         Change Line Format
           b         Change Margins and Tabs
           c         Change Page Format
           d         Change Header and Footer
           e         Change Alternating Headers and Footers

           f         Return All Formats to Starting Choice
           g         Return Line Format, Margins and Tabs to Starting Choice
           h         Return Typestyle to Starting Choice

           i         Begin Using Document Format
           j         Begin Using Alternate Format

     When finished with this menu, press ENTER.

     Type ID letter to choose ITEM; press ENTER: ¤
```

Figure 8.7 Format Change Menu

Items a, b, and c will take you to the same menus that you access through the Document or Alternate Format Menu.

Items d and e deal with headers and footers, which will be discussed in the next chapter.

Items f, g, and h return you to the original formats. When you are finished typing your page or pages using the special page format that has been set, you will need to return to the original format to type the remainder of your report. Item "f" tells the system to return all formats to the choices selected through the Document or Alternate Format Menu. Item "g" tells the system to return only the line format and margins and tabs to the choices made through the Document or Alternate Format Menu. Item "h" instructs the system to return only the typestyle to the starting choice.

STEPS FOR CHANGING PAGE FORMAT

1. Type to the position where the new format is to begin.

2. Press Ctrl--Page End. This moves your cursor to the upper left corner of the next page, as shown in Figure 8.8.

Figure 8.8   New Screen

3. Press Format (F7). The Format Change Menu displays.

4. Choose Change Page Format. The Page Format Menu will display. Make the necessary changes in the Page Format Menu.

5. Follow the prompt to press Enter to return to the typing area. A Page Format Change code is placed in the text (see Figure 8.9). It marks the beginning of the format change and stays in effect until you change it.

Figure 8.9   Page Format Change Code

6. Type the page or pages using the new format.

STEPS FOR RETURNING TO THE STARTING PAGE FORMAT

1. You have finished typing the page or pages in the new format, and you are now ready to return to the original format to continue typing the rest of the document.

2. Press Ctrl--Page End. This moves your cursor to the upper left corner of the next page.

3. Press Format (F7).

4. The Format Change Menu displays. Choose the appropriate item to return the settings to the starting choice.

5. Follow the prompt to press Enter to return to the typing area. A Format Return code is placed in the text as shown in Figure 8.10. It marks the end of a Page Format Change.

6. Continue typing the text using the original format.

7. Press End Task (F2).

8. Use Automatic Pagination to paginate the document.

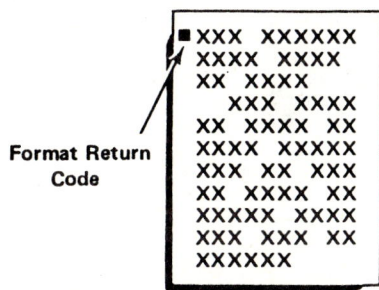

Figure 8.10   Format Return Code

EXERCISE 32

In Exercise 32, you will be recalling Exercise 31 to the screen and adding a second page to the document. Page 2 is a table that will need to be typed horizontally on the paper. In order to do this, you will need to insert a Change Page Format instruction.

PROCEDURES	COMMENTS
1. Recall the document b:Exerci31 to the screen.	
2. Press End.	This brings your cursor to the end of the page.
3. Press Ctrl--Page End (Ctrl--E).	This takes your cursor to the top left corner of the next page.
4. Press Format (F7).	The Format Change Menu displays.
5. Type c and press Enter.	This is to change Page Format.

Continued

Chapter 8   Formatting

PROCEDURES (Continued)		COMMENTS (Continued)
6.	Type c and press Enter.	This is to change Last Typing Line.
7.	Type 45 and press Enter.	Last Typing Line is now 45.
8.	Type d and press Enter.	This is to change the paper size.
9.	Type 4 and press Enter.	The paper size is now 11 by 8 1/2.
10.	Press Enter.	The Format Change Menu displays.
11.	Type b and press Enter.	This is to change the margins and tabs.
12.	Set the left margin at 10.	
13.	Set the right margin at 103.	
14.	Clear all tabs.	
15.	Set tabs at 30, 45, and 88.	
16.	Press Enter.	The Format Change Menu displays.
17.	Press Enter.	The typing area displays.
18.	Type the document as shown on page 127. Notice that the new center point is now 56. Center your titles at this point. Use the tab key to move from column to column.	
19.	Press F2.	This is to end the task.
20.	Print a copy of this document.	Remember to insert the paper sideways.

CHANGING TYPESTYLES

There may be times when you are typing documents in which you would want a character, a phrase, or a sentence printed in a different typestyle. An example of this might be when you are typing the titles of books and magazines. You may want a different typestyle so that the titles will be easier to distinguish.

A typestyle change allows you to change the typestyle from the one you originally set in the Document or Alternate Format Menu. Typestyles may be changed as often as you wish in a document. However, if you

TRI-COUNTY INCORPORATED

19-- Regional Vice Presidents

Name	Region	Address	Telephone
Marie Parzych	Northwest	210 Main St., Seattle, WA 98101-1221	206-555-8774
Thomas Boos	Southwest	55 Clover St., Irvine, CA 90042-0930	213-555-1264
Carol Reitmyer	Midwest	122 Grand Ave., Troy, MI 48224-0618	313-555-2410
Charles Hitch	Northeast	82 49th St., New York, NY 10017-1202	212-555-0933
Shirley Reile	Southeast	1663 Vail, Nashville, TN 37211-0611	615-555-1785
Sharon Schmidt	Plains	71 Center Rd., Omaha, NE 68106-0716	403-555-3101

change the typestyle in the middle of a line, the original and new typestyle must be the same pitch. The pitch can be changed, though, at the beginning of a line.

After you have made a typestyle change, you can choose another typestyle change or return to the original typestyle by selecting Return Typestyle to Starting Choice.

STEPS FOR CHANGING TYPESTYLES

1. Type to the first position where another typestyle is to begin.

2. Press Format (F7). The Format Change Menu displays. Depending on your cursor position, the Format Change Menu items that display on the screen will vary.

3. Select Change Line Format or select Typestyle Number.

4. If you select Change Line Format, select Typestyle Number in the Line Format Menu.

5. Type the number of the typestyle you want.

6. Press Enter to return to the typing area. A Typestyle Change code has been placed in the text. It marks the beginning of the Typestyle Change and stays in effect until you change it.

7. Type the word or words that are to be printed in the new typestyle.

STEPS FOR RETURNING TO THE STARTING TYPESTYLE

1. Type to the first position where the original typestyle is to begin again.

2. Press Format (F7). The Format Change Menu displays.

3. Select Return Typestyle to Starting Choice.

4. Press Enter to return to the typing area. A Typestyle Return code has been placed in the text. It marks the end of the Typestyle Change.

5. Continue typing the text in the original typestyle.

6. Press End Task.

7. Use Automatic Pagination to paginate the document.

EXERCISE 33

In Exercise 33, you will be typing the letter that is shown following Procedure 27. You will be making a typestyle change in the letter to make a portion of the letter stand out.

128   Chapter 8   Formatting

PROCEDURES	COMMENTS
1. Select Create Document in the Text Task Selection Menu.	
2. Name the document b:Exerci33.	
3. Choose Change Document Format in the Create or Revise Document Menu.	
4. Choose Change Margins and Tabs in the Document or Alternate Format Menu.	
5. Change right margin to 70.	
6. Press Enter.	The Document or Alternate Format Menu displays.
7. Choose Change Page Format.	The Page Format Menu displays.
8. Change First Typing Line, First Page to 13.	
9. Press Enter.	The Document or Alternate Format Menu displays.
10. Press Enter.	The Create or Revise Document Menu displays.
11. Press Enter.	The typing area displays.
12. Type the letter on page 131. Stop when you reach ⬡13.	
13. Return the carriage twice.	
14. Press Format (F7).	The Format Change Menu displays.
15. Type a and press Enter.	This is to choose Change Line Format.
16. Type c and press Enter.	This is to change Typestyle Number.

Continued

Chapter 8 Formatting

PROCEDURES (Continued)	COMMENTS (Continued)
17. Type 260 and press Enter.	This is to select 8.55 pitch.
18. Press Enter.	The Format Change Menu displays.
19. Press Enter.	The typing area displays.
20. Center and type BITS AND BYTES.	
21. Return the carriage twice.	
22. Press Format (F7).	The Format Change Menu displays.
23. Type c and press Enter.	This is to return typestyle and margins to starting choice.
24. Continue typing the rest of the letter.	
25. Press F2.	This is to end the task.
26. Paginate the document.	
27. Print the document.	

USING ALTERNATE FORMAT

An alternate format is a page format change that is stored for repetitive use. To illustrate when you might use an alternate format, consider this application:

You are creating a series of letters and envelopes, one right after the other (see Figure 8.11). Your letters would be created with the document format and your envelopes would be created using the alternate format. Then you would use the document format for the letter, go to the alternate format for the envelope, and then go back to the document format for another letter.

STEPS FOR CREATING AN ALTERNATE FORMAT

1. Select Create Document in the Text Task Selection Menu.

2. Select Change Alternate Format in the Create or Revise Document Menu.

3. The Document or Alternate Format Menu displays. Select the appropriate items and change the settings.

4. Press Enter to take you to the typing area.

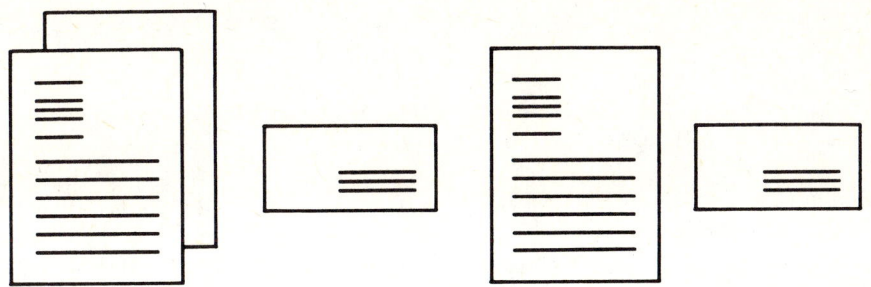

Figure 8.11   Letters and Envelopes

EXERCISE 33

February 15, 19--

Mr. Ronald VonSoosten
209 Alpine Drive
Seattle, WA 98102-1225

Dear Mr. VonSoosten:

We received your order with an enclosed check for $17.95 for our latest book: ⑬

BITS AND BYTES

We are in the process of printing the second edition of the book. The second edition will be ready for shipping in about three weeks. The second edition will contain the most up-to-date information with 36 additional color illustrations. It is certainly worth waiting for!

If you would rather have the first edition of the book, just return the enclosed card, and we will send it to you immediately.

Sincerely,

Richard Tanaka
Marketing Manager

xxx

Enclosure

STEPS FOR USING THE ALTERNATE FORMAT

1. Type the text up to the point where the alternate format is to begin.

2. Press Ctrl--Page End. This moves your cursor to the upper left corner of the next page.

3. Press Format (F7).

4. The Format Change Menu displays. Select Begin Using Alternate Format.

5. Press Enter to return to the typing area.

6. Type the text using the alternate format.

STEPS FOR RETURNING TO THE DOCUMENT FORMAT

1. Press Ctrl--Page End. This moves your cursor to the upper left corner of the next page.

2. Press Format (F7).

3. The Format Change Menu displays. Select Begin Using Document Format.

4. Press Enter to return to the typing area.

5. Type the text in the original format.

6. Press End Task.

7. Use Automatic Pagination to paginate the document.

EXERCISE 34

In Exercise 34, you will be creating an alternate format to type an envelope for the letter you created in Exercise 33.

PROCEDURES	COMMENTS
1. Select Revise Document from the Text Task Selection Menu.	
2. The document name is b:Exerci33.	
3. From the Create or Revise Document Menu, select Change Alternate Format.	
	Continued

PROCEDURES (Continued)	COMMENTS (Continued)
4. Press Enter.	The Document or Alternate Format Menu displays.
5. Choose Change Margins and Tabs.	
6. Set the left margin at 40.	
7. Set the right margin at 90.	
8. Press Enter.	
9. Select Change Page Format.	
10. Change First Typing Line, First Page to 15.	
11. Change Last Typing Line to 20.	
12. Change Paper or Envelope Size to 7.	The envelope is 9 1/2- by 4.13-inch paper.
13. Change Printing Paper Source to Manual feed.	If your printer has an envelope tray, Printing Paper Source should be changed to Envelope.
14. Press Enter.	The Document or Alternate Format Menu displays.
15. Press Enter.	The Create or Revise Document Menu displays.
16. Press Enter.	The document displays.
17. Press End.	This is to move to the end of the document.
18. Press Ctrl--Page End (Ctrl--E).	Page 2 is displayed.
19. Press Format (F7).	The Format Change Menu displays.
20. Choose Begin Using Alternate Format.	
21. Press Enter.	The typing area for alternate format displays.

Continued

Chapter 8 Formatting

PROCEDURES (Continued)	COMMENTS (Continued)
22. Type: Mr. Ronald VonSoosten 209 Alpine Drive Seattle, WA 98102-1225	This is the address for the envelope.
23. Press F2.	This will end the task.
24. Paginate the document.	
25. Print the document.	

REFORMATTING A DOCUMENT

REVISING FORMAT CHANGE CODES

You may have created a document with some format changes in it. Later, as you go back to revise the document, you may find that you will need to revise the format changes also.

To revise a format within a document, you alter the format change codes. To do this, you place the cursor under the format change code. The status line will identify the type of change (Page Format, Line Format, or Typestyle Change) the code represents. Press Continue (F10), and the Format Change Menu will display. Make your changes and follow the prompt to return to the typing area.

Format Return codes cannot be revised. They can only be moved, copied, or deleted.

REVISING FORMATS IN THE DOCUMENT OR ALTERNATE FORMAT MENU AND IN THE FORMAT CHANGE CODES

Keep in mind that revisions made through the Document or Alternate Format Menu are made before going to the typing area. Revisions to the Format Change codes are made in the typing area of the document.

If you make format changes to a document through the Document or Alternate Format Menu, these changes will not affect the Format Change codes within the document. Therefore, if you reformat a document, it is important to go to each Format Change code within the document, check it, and revise it if necessary.

STEPS FOR REVISING AN EXISTING FORMAT CHANGE

1. The document you need to revise should be displayed on the screen.

2. Turn on Display codes.

3. Move your cursor under the Format Change code.

4. Press Continue (F10). The Format Change Menu displays. The items in the Format Change Menu will vary according to the type of format change.

5. Make the necessary changes in the menu.

6. Follow the prompt to press Enter to return to the typing area.

7. Continue making the rest of your format revisions.

8. Press End Task (F10).

9. Use Automatic Pagination to paginate the document.

EXERCISE 35

For this exercise, you will need to recall Exercise 31 to the screen to make some revisions. You will be revising the Line Format Change code that was originally keyed into the document. We will change the Line Format code to single-spacing so that the tabulation incorporated in the letter will also be single-spaced.

PROCEDURES	COMMENTS
1. Recall the document b:Exerci31 to the screen.	
2. Page 1 of the document should be displayed on the screen.	
3. Turn on Display codes.	Use the Cmd (F6) to access the Display codes.
4. Highlight the first Line Format Change code.	Line Format Change will appear on the status line when the cursor is under the code.
5. Press Continue (F10).	The Format Change Menu displays.
6. Type a and press Enter.	The Line Format Menu displays.
7. Change Line Spacing to Single.	
8. Press Enter.	The Format Change Menu displays.
9. Press Enter.	The typing area displays.
10. Highlight the Required Carrier Return following the word "Treasurer."	Your screen should look like this: Jane Leonard Treasurer◄

Continued

Chapter 8 Formatting

11.	Press the carrier return.	This will insert another carrier return so that you will still have two carrier returns separating the table from the next paragraph.
12.	Press F2.	This is to end the task.
13.	Paginate the document.	
14.	Print page 1 of the document.	The table in the letter should now be single-spaced.

CHAPTER SUMMARY

A. Changing Line Format

1. Place your cursor at the beginning of the line where the new format is to begin.
2. Press Format (F7). The Format Change Menu displays.
3. Select Change Line Format. The Line Format Menu will display. Make the necessary changes in this menu.
4. Press Enter to return to the typing area.

B. Returning to Starting Line Format

1. Place cursor at the beginning of the line where original format will begin again.
2. Press Format (F7).
3. Choose the item in the Format Change Menu to return the settings to starting choices.
4. Press Enter.

C. Changing Page Format

1. Type to the position where the new format is to begin.
2. Press Ctrl--Page End.
3. Press Format. The Format Change Menu displays.
4. Choose Change Page Format. The Page Format Menu will display. Make the necessary changes in this menu.
5. Press Enter.

D. Returning to Starting Page Format

1. After you have finished typing the pages in the new page format, press Ctrl--Page End.
2. Press Format. The Format Change Menu displays.
3. Choose Return Settings to Starting Choice.
4. Press Enter.

E. Changing Typestyles

1. Type to the first position where another typestyle is to begin.
2. Press Format. The Format Change Menu displays.
3. Select Change Line Format or select Typestyle Number. If you select Change Line Format, select Typestyle Number in the Line Format Menu.
4. Type the number of the typestyle you want.
5. Press Enter.

F. Returning to Starting Typestyle

1. Type to the first position where the original typestyle is to begin again.
2. Press Format.
3. Select Return Typestyle to Starting Choice.
4. Press Enter to return to the typing area.

G. Creating an Alternate Format

1. Select Create Document in the Text Task Selection Menu.
2. Select Change Alternate Format in the Create or Revise Document Menu.
3. Select the appropriate items in the Document or Alternate Format Menu and change the settings.
4. Press Enter to take you to the typing area.

H. Using the Alternate Format

1. Type the text up to the point where the alternate format is to begin.
2. Press Ctrl--Page End.
3. Press Format.
4. Select Begin Using Alternate Format.
5. Press Enter to return to the typing area.

I. Returning to the Document Format

1. Press Ctrl--Page End.
2. Press Format.
3. Select Begin Using Document Format.
4. Press Enter to return to the typing area.

J. Revising an Existing Format Change

1. Turn on Display codes.
2. Move cursor under the Format Change code.
3. Press Continue (F10).
4. Make the necessary changes in the menu.
5. Press Enter to return to the typing area.

Chapter 8   Formatting

Chapter 9

MODIFYING TEXT APPEARANCE

When you complete this chapter, you will be able to:

1. Justify text.

2. Use the line adjust key to get a more even right margin.

3. Insert keep instructions to keep text together on a page.

4. Insert required spaces to keep words together on a line.

5. Use the indent key to set up a temporary left margin when typing indented paragraphs.

JUSTIFYING TEXT

The Line Alignment option in the Line Format Menu controls how the lines of text are aligned, or arranged, between the left and right margins.

Usually text is aligned at the left margin. Line Alignment, however, gives you the choice of having text aligned in the three ways illustrated in Figure 9.1.

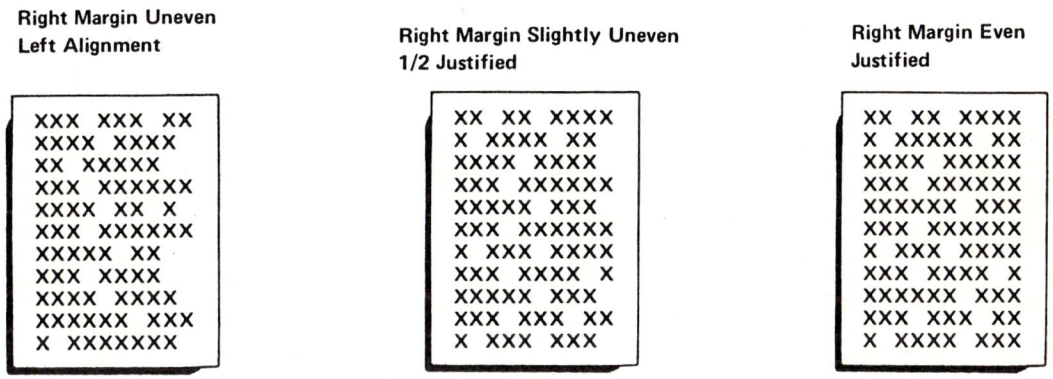

Figure 9.1   Line Alignment Choices

Note: As you type or revise, the text displayed on the screen does not look justified or 1/2 justified. Justification and 1/2 justification occur only during printing.

Read Steps 1-9. The steps and Figure 9.2 illustrate justifying the right margin.

1. Choose Create Document in the Text Task Selection Menu.

2. Choose Change Document Format in the Create or Revise Document Menu.

3. Choose Change Line Format in the Document or Alternate Format Menu.

4. Choose Line Alignment and set it to Justify or 1/2 Justify in the Line Format Menu.

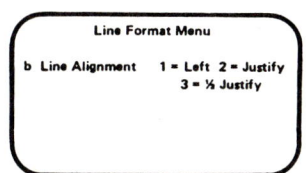

Figure 9.2   Line Format Menu

5. Press Enter to go to the typing area.

6. Type the document. Remember, the document will not look justified on the screen.

Chapter 9   Modifying Text Appearance   139

7. Press End Task.

8. Use Automatic Pagination to paginate the document.

9. Print the document.

EXERCISE 36

In Exercise 36, you will type the short document that is displayed at the end of this exercise. Prior to typing the document, you will need to tell the system to justify the document. The text will not appear justified on the screen, but it will print justified on your paper.

PROCEDURES	COMMENTS
1. Choose Create Document in the Text Task Selection Menu.	
2. Name the document b:Exerci36.	
3. Choose Change Document Format in the Create or Revise Document Menu.	
4. Choose Change Line Format in the Document or Alternate Format Menu.	The Line Format Menu displays.
5. Type b and press Enter.	This will change the line alignment.
6. Type 2 and press Enter.	This is to choose justify.
7. Press Enter.	The Document or Alternate Format Menu displays.
8. Press Enter.	The Create or Revise Document Menu displays.
9. Press Enter.	The typing area displays.
10. Type the document that follows this exercise.	
11. Press F2.	This is to end the task.
12. Paginate the document.	
13. Print the document.	

Chapter 9   Modifying Text Appearance

JUSTIFY

Having a justified right margin can greatly enhance the appearance of your document. Documents that are often justified are brochures, newsletters, magazine articles, proposals, and some reports.

DisplayWrite 3 makes it easy to justify text. You simply tell the system to change the line format to justify. The system will either add or delete spaces between characters and/or words to make each line end evenly.

The text does not appear justified on the screen, but it will print justified on your paper.

ADJUSTING LINE ENDINGS

The Line Adjust key can be used to give your document a more even right margin. The Line Adjust is typematic; that is, once the key has been pressed, it repeats until you release it.

The Line Adjust is limited to page boundaries. When the cursor reaches the end of a page, it stops at the Page End code. Therefore, Line Adjust does not take the place of pagination. Line Adjust should only be used within a short document or for a portion of a document.

In the Line Format Menu, there is an item called Zone Width. The system default for Zone Width is 6. This means that the system will end all lines within six spaces of the right margin, if possible. If you want a tighter right margin, make the Zone Width setting smaller. A smaller Zone Width will probably result in more hyphenation decisions. If the system cannot end the line because of a long word within the zone, it prompts you for a hyphenation decision.

1. The document to be adjusted should be displayed on the screen.

2. Move your cursor to the beginning of the first line to be adjusted.

3. Press Line Adjust once for each line that needs to be adjusted. If you need to adjust a block of lines in a document, move the cursor to the beginning of the block of lines. Then hold down the Line Adjust continually while the lines adjust on the display.

4. If the prompt "Hyphenate where?" displays on the screen, you must make a line ending choice. In Figure 9.3, your choices are illustrated and explained.

5. Repeat Steps 2 through 4 for each line to be adjusted.

6. Press End Task.

- To accept the system's point of hyphenation, press Enter.

- To keep the entire word on the *same* line, place the cursor one space *past* the last character of the word, and press Enter.

- To change the system's point of hyphenation, place the cursor where you want the hyphen to be and press Enter.

- To move the entire word to the next line, place the cursor under the first character of the word, and press Enter.

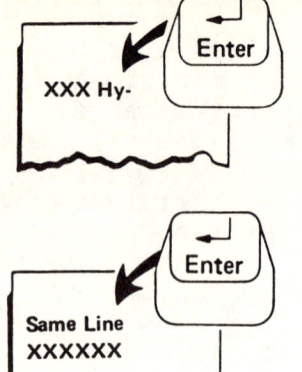
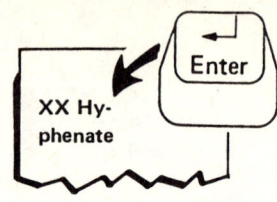
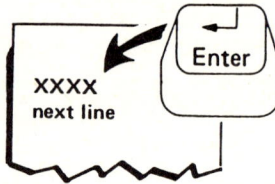

Figure 9.3   Hyphenation Choices

EXERCISE 37

In Exercise 37, you will type a paragraph and then use the Line Adjust key to make the right margin more even. The system will ask you for hyphenation decisions.

PROCEDURES	COMMENTS
1. Select Create Document in the Text Task Selection Menu.	
2. Name the document b:Exerci37.	
3. Type the following paragraph as shown. A balanced diet is the key to good eating habits. Unfortunately, to many people the term "diet" brings an immediate image of "reducing diet" or "ulcer diet" or some other self-sacrificing regime. This is not true. A balanced diet is the daily selection of a variety of foods that fulfills the body's needs for essential nutrients such as proteins, carbohydrates, fats, vitamins, minerals, and water.	
4. Press the Home key.	The cursor moves to the home position.
5. Press the Line Adjust key (F5) four times.	The cursor will move down the page.

Continued

PROCEDURES (Continued)	COMMENTS (Continued)
6. The cursor will stop under the "b" in balanced.	A prompt, "Hyphenate where?" appears on the screen.
7. Move the cursor under the second "a" in balanced.	This is where you want the word hyphenated.
8. Press Enter.	The word is hyphenated.
9. Press Line Adjust continually until the cursor is at the end of the paragraph.	The rest of the line endings in the paragraph will adjust.
10. Press F2.	This will end the task.
11. Print the document.	The word "balanced" should be hyphenated on your printout.

STEPS FOR INSERTING KEEP CODES

Sometimes you type certain lines of text that must stay on the same page, such as headings over a table. Without a way to tell the system that this text must stay together, the table could get separated after pagination, as shown in Figure 9.4.

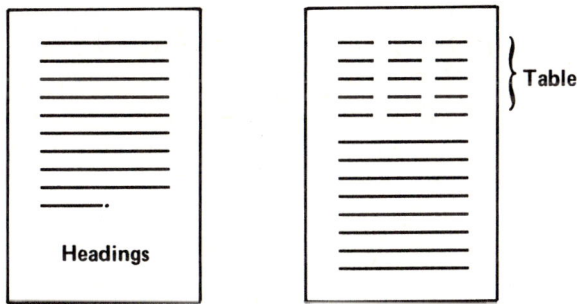

Figure 9.4   No Keep Codes

To ensure that text is not split by pagination, use the Begin Keep and End Keep codes. The Begin Keep code identifies the beginning of the text to be kept together. The End Keep code identifies the end of the text to be kept together. Figure 9.5 illustrates the result of pagination using Keep codes.

You select the Begin and End Keep codes by pressing Instr (F8). This causes the prompt line choices to display.

When revising, the Begin and End Keep codes are deleted in the same way you delete any other text or codes.

Chapter 9   Modifying Text Appearance

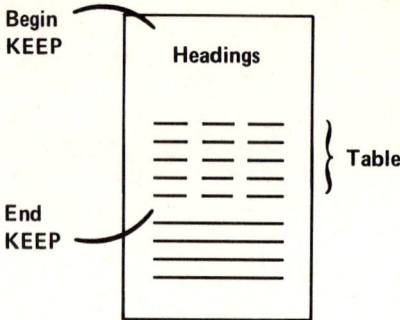

Figure 9.5   Keep Codes

Notes:

--If the text between the Begin and End Keep codes is too long to fit on a single page, the text will be split regardless of the Keep codes.

--When a Required Page End code is in the text between the Begin and End Keep codes, the Required Page End code causes the page to break during pagination.

--Begin and End Keep codes are ignored when the Adjust Page Endings is set at "No" in the Paginate Document Menu.

1. In the typing area, type to the first character or code of the text to be kept together, as shown in Figure 9.6. Include any formatting codes, such as tabs, that are part of the text.

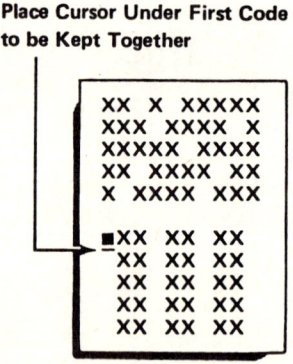

Figure 9.6   Begin Keep Code

2. Press Instr (F8) to display the prompt line choices.

3. Choose Begin.

4. Choose Keep.

5. Type to the first space after the last character or code of the text to be kept together. Include any punctuation or formatting codes, such as Carrier Return codes, that are part of the text.

6. Press Instr (F8). The prompt line choices will display.

7. Choose End.

8. Choose Keep.

9. Continue typing the rest of the document.

10. Press End Task.

11. Use Automatic Pagination to paginate the document.

STEPS FOR INSERTING A REQUIRED SPACE

There may be times when you want to make sure that certain words, names, or numbers stay together on the same line. Examples of this might be as follows:

Washington, D. C.	not	Washington, D. C.
Mr. R. C. Jones	not	Mr. R. C. Jones
June 5, 19--	not	June 5, 19--

When the text was originally created, you may have typed the date, for example, all on one line. After you made additions and deletions and paginated the document, however, the date could be separated. When you do not want words or numbers to be separated, type a Required Space between them. The Required Space is used in place of a normal space. A Required Space is typed by pressing the Ctrl key and the Required Space key (Ctrl--B) at the same time.

The Required Space code looks like this ▼ on your display. On your screen, the date, typed with required spaces, should look like the example following this paragraph. (In order to see the Required Space symbol, you will need to use the cursor movement keys to place the cursor on the Required Space.)

June▼5,▼19--

A Required Space can also be used between words so that a single Word Underscore instruction (Ctrl--U) will underscore several words and the spaces between them.

underscore▼these▼words

1. In the typing area, type to the first character or group of words to be kept together.

2. Press Ctrl--Reqd Space.(Ctrl--B). A Required Space code is inserted.

3. Type the next character or word.

4. Press Ctrl--Reqd Space.

5. Repeat Steps 2 and 3 until you have typed a Required Space between all of the words you want on the same line.

6. Continue typing the rest of the document.

7. Press End Task.

8. Use Automatic Pagination to paginate the document.

EXERCISE 38

In Exercise 38, you will be typing a report with a table incorporated in it. You will be asked to insert Keep instructions before and after the table. The purpose of the Keep instructions is to keep the entire table together so that it will not be printed on two pages. Keeping it on one page makes it easier to read.

The report that you will be typing for Exercise 38 takes up more than 60 lines of typing. According to the document format, 60 is the maximum number of lines that can be printed on a page. When you print the document, you will find that the entire table will be printed on page 2. This is because you inserted Keep instructions around the table. The system needs to keep the table together and not print below line 60. The only solution, therefore, is to move the entire table to page 2.

PROCEDURES	COMMENTS
1. Select Create Document in the Text Task Selection Menu.	
2. Name the document b:Exerci38.	
3. Select Change Document Format.	
4. Select Change Line Format.	
5. Change Line Spacing to Double.	
6. Press Enter.	The Document or Alternate Format Menu displays.
7. Select Change Margins and Tabs.	
8. Delete all tabs.	
Continued	

PROCEDURES (Continued)	COMMENTS (Continued)
9. Set tabs at 20 and 55.	
10. Press Enter.	The Document or Alternate Format Menu displays.
11. Select Change Page Format.	
12. Change First Typing Line, First Page to 13.	
13. Press Enter enough times to reach the typing area.	
14. In the typing area, type until you reach ⬡15.	
15. Return the carriage once.	
16. Press Instr (F8).	The prompt line choices display.
17. Choose Begin.	
18. Choose Keep.	A Begin Keep instruction has been inserted.
19. Continue typing up to the ⬡20.	Type the first column of the table at 20 and the second column at your tab of 55.
20. Type **Toxic**. Press Ctrl--B. Type **Part**. Press Ctrl--U.	This types the column head, Toxic Part, with a continuous underscore.
21. Continue typing up to ⬡22.	
22. Press Instr (F8).	The prompt line choices display.
23. Choose End.	
24. Choose Keep.	An End Keep instruction has been inserted.
25. Press (F2).	This will end the task.
26. Use Automatic Pagination to paginate the document.	
27. Print the document.	This will be a two-page document.

PLANTS AND POISONING

With the increasing popularity of indoor and outdoor plants, the number of accidental poisonings associated with plants has also increased. In fact, household plants recently edged out household products as the nation's number one cause of poisoning in children under five. Pets are frequent victims of plant poisoning.

It is vitally important that you know the names of all plants in your home and yard. It is a good idea to keep with your plants the name tabs that come with them when purchased.

Take unfamiliar plants to a reputable nursery or plant store and have them identified accurately. ⬡15

VEGETABLES

Name	⬡20 Toxic Part
Potato	All green parts
Rhubarb	Leaf blade
Tomato	Green parts

2 carrier returns

TREES

Name	Toxic Part
Apple	Seeds
Black Locust	Bark, sprouts
Cherry	Leaves, twigs, seeds
Fir tree	Nontoxic ⬡22

MAKING TEXT BOLD

DisplayWrite 3 gives you the capability of printing a single character, an entire word, or a series of words in bold type.

You need to insert a Begin Bold code at the beginning of the text and an End Bold code at the end of the text to be printed in bold. You select the Begin and End Bold codes by pressing Instr (F8), which causes the prompt line choices to display.

1. In the typing area, type to the first character or word that you want in bold.

2. Press Instr (F8). The prompt line choices display.

3. Choose Begin.

4. Choose Bold.

5. Type all of the characters you want to be printed in bold.

6. Press Instr (F8). The prompt line choices will display.

7. Choose End.

8. Choose Bold.

9. Continue typing the document.

10. Press End Task.

EXERCISE 39

For Exercise 39, you will be recalling the document Exerci36 to the screen. You will be making some revisions to the document by making certain words bold to make them stand out.

PROCEDURES	COMMENTS
1. Recall the document b:Exerci36 to the screen.	
2. Place the cursor under the "J" in JUSTIFY.	This is where you want the bold type to begin.
3. Press Instr (F8).	The prompt line choices display.
4. Type b.	This is to select Begin.
5. Type b.	This is to select Bold.

Continued

Chapter 9 Modifying Text Appearance

PROCEDURES (Continued)	COMMENTS (Continued)
6. Place the cursor one space past the "Y" in JUSTIFY.	This is where you want the bold type to end.
7. Press Instr (F8).	The prompt line choices display.
8. Type e.	This is to select End.
9. Type b.	This is to select Bold.
10. Place the cursor under the "D" in DisplayWrite 3.	This is where you want the bold type to begin.
11. Press Instr (F8).	The prompt line choices display.
12. Type b.	This is to select Begin.
13. Type b.	This is to select Bold.
14. Move the cursor to the blank space following the "3" in DisplayWrite 3.	This is where you want the bold type to end.
15. Press Instr (F8).	The prompt line choices display.
16. Type e.	This is to select End.
17. Type b.	This is to select Bold.
18. Press F2.	This will end the task.
19. Print the document.	

INDENTING PARAGRAPHS

You may want to type paragraphs that are indented from the left margin. This format is used for outlines or anytime several consecutive lines of text are indented from the left margin.

Instead of using the tab to type indented paragraphs, you will press Ctrl and Indent at the beginning of the first line of the text to be indented. This sets up a temporary left margin. As you type, automatic carrier returns move the cursor to the temporary left margin so you do not have to type a tab before each line (see Figure 9.7).

Using Indent saves you typing time; but more importantly, it saves you time when revising your document. When a regular tab is typed on every line, adding or deleting text rearranges those tab positions and the text will not realign correctly. When you use Indent, adding or deleting text will not change the position of any tabs and the indented text realigns correctly.

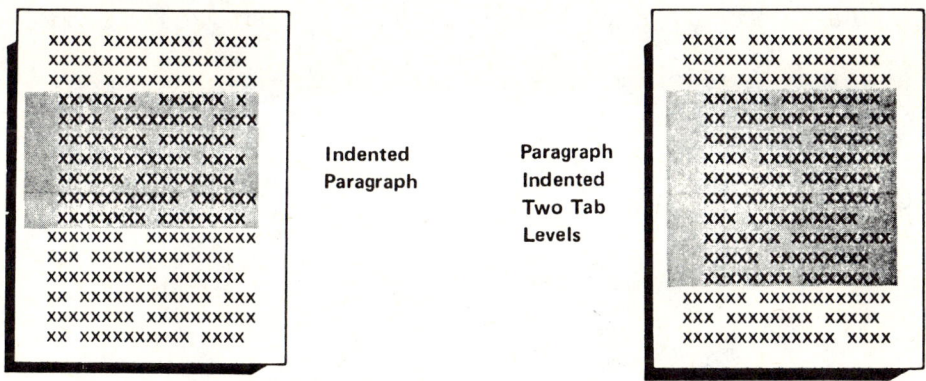

Figure 9.7   Indented Paragraphs

If lines of text are indented more than one tab level from the left margin, press Ctrl and Indent for each tab level you want to indent (see Figure 9.8). A temporary left margin can be set up at any tab setting.

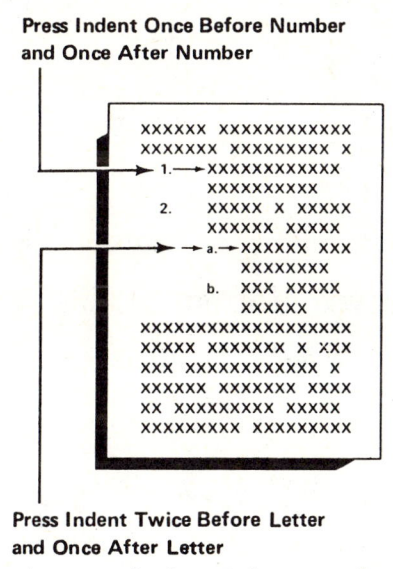

Figure 9.8   Tab Levels

The temporary left margin can be canceled by pressing the carrier return. This cancels the indent and returns the cursor to the original left margin. Using a Page Format Change, a Line Format Change, and a Format Return also cancels the Indent code. Indent codes are deleted by pressing the Del key.

STEPS FOR CREATING INDENTED PARAGRAPHS

1. Decide where tabs need to be set for each level of indentation. If the default tab settings are usable, you can skip Steps 3, 4, and 5.

Chapter 9   Modifying Text Appearance

2. Choose Create Document in the Text Task Selection Menu.

3. Choose Change Document Format in the Document or Alternate Format Menu.

4. Choose Change Margins and Tabs in the Format Selection Menu.

5. Set tabs for the document. Return to the typing area.

6. Type your document. When you reach the indented paragraphs, press Ctrl--Indent (see Figure 9.9) once for each level of tab needed.

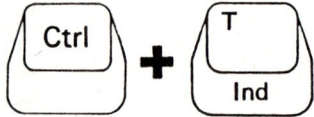

Figure 9.9   Ctrl--Indent

7. Type the indented paragraph. You should find that as the system carrier returns, the cursor returns to the temporary left margin.

8. Press carrier return at the end of the last indented line. This cancels the Indent and returns the cursor to the original left margin.

9. Continue typing the text using Indent when needed.

10. Press End Task.

11. Use Automatic Pagination to paginate the document.

STEPS FOR CHANGING INDENTATION OF PARAGRAPHS

1. If there are tabs or Indent codes in the text to be indented, delete the tabs and the Indent codes. The lines following the deleted Indent code readjust automatically.

2. If the text had Indent codes, you will also need to delete the Required Carrier Return codes following the indented text.

3. If it is necessary to add a level of indentation, set a tab in the Margins and Tabs Menu. Then use Ctrl--Indent on the first line of text you wish to indent.

4. Insert Required Carrier Returns at the end of the indented text.

5. Press End Task.

6. Use Automatic Pagination to paginate the document.

EXERCISE 40

In Exercise 40, you will be creating the document that is shown following this exercise. In order to type the indented paragraphs, you will need to set up a temporary left margin. This is done by pressing Ctrl--T.

PROCEDURES	COMMENTS
1. Select Create Document in the Text Task Selection Menu.	
2. Name the document b:Exerci40.	
3. Select Change Document Format.	
4. Select Change Page Format.	
5. Change First Typing Line, First Page to 13.	
6. Press Enter until you reach the typing area.	
7. Type the document on the next page. Stop when you reach the ⟨8⟩.	
8. Press Ctrl--T.	
9. Type 1.	
10. Press Ctrl--T.	This sets your temporary left margin.
11. Continue typing up to ⟨12⟩.	Do not type the carrier returns. Use the automatic carrier return.
12. Press the carrier return twice.	This returns your cursor back to the left margin.
13. Press Ctrl--T.	
14. Type 2.	
15. Press Ctrl--T.	This sets your temporary left margin.

Continued

Chapter 9 Modifying Text Appearance

PROCEDURES (Continued)	COMMENTS (Continued)
16. Continue typing up to ⟨17⟩.	Do not type the carrier returns. Use the automatic carrier return.
17. Press the carrier return twice.	This returns your cursor to the left margin.
18. Type the next paragraph.	
19. Repeat the previous procedures for typing the last set of indented paragraphs.	
20. Press F2.	This will end the task.
21. Print the document.	

FOOTNOTES

The writer of a term paper or report should credit the source of his/her quotations by means of footnotes.

Footnotes may be constructed in either of the following ways:

⟨8⟩ 1. In complete form--giving all available facts of publication such as authors, title of publication, publishing company, date, and page.⟨12⟩

2. In brief form--giving only the author's name, the publication title, and a page reference. This is used only when a formal bibliography is included.⟨17⟩

A footnote is typed at the bottom of the page on which its reference figure appears. A footnote is separated from the last line of a manuscript as follows:

1. After typing the last manuscript line, single-space and type an underscore 1 1/2 inches long beginning at the left margin.

2. Following the underscore, double-space, indent five spaces from the left margin, and type the appropriate superscript. Without spacing, type the footnote single-spaced. Double-space between footnotes.

154   Chapter 9 Modifying Text Appearance

CHAPTER SUMMARY

A. Justifying the Right Margin

   1. Choose Change Document Format in the Text Task Selection Menu.
   2. Choose Change Line Format in the Format Selection Menu.
   3. Choose Line Alignment and set it to Justify.
   4. Press Enter to go to the typing area.

B. Using Line Adjust

   1. Move your cursor to the beginning of the first line to be adjusted.
   2. Press Line Adjust once for each line that needs to be adjusted.
   3. Make line ending choices if the prompt "Hyphenate where?" displays on the screen.

C. Inserting Begin and End Keep Codes

   1. Type to the first character or code of the text to be kept together.
   2. Press Instr (F8).
   3. Choose Begin.
   4. Choose Keep.
   5. Type to the first space after the last character or code of the text to be kept together.
   6. Press Instr.
   7. Choose End.
   8. Choose Keep.
   9. Continue typing the rest of the document.

D. Inserting a required space involves pressing Ctrl--Reqd Space (Ctrl--B).

E. Making Text Bold

   1. Type to the first character or word to be typed in bold print.
   2. Press Instr.
   3. Choose Begin.
   4. Choose Bold.
   5. Type all the characters that need to be typed in bold print.
   6. Press Instr.
   7. Choose End.
   8. Choose Bold.

F. Typing Indented Paragraphs

   1. To type indented paragraphs, press Ctrl--Indent (Ctrl--T) once for each level of tab needed.
   2. Press the carrier return at the end of the last indented line to cancel the indent and return the cursor to the original left margin.

Chapter 10

CREATING HEADERS AND FOOTERS

When you complete this chapter, you will be able to:

1. Type superscripts and subscripts.

2. Create headers and footers.

3. Create alternating headers and footers.

CHAPTER SUMMARY

A. Justifying the Right Margin

    1. Choose Change Document Format in the Text Task Selection Menu.
    2. Choose Change Line Format in the Format Selection Menu.
    3. Choose Line Alignment and set it to Justify.
    4. Press Enter to go to the typing area.

B. Using Line Adjust

    1. Move your cursor to the beginning of the first line to be adjusted.
    2. Press Line Adjust once for each line that needs to be adjusted.
    3. Make line ending choices if the prompt "Hyphenate where?" displays on the screen.

C. Inserting Begin and End Keep Codes

    1. Type to the first character or code of the text to be kept together.
    2. Press Instr (F8).
    3. Choose Begin.
    4. Choose Keep.
    5. Type to the first space after the last character or code of the text to be kept together.
    6. Press Instr.
    7. Choose End.
    8. Choose Keep.
    9. Continue typing the rest of the document.

D. Inserting a required space involves pressing Ctrl--Reqd Space (Ctrl--B).

E. Making Text Bold

    1. Type to the first character or word to be typed in bold print.
    2. Press Instr.
    3. Choose Begin.
    4. Choose Bold.
    5. Type all the characters that need to be typed in bold print.
    6. Press Instr.
    7. Choose End.
    8. Choose Bold.

F. Typing Indented Paragraphs

    1. To type indented paragraphs, press Ctrl--Indent (Ctrl--T) once for each level of tab needed.
    2. Press the carrier return at the end of the last indented line to cancel the indent and return the cursor to the original left margin.

Chapter 10

CREATING HEADERS AND FOOTERS

When you complete this chapter, you will be able to:

1. Type superscripts and subscripts.

2. Create headers and footers.

3. Create alternating headers and footers.

SUPERSCRIPTS AND SUBSCRIPTS

Superscripts and subscripts are often used in mathematical or scientific material. Superscripts are characters printed a half space above the normal line of printing. You have probably typed superscripts when you typed footnotes. Subscripts are characters printed a half space below the normal printing line.

To create a superscript, press Ctrl--1/2 Up and type the characters. To create a subscript, press Ctrl--1/2 Down and type the characters. The screen will not show the characters as being 1/2 up or 1/2 down. The printer, though, will print the characters above and below the lines.

STEPS FOR CREATING SUPERSCRIPTS

1. Type to the first position where a superscript is to begin in your document.

2. Press Ctrl--1/2 Up as shown in Figure 10.1.

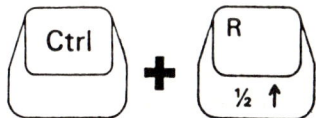

Figure 10.1   Ctrl--1/2 Up

3. Type the characters for the superscripts. Remember that the screen will not show the superscripts as being above the line.

4. Press Ctrl--1/2 Down, as shown in Figure 10.2, to return to the typing line.

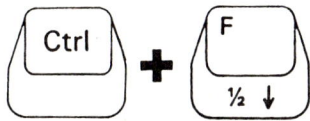

Figure 10.2   Ctrl--1/2 Down

5. Continue typing the rest of the document.

6. Press End Task.

7. Use Automatic Pagination to paginate the document.

STEPS FOR CREATING SUBSCRIPTS

1. Type to the first position where a subscript is to begin in your document.

2. Press Ctrl--1/2 Down.

3. Type the characters for the subscript.

Chapter 10   Creating Headers and Footers

4. Press Ctrl--1/2 Up to return to the typing line.

5. Continue typing the rest of the document.

6. Press End Task.

7. Use Automatic Pagination to paginate the document.

STEPS FOR DELETING SUPERSCRIPTS AND SUBSCRIPTS

1. Place the cursor under the 1/2 Up or 1/2 Down code that precedes the superscript or subscript characters. The words "Half Index Up" or "Half Index Down" display on the status line to help you position your cursor.

2. Delete the 1/2 Up and 1/2 Down codes by using the Del key.

3. Move the cursor to the 1/2 Up or 1/2 Down following the superscript or subscript and delete.

4. Press End Task.

5. Use Automatic Pagination to paginate the document.

EXERCISE 41

You will be typing the document that appears at the end of this exercise. The document will give you practice in typing superscripts and subscripts, as well as making a line format change.

PROCEDURES	COMMENTS
1. Select Create Document in the Text Task Selection Menu.	
2. Name the document b:Exerci41.	
3. Select Change Line Format.	
4. Change Line Spacing to Double.	
5. Continue to press Enter until you reach the typing area.	
6. Type the document. Stop typing when you reach ⑦.	
7. Type H.	
Continued	

PROCEDURES (Continued)	COMMENTS (Continued)
8. Press Ctrl--1/2 Down (Ctrl--F).	You are now a half space below the line of typing.
9. Type 2.	The 2 will be a subscript.
10. Press Ctrl--1/2 Up (Ctrl--R).	This will return you to the normal line of typing.
11. Type 0.	
12. Return the carriage.	
13. Type 10.	
14. Press Ctrl--1/2 Up.	You are now a half space above the line of typing.
15. Type (n-3).	The (n-3) will be a superscript.
16. Press Ctrl--1/2 Down.	This will return you to the normal line of typing.
17. Type +y=120.	This will finish the equation.
18. Continue typing until you reach ⬡19.	
19. Press Fmt (F7).	This will change the format.
20. Select Change Line Format.	
21. Change Line Spacing to Single.	Footnotes are typed single-spaced.
22. Press Enter twice to return to the typing area.	
23. Press Tab once.	
24. Press Ctrl--1/2 Up.	You are now a half space above the typing line.
25. Type 1.	The 1 will be a superscript.
26. Press Ctrl--1/2 Down.	You are now back on the normal typing line.
27. Continue typing the rest of the document.	
28. Press F2.	This is to end the task.

Continued

Chapter 10 Creating Headers and Footers

> PROCEDURES (Continued)
>
> COMMENTS (Continued)
>
> 29. Print the document.

Superscripts and subscripts are often used in mathematical and scientific material. Here are some examples:

$$\langle 7 \rangle \; H_2O$$
$$10^{(n-3)} + y = 120$$

Superscripts are also used in footnotes:

⟨19⟩ [1]Thomas M. Jones, <u>Word Processing Handbook</u>, (2d ed., Cleveland: Northern Publishing Co., 1974), p. 23.

CREATING HEADERS AND FOOTERS

Headers and footers allow us to have various types of information automatically printed on every page of the document. A few examples would be page numbers, a date, chapter titles, and so on.

A header could contain any of the previously mentioned information typed in the top margin of every page in the document. A footer could contain any of this same information typed in the bottom margin of every page in the document (see Figure 10.3).

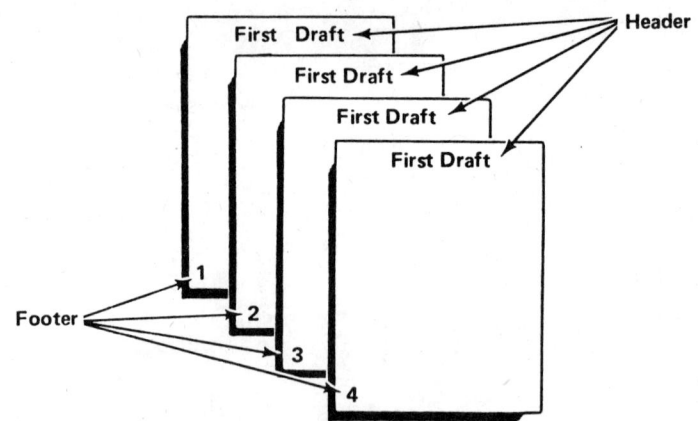

Figure 10.3 Headers and Footers

Even though headers and footers appear on every page, you only need to type them once. The text is typed in a typing area which is accessed only through the Header and Footer Menu.

The system automatically sets Line Spacing to single-spacing and sets Auto Carrier Return and Adjust Line Endings to "No" when printing headers and footers. The margins and tabs for headers and footers use the same default settings that are established in the Document or Alternate Format Menu. If changes in margins and tabs are made to the document, the margin and tab settings in the header or footer typing area will not change automatically.

INCORPORATING PAGE NUMBERS IN HEADERS AND FOOTERS

There are two types of page numbers available for use in headers and footers.

1. System Page Numbers are assigned by the system as you type the document or during Automatic Pagination. It is the page number that is displayed on the status line while you are typing the document.

   System Page Numbers are used when the document begins on page 1 and is numbered consecutively to the last page, as shown in Figure 10.4. When using System Page Numbers, you should always paginate the document before printing. Pagination removes any inconsistencies in page numbering that may occur while creating or revising a document.

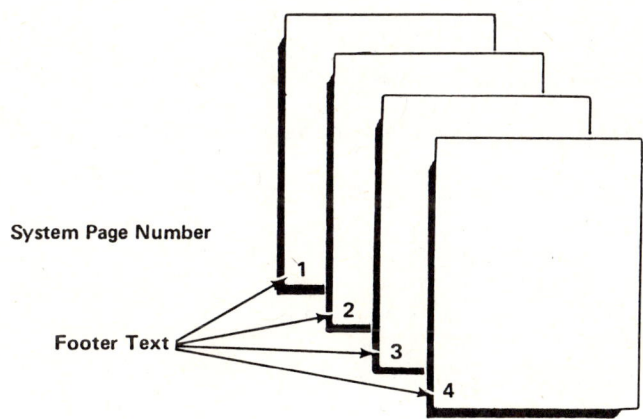

Figure 10.4   System Page Numbers

2. Page Numbers are numbers that are assigned by the typist and can be any number between 1 and 9999. The system then increments the number for each subsequent page typed. The following is an example of where you would choose to use Page Numbers. If you were writing several chapters for a book, each chapter would have been inputted as a new document. If your previous chapter contained 40 pages, you would want the subsequent chapter to begin with page 41. In order to do this, you would need to choose Page Number in the Page Number Menu and type 41, as shown in Figure 10.5. Otherwise, the system would begin numbering this chapter with page 1 since it sees it as a new document.

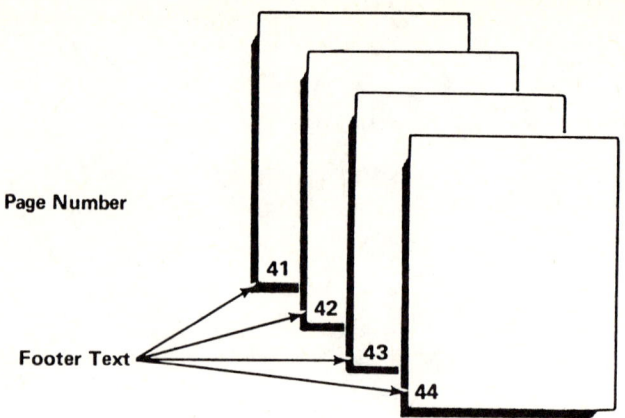

Figure 10.5   Page Number

STEPS FOR CREATING HEADERS AND FOOTERS

1. Select Create Document in the Text Task Selection Menu.

2. Select Change Document Format in the Create or Revise Document Menu.

3. Select Change Header and Footer in the Document or Alternate Format Menu.

4. Select Create or Revise Header in the Header and Footer Menu.

5. Type the header text and then press Continue (F10).

6. Select Create or Revise Footer in the Header and Footer Menu.

7. Type the footer text and then press Continue (F10). The footer text prints under the margin scale on your screen, but it will print at the bottom of the page on your paper.

8. Change the following items in the Header and Footer Menu, if necessary:

   --First Header Line
   --Print Header On
   --First Footer Line
   --Print Footer On

   These items must be compatible with the choices made through the Format Selection Menu. For example, if your First Typing Line is seven, your First Header Line must be smaller than seven.

9. Press Enter to return to the Document or Alternate Format Menu.

10. Press Enter to return to the Create or Revise Document Menu.

11. Press Enter to go to the typing area.

12. Type the document.

13. Press End Task (F2).

14. Use Automatic Pagination to paginate the document.

STEPS FOR NUMBERING PAGES

1. Select Create or Revise Header or Footer in the Header and Footer Menu.

2. Tab or space to the location where the page number is to print.

3. Press Instr (F8) to display prompt line choices.

4. Select Page Number. The Page Number Menu is illustrated in Figure 10.6.

5. Select System Page Number or Page Number. If you select Page Number, type the number with which the document is to begin.

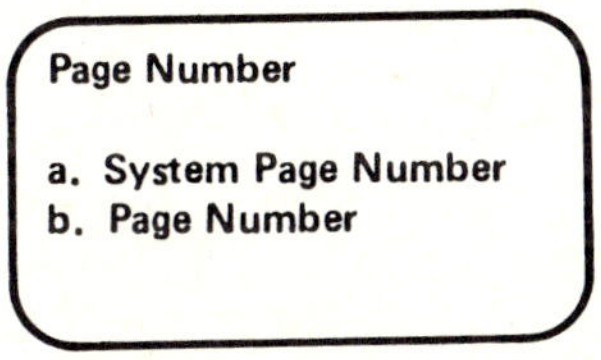

```
Page Number

a. System Page Number
b. Page Number
```

Figure 10.6   Page Number Menu

6. Press Continue. Make any other necessary changes in the Header and Footer Menu.

7. Press Enter to go to the typing area.

8. Type the document.

9. Press End Task (F2).

10. Use Automatic Pagination to paginate the document.

STEPS FOR REVISING HEADERS AND FOOTERS

1. Select Create or Revise Header or Footer from the Header and Footer Menu.

2. In the typing area for headers and footers, revise or delete the header or footer text the same way you do for any text or codes.

3. Press Continue (F10).

4. Press Enter to return to the typing area.

5. Press End Task (F2).

6. Use Automatic Pagination to paginate the document.

Chapter 10   Creating Headers and Footers

EXERCISE 42

In Exercise 42, you will be recalling the document b:VisitLA. You will revise this document by adding a header and footer to it.

PROCEDURES	COMMENTS
1. Select Revise Document in the Text Task Selection Menu.	
2. Type b:VisitLA.	This is the name of the document to be revised.
3. Select Change Document Format in the Create or Revise Document Menu.	
4. Select Change Header and Footer in the Document or Alternate Format Menu.	The Header and Footer Menu will display.
5. Type a.	This is to select Create or Revise Header.
6. Press Enter.	The Create or Revise Header typing area displays.
7. At the upper left corner of the screen, type Chapter 1.	
8. Press Continue (F10).	The Header and Footer Menu displays.
9. Type d.	This is to select Create or Revise Footer.
10. Press Enter.	The Create or Revise Footer typing area displays.
11. Space over to the center of the typing line.	Place your cursor on the pyramid-shaped symbol.
12. Press Instr (F8).	The prompt line choices display.
13. Press Enter.	This is to choose Page Number.
14. Type a and press Enter.	This is to choose System Page Number.
15. Press Continue (F10).	The Header and Footer Menu displays.

Continued

PROCEDURES (Continued)	COMMENTS (Continued)
16. Press Enter.	The Document or Alternate Format Menu displays.
17. Press Enter.	The Create or Revise Document Menu displays.
18. Press Enter.	The document displays.
19. Press F2.	This is to end the task.
20. Paginate the document.	
21. Print the document. The first page of your document will look like Figure 10.8.	

CREATING ALTERNATING HEADERS AND FOOTERS

The headers and footers that we have created thus far have printed in identical form and position on every page. However, documents that are printed on both sides of the paper often have different headers and footers on the facing pages. An example of this would be to have the title of a book or report as a header on the left-hand (even-numbered) pages and have chapter titles on the right-hand (odd-numbered) pages. Alternating headers and footers would allow you to have a set of headers and footers for all even-numbered pages and a different set for all odd-numbered pages, as shown in Figure 10.7.

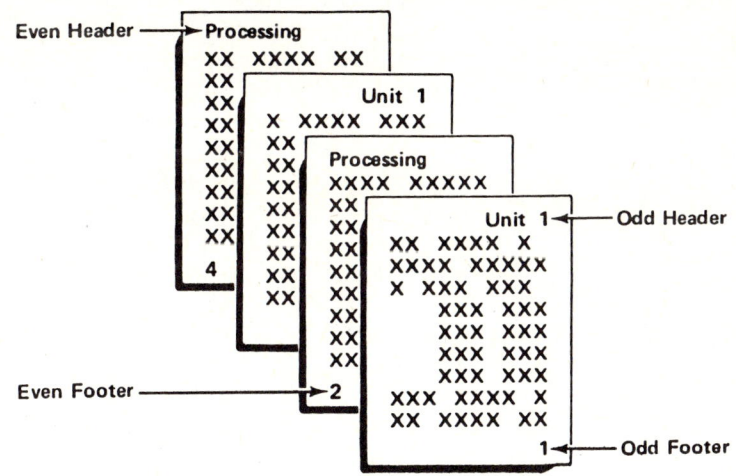

Figure 10.7 Alternating Headers and Footers

Alternating headers and footers are created and revised the same way as regular headers and footers. The only difference with alternating headers and footers is that you have two headers and two footers to create or revise.

Chapter 10 Creating Headers and Footers

Chapter 1

VISITING LOS ANGELES

     Today's TV image of L.A. is set by the westside---the broad
shady streets of Beverly Hills, the Rolls-lined sidewalks of
Rodeo Drive, and the pool-studded homes in the hills above Sunset
Boulevard. For much of the world, the "good life" in America has
become synonymous with the elegance of places like Beverly Hills,
Brentwood, and Westwood. This is where the stars live--and most
of the affluent in L.A. county.
POINTS OF INTEREST
     Star-gazing is very popular in L.A., and there are a number
of tours that will guide you past the homes of the stars.
     Westwood is the home of the University of California at L.A.
and the spot where most of Hollywood's new films open. Westwood
is a spirited college town with a gala of theaters, bookshops,
clothing stores, and restaurants.
WINING AND DINING
     The influx of young, ambitious, and creative chefs and
restaurateurs have found in L.A. an eager clientele to challenge
their talents. Because dining in L.A. is an important part of
the social life, restaurants tend to be exciting and imaginative
as well as intensely competitive in the quality of their cooking.
     La Cienega's Restaurant Row still illustrates some of the
diversity of L.A. eating. From Lawry's Prime Rib and Gitanjali's

                                1

         Figure 10.8   Exercise 42 Printout

TYPING PAGE NUMBERS ON ALTERNATING HEADERS AND FOOTERS

Typing page numbers on alternating headers and footers is similar to typing page numbers on regular headers and footers, except for the following minor changes:

1. If you use System Page Numbers, you must type the entry in both the odd pages' and even pages' header/footer typing areas.

2. If you use Page Number to print page numbers other than system-generated numbers, you must type the same number in both the odd pages' and the even pages' header/footer typing areas. The number you choose for Page Number determines if an odd or even header/footer is used first. When you type an odd number, the odd page header/footer is used first. When you type an even number, the even page header/footer is used first.

STEPS FOR CREATING ALTERNATING HEADERS AND FOOTERS

1. Select Create Document in the Text Task Selection Menu.

2. Select Change Document Format in the Create or Revise Document Menu.

3. Select Change Alternating Headers and Footers in the Document or Alternate Format Menu.

4. Select all of the following items listed in the Alternating Headers and Footers Menu.

    --Create or Revise Odd Pages Header
    --Create or Revise Even Pages Header
    --Create or Revise Odd Pages Footer
    --Create or Revise Even Pages Footer

    Each of the items takes you to a header or footer typing area. The order in which you select them does not matter.

5. Type the header or footer text in the four typing areas. Press Continue (F10) when you finish typing in each area.

6. Change these other items in the Alternating Headers and Footers Menu, if necessary:

    --First Header Line
    --Print Headers On
    --First Footer Line
    --Print Footers On

7. Press Enter to go to the typing area.

8. Type the document.

9. Press End Task.

10. Use Automatic Pagination to paginate the document.

STEPS FOR REVISING ALTERNATING HEADERS AND FOOTERS

1. Select Change Alternating Headers and Footers in the Document or Alternate Format Menu.

2. Select Create or Revise Odd/Even Pages Header or Footer in the Alternating Headers and Footers Menu.

3. In the typing area for headers and footers, revise or delete the alternating header or footer text the same way that you do any other text or codes.

4. Press Continue (F10).

5. Press Enter to return to the typing area.

6. Press End Task (F2).

7. Use Automatic Pagination to paginate the document.

EXERCISE 43

In Exercise 43, you will be revising the document b:VisitLA by adding alternating headers and footers to the document.

PROCEDURES	COMMENTS
1. Select Revise Document in the Text Task Selection Menu.	
2. Type b:VisitLA.	This is the name of the document to be revised.
3. Select Change Document Format in the Create or Revise Document Menu.	
4. Select Change Alternating Headers and Footers in the Document or Alternate Format Menu.	The Alternating Header and Footer Menu will display.
5. Type a.	This is to select Create or Revise Odd Pages Header.
6. Press Enter.	The Create/Revise Header typing area displays.
7. Move the cursor to 65.	
8. Type Chapter 1.	
9. Press Continue (F10).	
	Continued

PROCEDURES (Continued)	COMMENTS (Continued)
10. Type b.	This is to select Create or Revise Even Pages Header.
11. Press Enter.	The Create/Revise Header typing area displays.
12. Type **TOURING USA**.	
13. Press Continue (F10).	
14. Type e.	This is to select Create or Revise Odd Pages Footer.
15. Press Enter.	The typing area displays.
16. Move the cursor to 72.	
17. Press Instr (F8).	The prompt line choices displays.
18. Press Enter.	This is to choose Page Number.
19. Type a.	This is to select System Page Number.
20. Press Enter.	The typing area displays with the System Page Number symbol at 72.
21. Press Continue (F10).	
22. Type f.	This is to select Create or Revise Even Pages Footer.
23. Press Enter.	The Create/Revise Footer typing area displays.
24. At the left margin, press Instr (F8).	The prompt line choices display.
25. Press Enter.	This is to choose Page Number.
26. Type a.	This is to select System Page Number.
27. Press Enter.	The Create/Revise Footer typing area displays with the System Page Number symbol at the left margin.
28. Press Continue (F10).	The Alternating Headers and Footers Menu displays.

Continued

PROCEDURES (Continued)	COMMENTS (Continued)
29. Press Enter.	The Document or Alternate Format Menu displays.
30. Press Enter.	The Create or Revise Document Menu displays.
31. Press Enter.	The document displays.
32. Press F2.	This is to end the task.
33. Paginate the document.	
34. Print the document. Your first two pages should look like Figures 10.9 and 10.10.	

                                                            Chapter 1

                        VISITING LOS ANGELES

     Today's TV image of L.A. is set by the westside--the broad
shady streets of Beverly Hills, the Rolls-lined sidewalks of
Rodeo Drive, and the pool-studded homes in the hills above Sunset
Boulevard. For much of the world, the "good life" in America has
become synonymous with the elegance of places like Beverly Hills,
Brentwood, and Westwood. This is where the stars live--and most
of the affluent in L.A. county.
POINTS OF INTEREST
     Star-gazing is very popular in L.A., and there are a number
of tours that will guide you past the homes of the stars.
     Westwood is the home of the University of California at L.A.
and the spot where most of Hollywood's new films open. Westwood
is a spirited college town with a gala of theaters, bookshops,
clothing stores, and restaurants.
WINING AND DINING
     The influx of young, ambitious, and creative chefs and
restaurateurs have found in L.A. an eager clientele to challenge
their talents. Because dining in L.A. is an important part of
the social life, restaurants tend to be exciting and imaginative
as well as intensely competitive in the quality of their cooking.
     La Cienega's Restaurant Row still illustrates some of the
diversity of L.A. eating. From Lawry's Prime Rib and Gitanjali's

                                                                  1

            Figure 10.9   Exercise 43 Printout

TOURING USA

award-winning Indian fare to Benihana's chef floor show, every nationality and taste sensation is represented within a few blocks between Wilshire and San Vicente.

NIGHTLIFE

When people speak of the nightlife in L.A., it is usually the westside's haunts that do the attracting. In Beverly Hills, you can spend a wonderful evening just window-shopping along the streets. This is one of the few neighborhoods in L.A. besides Westwood where walking is the main form of transportation.

The scene in Century City is also for walkers but is more sedate. All the restaurants have lovely saloons for the after-theater crowd. In L.A., theaters, movie houses, and the famous Shubert Theatre are all found here on the west side. THE CITIES OF THE HARBOR

The big, bustling, side-by-side harbors of L.A. and Long Beach were, like much of L.A., the product of much sweat and hard work rather than gifts of nature. Today, two harbors constitute the shipping hub of the Pacific Coast, moving more than 125,000 tons of cargo daily along miles of dock that can berth 100 ships. San Pedro, annexed by L.A. to gain a seaport, lies at the gateway to the L.A. Harbor and forms the western tip of the harbor area crescent. The entire harbor area is married to the sea, and the tourists who come to make use of the harbors' recreation are as critical to the region's economy as fishing and shipping.

Long Beach is the home of the world's largest passenger ship, the Queen Mary, and the world's largest passenger wooden airplane, the Spruce Goose. Long Beach has undergone a dramatic,

2

Figure 10.10 Exercise 43 Printout

CHAPTER SUMMARY

A. Creating Superscripts

   1. Press Ctrl--1/2 Up (Ctrl--R).
   2. Type the characters for the superscript.
   3. Press Ctrl--1/2 Down (Ctrl--F) to return to the typing line.

B. Creating Subscripts

   1. Press Ctrl--1/2 Down.
   2. Type the characters for the subscript.
   3. Type Ctrl--1/2 Up to return to the typing line.

C. Creating Headers and Footers

   1. Select Change Document Format in the Create or Revise Document Menu.
   2. Select Change Header and Footer in the Format Selection Menu.
   3. Select Create or Revise Header in the Header and Footer Menu.
   4. Type the header text and then press Continue (F10).
   5. Select Create or Revise Footer in the Header and Footer Menu.
   6. Type the footer text and then press Continue (F10).
   7. Make the necessary changes in the Header and Footer Menu.
   8. Press Enter to go to the typing area.

D. Numbering Pages

   1. Select Create or Revise Header or Footer in the Header and Footer Menu.
   2. Tab or space to the location where the page number is to print.
   3. Press Instr (F8).
   4. Select Page Number.
   5. Select System Page Number or Page Number. If you select Page Number, type the number with which the document is to begin.
   6. Press Continue. Make any necessary changes in the Header and Footer Menu.
   7. Press Enter to go to the typing area.

E. Creating Alternate Headers and Footers

   1. Select Change Document Format in the Create or Revise Document Menu.
   2. Select Change Alternating Headers and Footers in the Format Selection Menu.
   3. Select all of the following items in the Alternating Headers and Footers Menu:
      --Create or Revise Odd Pages Header
      --Create or Revise Even Pages Header
      --Create or Revise Odd Pages Footer
      --Create or Revise Even Pages Footer
   4. Type the header or footer text in the four typing areas. Press Continue when you finish typing in each area.
   5. Make the necessary changes in the other items in the Alternating Headers and Footers Menu, if necessary.
   6. Press Enter to go to the typing area.

Chapter 11

CREATING ENVELOPES

When you complete this chapter, you will be able to:

1. Create a document consisting of envelopes only.

2. Store and recall a document using block save.

STEPS FOR CREATING ENVELOPES

In this chapter, we will discuss two procedures for creating envelopes. The first procedure explains the steps for creating a document made up only of envelopes. The second procedure explains how to create a letter with an envelope in the same document.

In a previous chapter, we discussed how to set up an alternate format to create envelopes. If you create envelopes frequently, it will be to your advantage to set up an alternate format for envelopes.

1. Select Create Document in the Text Task Selection Menu.

2. Select Change Document Format in the Create or Revise Document Menu.

3. Select Change Page Format in the Document or Alternate Format Menu.

4. Change all of the following items for proper placement for your envelope size:

   --First Typing Line
   --First Typing Line, Following Pages (the following pages are also envelopes)
   --Last Typing Line
   --Paper or Envelope Size
   --Printing Paper Source (Select "Manual Feed." If your printer has an envelope tray, select "Envelope.")

5. Press Enter to return to the Document or Alternate Format Menu.

6. Select Margins and Tabs in the Document or Alternate Format Menu.

7. Change the left and right margins for proper placement on your envelope.

8. Press Enter to return to the Document or Alternate Format Menu.

9. Press Enter to return to the Create or Revise Document Menu.

10. Press Enter to go to the typing area.

11. Type the name and address for the envelope.

12. Press Ctrl--Page End.

13. Continue typing the rest of the names and addresses for each envelope using Steps 11 and 12. Do not press Ctrl--Page End after the last envelope.

14. After the last envelope, press End Task to store the document. Do not use Automatic Pagination for a document of envelopes.

15. Make the necessary changes on the Print Menu before printing the document. (You may need to change Paper Handling in the Printer Description Menu.)

EXERCISE 44

In Exercise 44, you will be creating a document that consists of envelopes only. You will be treating each envelope as a new page of the document.

PROCEDURES	COMMENTS
1. Select Create Document in the Text Task Selection Menu.	
2. Name the document b:Exerci44.	
3. Select Change Document Format in the Create or Revise Document Menu.	
4. Select Change Page Format in the Format Selection Menu.	
5. Change First Typing Line, First Page to 15.	Begin typing business envelopes on line 15.
6. Change First Typing Line, Following Pages to 15.	Each page is an envelope.
7. Change Last Typing Line to 20.	
8. Change Paper or Envelope Size to Choice 7.	This is the standard-size business envelope.
9. Change Printing Paper Source to Choice 4.	If you have an envelope tray, choose "5 Envelopes."
10. Press Enter.	The Document or Alternate Format Menu displays.
11. Select Change Margins and Tabs.	
12. Set the left margin at 40.	
13. Set the right margin at 90.	
14. Press Enter.	The Document or Alternate Format Menu displays.

Continued

PROCEDURES (Continued)	COMMENTS (Continued)
15. Press Enter.	The Create or Revise Document Menu displays.
16. Press Enter.	The typing area displays.
17. Type: MS MARIE PARZYCH 210 MAIN ST SEATTLE WA 98101-8320	This is the name and address for the first envelope.
18. Press Ctrl--Page End.	The next page displays.
19. Type: MR THOMAS BOOS 7 BEVERLY BLVD LOS ANGELES CA 90042-1372	This is the name and address for the second envelope.
20. Press Ctrl--Page End.	The next page displays.
21. Type: MS CAROL REITMYER 1222 GRAND AVE DETROIT MI 48224-5614	This is the name and address for the third envelope.
22. Press F2.	The Text Task Selection Menu displays.
23. Select Print Document.	Make any necessary changes to the Print Document Menu and Printer Description Menu.

BLOCKS OF TEXT

The remainder of this chapter will explain blocks of text. You will learn how to save and recall a block of text. You will also learn how to create an envelope by copying it from the inside address of a letter.

STEPS FOR SAVING A BLOCK OF TEXT

1. In the typing area, place the cursor under the first character or code to be saved.

2. Press Block (F4). The prompt line choices will appear. Select Save or ASCII_save.

3. Follow the prompt to move the cursor to the end of the block and press Enter. The block of text is highlighted.

4. If you selected Save in Step 2, the prompt "Type document name; press ENTER" displays. The system will supply a default document name of SAVEDOC.TXT. You may type another name if you wish.

5. If you selected ASCII_save, the prompt "Type name of file; press ENTER" displays. The system will not supply a default file name; you will need to type the file name. It will supply a default extension of .ASC unless you type another.

6. Press Enter. The highlighted text is saved in the document or file you specified. It also remains in your original document.

STEPS FOR RECALLING A BLOCK OF SAVED TEXT

1. In the typing area, place the cursor under the first character or code that the recalled block is to precede.

2. Press Block (F4). Select Recall. The prompt "Type document name; press ENTER" displays. The system default is to display the name used in the last Save or ASCII_save operation. If there was no previous save operation, the default name is SAVEDOC.

3. Press Enter to recall the default document name. If the default document is not the one you wish to recall, then press Esc to clear the name on the prompt line. Type the name of the document you want to recall and then press Enter.

4. The document or file is inserted at the cursor position. When you have finished making all of your changes, paginate the document.

STEPS FOR CREATING AN ENVELOPE WITH A LETTER

1. After typing the last page of the letter, press Ctrl--Page End.

2. Press Format.

3. The Page Format Change Menu displays. Select Change Page Format.

4. Make the page format changes required for an envelope. Change the following items for proper placement of the address for your envelope:

    --First Typing Line
    --Last Typing Line
    --Envelope Size
    --Printing Paper Source (Select "Manual Feed." If your printer
      has an envelope tray, select "Envelope.")

5. Press Enter to return to the Page Format Change Menu.

6. Select Change Margins and Tabs in the Page Format Change Menu.

7. Change the left and right margins so that the address will be properly placed on the envelope.

8. Press Enter to return to the Page Format Change Menu.

9. Press Enter to go to the typing area.

10. Type the name and address for the envelope.

11. Press End Task.

12. Make the necessary changes to print the document.

EXERCISE 45

In Exercise 45, you will be creating a document consisting of a letter and an envelope. Page 1 of the document will be a letter. After typing the letter, you will ask the system to save the inside address. Page 2 of the document will be the envelope for the letter. You will request a page format change on page 2 and ask the system to recall the inside address and place it on the envelope.

PROCEDURES	COMMENTS
1. Select Create Document in the Text Task Selection Menu.	
2. Name the document b:Exerci45.	
3. Request Change Document Format from the Create or Revise Document Menu.	The Document or Alternate Format Menu displays.
4. Select Change Margins and Tabs.	The Margins and Tabs Menu displays.
5. Change right margin to 70.	
6. Press Enter.	The Document or Alternate Format Menu displays.
7. Select Change Page Format.	The Page Format Menu displays.
8. Change First Typing Line, First Page to 15.	
9. Press Enter.	The Document or Alternate Format Menu displays.
10. Press Enter.	The Create or Revise Document Menu displays.
11. Press Enter.	The typing area displays.
12. Type the letter that follows the procedures in this exercise.	

Continued

Chapter 11 Creating Envelopes

PROCEDURES (Continued)

13. Place the cursor under the first character in the inside address.

14. Press Block (F4).

15. Select Save.

16. Place the cursor under the last digit in the ZIP code.

17. Press Enter.

18. Press Enter.

19. Press End.

20. Press Ctrl--Page End.

21. Press Format (F7).

22. Select Change Page Format.

23. Change First Typing Line, First Page to 15.

24. Change Last Typing Line to 20.

25. Change Paper or Envelope Size to Choice 7.

26. Change Printing Paper Source to Choice 4.

27. Press Enter.

28. Select Change Margins and Tabs.

29. Change the left margin to 40.

30. Change the right margin to 90.

COMMENTS (Continued)

The cursor should be under the "M" in Mr.

The prompt line choices appear.

The prompt appears asking you to move the cursor to the end of the block.

Your screen should look like this:
    CA 90740-805<u>6</u>

The system supplies a default document named SAVEDOC.

The text is saved.

This is to move the cursor to the end of the document.

Page 2 displays.

The Format Change Menu displays.

Select Choice 5 if you have an envelope tray.

The Format Change Menu displays.

Continued

PROCEDURES (Continued)	COMMENTS (Continued)
31. Press Enter.	The Format Change Menu displays.
32. Press Enter.	The typing area displays.
33. Press Block (F4).	
34. Select Recall.	The document name, SAVEDOC.TXT, appears in the prompt line.
35. Press Enter.	The inside address appears on the envelope.
36. Press F2.	The Text Task Selection Menu displays.
37. Print the document.	The letter and the envelope will be printed.

May 25, 19--

Mr. William Brown
22 E. Fourth St.
Seal Beach, CA   90740-8056

Dear Mr. Brown:

We have finished making the repairs you requested to your IBM Personal Computer.

The bill for $73.25 includes parts and labor. Please make your payment within the next 30 days.

We appreciate your patronage. Our workmanship is guaranteed for 30 days.

Sincerely,

John Craft

xxx

CHAPTER SUMMARY

A. Creating a Document of Envelopes

   1. Select Create Document in the Text Task Selection Menu.
   2. Select Change Document Format in the Create or Revise Document Menu.
   3. Select Change Page Format in the Format Selection Menu.
   4. Change all of the following items for proper placement for your envelope size:
      --First Typing Line
      --First Typing Line, Following Pages
      --Last Typing Line
      --Paper or Envelope Size
      --Printing Paper Source
   5. Press Enter to return to the Format Selection Menu.
   6. Change the left and right margins in the Margins and Tabs Menu.
   7. Press Enter three times to return to the typing area.
   8. Type the names and addresses for each envelope. Press Ctrl--Page End after typing each envelope, except the last one.
   9. Press End Task after typing the last envelope.

B. Creating an Envelope with a Letter

   1. After typing the last page of the letter, press Ctrl--Page End.
   2. Press Format.
   3. Select Change Page Format.
   4. Change the following items for proper placement of the address for your envelope:
      --First Typing Line
      --Last Typing Line
      --Envelope Size
      --Printing Paper Source
   5. Press Enter.
   6. Change the left and right margins in the Margins and Tabs Menu so that the address will be placed properly on the envelope.
   7. Press Enter enough times to bring you back to the typing area.
   8. Type the name and address for the envelope.

C. Using Block Copy to copy the Inside Address onto the Envelope

   1. In the typing area, place the cursor under the first character or code to be saved.
   2. Press Block (F4). The prompt line choices will appear. Select Save or ASCII_save.
   3. Follow the prompt to move the cursor to the end of the block and press Enter. The block of text is highlighted.
   4. If you selected Save in Step 2, the prompt "Type document name; press ENTER" displays. The system will supply a default document name of SAVEDOC.TXT. You may type another name if you wish.

If you selected ASCII_save, the prompt "Type name of file; press ENTER" displays. The system will not supply a default file name; you will need to type the file name. It will supply a default extension of .ASC unless you type another.

5. Press Enter. The highlighted text is saved in the document or file you specified. It also remains in your original document.

6. In the typing area, place the cursor under the first character or code that the recalled block is to precede.

7. Press Block (F4). Select Recall. The prompt "Type document name; press ENTER" displays. The system default is to display the name used in the last Save or ASCII_save operation. If there was no previous save operation, the default name is SAVEDOC.

8. Press Enter to recall the default document name. If the default document is not the one you wish to recall, then press Esc to clear the name on the prompt line. Type the name of the document you want to recall and then press Enter.

9. The document or file is inserted at the cursor position. When you have finished making all of your changes, paginate the document.

Chapter 12

SPELLING

When you complete this chapter, you will be able to:

1. Verify spelling while creating or revising a document using Spell Word.

2. Verify spelling while creating or revising a document using Spell Page.

3. Correct spelling errors that are left highlighted after using Spell Page.

4. Spell Check documents through prompted mode and convert words in the system supplement to a supplement dictionary program.

5. Spell Check automatically.

6. Correct spelling errors that are left highlighted after using automatic spell checking.

7. Use Begin and End Spell Check to cause the system to skip words during spell checking.

8. Create and use a supplement dictionary program.

9. Revise a supplement dictionary program.

INTRODUCTION TO SPELL CHECKING

Although nothing can take the place of a command of the English language, the DisplayWrite 3 spelling program, found on Volume 4, can catch many spelling errors, and in most cases, "typos."

Because the dictionary program works by matching the words in your document to the words in the dictionary and the supplement, it will highlight errors when those items do not match. Legal and medical dictionaries are also available for purchase. You may create your own supplement dictionary programs containing words that are used in specialized fields. You can store these little dictionaries on the dictionary diskette to be called into the supplement whenever you need them. If you write papers for several kinds of classes such as anthropology, sociology, and economics, terms can be put into separate personal dictionaries to be used when spell checking documents in any of these disciplines. The dictionary will not highlight words with capitalization errors, letters that are not surrounded by other letters (such as letters used in an outline to designate different divisions), correctly hyphenated words, graphics, or numbers.

It will not highlight homonyms used incorrectly. An example of this would be "blew" instead of "blue." The dictionary program will not highlight "blew" because the word matches the dictionary spelling program.

You can paginate your document while you are spell checking. Also, it is possible for the system to skip text during a spelling check. Any sections you do not wish to be verified should be preceded by an End Spell code and followed by a Begin Spell code. For instance, a passage in a foreign language could easily be skipped this way. The Begin Spell code is placed in the text by pressing F8, selecting End from the prompt line choices, and then Spelling_Check from the second prompt line choices you view. The Begin Spell code is put in your text by pressing the Instruction key, choosing Begin from the prompt line, and then Spelling_Check.

KINDS OF SPELLING CHECKS

You have four spell checking options from which to choose. They are as follows: Spell Word, Spell Page, Prompted Mode, and Automatic Mode.

SPELL WORD AND SPELL PAGE

Two options are available for spell checking without leaving the typing area. These do not involve the entire document. They are Spell Word and Spell Page. If you are not sure whether your spelling of a word is correct, you may check a single word at a time. The system will check your spelling against that in the dictionary program and the words in the supplement. If your spelling is correct, the message "Word Spelled Correctly" will appear. If the system does not find a match, it will attempt to determine what word you are trying to spell by offering up to seven choices of words that can be used to replace the word you are spell checking. If one of these is the correct spelling, you can substitute it in your text by choosing the ID letter in front of the word you want and entering it. This can be done during the creation or revision of a document. If you want to leave the word unchanged, just press Esc. If there are no possible candidates for the word you are checking, you will see the message "No Possible Words Found." Spell Word does not work in column mode or in headers or footers. Placing the cursor under the word to be checked and pressing F9 will start Spell Word. The dictionary disk must be inserted for Spell Word to be in effect.

EXERCISE 46

PROCEDURES	COMMENTS
1. Create a document and name it b:change.txt.	This is a document with deliberate spelling errors.
2. Go to the typing area and type the following document exactly as it appears with the errors.

Change is caused by influences inside and outside a business. The ability to chagne requires patience, pragmatism, and participatin. Moreover, change management requires the people skills to lead the business through teh unfreezing, chagne and freezing stages.

Proper change management involves planning for change. This will prevent failures and allow one to implement systems effectively. You msut make use of management and technical skills to implement change.

3. When you have finished typing, Press F9 for spell check.	The prompt "Insert Default Dictionary program; press ENTER" will appear on the screen.
4. Remove Volume 2 and replace it with the dictionary disk (Volume 4). Press Enter. Place the cursor under the word "chagne." Press F9.	A rectangle will appear on the screen containing words from which you may select.
5. Type the ID letter of the correct spelling of change and Enter.	

Continued

PROCEDURES (Continued)

6. Follow this procedure for the word "participatin" and the rest of the misspelled words. When you are finished, go to the end of the document and press Page End.
Type the following paragraph exactly as it appears.

COMMENTS (Continued)

Electronic mail is the transmission and recpetion of text in electronic form instead of paper. Advanced electronic mail systems provide capabilities for store and forward processing and electronic mailboxes to manage message receipt.

EXERCISE 47

PROCEDURES

1. When you have finished typing the material, move to the top of the page. (Remember, you should be on page 2.) Insert Volume 2 again and press Control--F9 to start Spell Page.

2. Put the dictionary disk in drive A and Enter.

3. When you have finished the Spell Page, put Volume 2 back in drive A and press F9 to verify the spelling of each word.

4. Reinsert the dictionary disk in drive A. Use Find and Spell Word to verify the remaining highlighted words. When you are finished, press F2.

COMMENTS

The system will spell check the words automatically from where your cursor was at the time you pressed Spell Page to the end of the document.

The cursor will find the first misspelled word.

To use Find and Spell Word, depress Ctrl--Find. When the system prompts "Find what?" depress F9 and Enter. This will move you more quickly to the highlighted words.

Chapter 12 Spelling

SPELL CHECKING IN PROMPTED MODE AND CONVERTING WORDS IN THE SYSTEM SUPPLEMENT TO A SUPPLEMENT DICTIONARY PROGRAM

Since your training may span several sessions at the computer, the procedures start in the Text Task Selection Menu. You may skip the directions guiding you to the Spelling Tasks Menu if you are already there.

At the end of the spell check, you will convert the words in the system supplement to a supplement dictionary program. To learn how to use the dictionary initially, you will spell check the document named b:Rivera.txt.

EXERCISE 48

PROCEDURES	COMMENTS
1. If you are in the Text Task Selection Menu, select Spelling Tasks and Enter. At the prompt, "Insert Default Dictionary program; press ENTER," remove the volume in drive A and insert the dictionary disk, Volume 4. Press Enter.	The dictionary disk must remain in the drive until all of the spelling tasks are finished.
2. In the Spelling Tasks Menu, choose Check Document. Enter.	This is choice a.
3. Type b:Rivera and Enter.	
4. In the Check Document Menu, type A and Enter. Type 1 and Enter. Enter again.	This tells the system that you want to use the prompted mode of spell checking as opposed to the automatic default.
5. When prompted for the word "McDonald," choose Add_to_supplement from the prompt line to add the word to the supplement.	The choices you will have are Add_to_supplement, Retype_word, Highlight_and_continue, and List_possible_words. After the highlighted words have been entered into the supplement, they will not be highlighted again.

Continued

188   Chapter 12 Spelling

PROCEDURES (Continued)	COMMENTS (Continued)
6. Choose Add_to_supplement to add the words "Erwood" and "Norwalk" to the supplement as well.	
7. When "yor" is highlighted, choose Retype_word and then retype the word on the prompt line.	You can consult the directions on the screen for quick reference.
8. When the words "propose," "firrst," "faver," and "responce" are highlighted, either choose List_possible_words or choose Retype_word, and retype the words.	Do not store an incorrectly spelled word in the supplement. Instead, correct the spelling. If you choose List_possible_words, choose the correct spelling from the list. If you choose Retype_word, you must retype the word with the correct spelling. On the job you would highlight correct words so that you can remember to add them to a supplement dictionary program if you use them frequently.
9. When "Reinaldo," "Rivera," and "RR:et" are highlighted, press Enter to place the words in the supplement. Continue with the spelling program until you see the message that the spelling check is complete.	
10. In the Spelling Tasks Menu, select Store Supplement on Disk and press Enter.	
11. Return to the Text Task Selection Menu.	
12. Print a corrected version of b:Rivera.txt.	

If you want to check only certain pages of a document, you may select System Page Numbers and type the numbers of the pages you want checked and leave a space after each page number. Ten pages may be spell checked at a time using this method.

Chapter 12 Spelling

Pagination is also possible while you are spell checking and can be requested by selecting ID C, Choice 1 in the Check Document screen. If you choose to have your document paginated, you cannot take advantage of System Page Number spell checking.

AUTOMATIC SPELL CHECKING

The document you will spell check automatically is named b:Spellos.txt. During automatic spell checking, the system goes through the document and marks misspelled words by highlighting them. Later you can edit the document and rapidly find the marked words using the Find and Spell keys. As you come to each marked word, you can correct it, leave it marked, Word Spell or just remove the highlighting. Follow the steps to check automatically the document named b:Spellos.txt for errors.

EXERCISE 49

PROCEDURES	COMMENTS
1. If you are in the Text Task Selection Menu, select Spelling Tasks.	
2. At the prompt, remove Volume 2 and replace it with the dictionary diskette. Enter.	This will take you to the Spelling Tasks Menu.
3. In the Spelling Tasks Menu, select Check Document and Enter.	
4. At the prompt, type b:Spellos.txt and Enter.	
5. In the Check Document Menu, press Enter. When the spelling check is finished, you will see the prompt "Spelling check complete." It will also tell you how many words have been marked.	The default is an automatic check. The system will now check the document without prompting. The "marked" words are those that are highlighted and do not match the system dictionary.
6. Return to the Text Task Selection Menu and remove the dictionary program disk from drive A and insert Volume 2.	

Continued

PROCEDURES (Continued)	COMMENTS (Continued)
7. Choose Revise Document and go to the typing area and correct the words that are misspelled. Remove the highlighting from the words that are not misspelled but are highlighted because they do not match the dictionary.	Remember to use Find and F9 to go to the spell marks and use Esc to remove highlighting.

BEGIN AND END SPELLING CHECK CODES

When words occur in your documents that you feel will not match the dictionary, such as foreign words or unusual terms, you may place an End Spelling_Check code before the words and a Begin Spelling_Check code after them. The system will, in effect, "skip" them. In the following exercise, you will type a paragraph using End and Begin Spelling_Check codes so that two terms will not be checked during Spell Page. An End Spelling_Check code is placed in the document by pressing F8 and selecting End from the prompt line choices. From the second set of prompt line choices, select Spelling_Check. A Begin Spelling_Check code is placed in the document by pressing F8 and selecting Begin from the prompt line choices. From the second set of choices, choose Spelling_Check.

EXERCISE 50

PROCEDURES	COMMENTS
1. Create a document and name it b:Dinosaur.txt.	This document will contain names that would not be found in the standard dictionary of a word processing program.
2. Go to the typing area and type the following paragraph.	

Dinosaurs once roamed the earth in great numbers. We have never seen many of the varieties which we have drawn. Although no living artist has laid eyes upon either the (insert End Spelling_Check code here) triceratops or the stegosaurus, (insert Begin Spelling_ Check code here) they have been rendered on canvas many times because we can surmise their appearance from their remains.

3. Go to the top of the page and use Spell Page to spell check this paragraph.	The names of the dinosaurs did not highlight because they were not checked by the system.

Continued

Chapter 12 Spelling

PROCEDURES (Continued)	COMMENTS (Continued)
	If they were highlighted, check to make sure that you did not start with a Begin Spelling_Check code.

WORKING WITH THE SUPPLEMENT DICTIONARY PROGRAM

The system supplement is merely an area set aside in memory to store words temporarily. The words in the document you are checking are compared with these words as well as the words in the dictionary program.

If you wrote memos to the same personnel often, you would want to store the words in a supplement dictionary program on the spelling program diskette so that it could be brought into the system supplement whenever you needed it.

We will now explore creating and using a supplement dictionary program. In the next exercise, you will type a list that contains words which would be considered misspellings (proper names and one unusual word). They will be stored in the form of a supplement dictionary program.

EXERCISE 51

PROCEDURES	COMMENTS
1. From the Text Task Selection Menu, select Create Document and name it b:Words.	You are now creating the document containing the words you will load into the system supplement when you spell check the first document.
2. In the typing area, type the following list of names:	You will add these names because many proper names do not appear in a dictionary.
3. Atkinson Axline Brown Capsuto Cody Doll Johnson Margo Mattingly Plummer Riedel Rowena Tyrrell	

Continued

Chapter 12 Spelling

PROCEDURES (Continued)

4. The word palmiped should be typed as follows:

5. Type pal. Hold down the control key and strike the hyphen.

6. Type mi. Hold down the control key and strike the hyphen.

7. Type ped.

8. Press Enter.

9. Press End Task.

10. Print b:Words.txt.

11. In the Text Task Selection Menu, select Spelling Tasks and Enter.

12. In response to the prompt, place the dictionary disk in drive A and press Enter.

13. In the Spelling Tasks Menu, select Change Spelling Dictionary.

14. In the Change Spelling Dictionary Menu, choose Supplement Dictionary Program Name.

15. Respond to the prompt by typing a:Words. DO NOT ADD AN EXTENSION TO THIS NAME. The system will put it in for you automatically.

COMMENTS (Continued)

You are putting syllable hyphens in this word so that the system will be able to hyphenate it when necessary.

You will not see the hyphens unless the cursor is on them or Display codes is on. The system will, however, be able to hyphenate the word according to where you place the syllable hyphens. To make a syllable hyphen, hold down the control key and press the hyphen key.

This printed copy will serve as a reference copy of what is in the supplement dictionary program.

Continued

Chapter 12 Spelling

PROCEDURES (Continued)	COMMENTS (Continued)
16. Enter enough times to get back into the Spelling Tasks Menu.	
17. Select Add Words to Supplement.	
18. At the prompt, type b:Words.txt (if it does not already appear on the prompt line) and Enter.	
19. Select Store Supplement on Disk and Enter.	A message telling you that the words are now in the supplement can be seen on the screen.
20. Return to the Text Task Selection Menu.	

In the next exercise, you will type a document that can be spell checked automatically using the supplement dictionary program you just created.

EXERCISE 52

PROCEDURES	COMMENTS
1. From the Text Task Selection Menu, select Create Document and name it b:Business.txt. Type the memo as it appears on page 195 and then continue with Procedure 2.	Volume 2 should be inserted in drive A.
2. When you finish typing the memorandum, press End Task (F2).	
3. Print b:Business.txt.	

You may now change dictionary programs and use the words contained in Words.sdc (the extension was changed to .sdc when it was stored on the disk) as well as the standard dictionary program to spell check your document named b:Business.txt. Follow the steps in Exercise 53.

```
        TO:   Thomas Atkinson
              Donna Axline
              John Brown
              Mike Capsuto
              Margo Doll
              Rowena Johnson
              Jack Long
              Lynn Mattingly
              William Nelson
              Cody Plummer
              Alan Ransom
              Donna Riedel

      FROM:   Don Tyrrell

      DATE:   (Use the current date)

   SUBJECT:   Sales Meeting
```

We will have our usual sales meeting the third Wednesday of this month at 9:00 a.m. to examine our goals and progress. We will also be briefed on a new product we will be carrying, palmiped repellent.

EXERCISE 53

PROCEDURES	COMMENTS
1. Go to the Spelling Tasks Menu.	In response to the prompt, insert the dictionary disk.
2. In the Spelling Tasks Menu, choose Change Spelling Dictionary and Enter.	You are going to check b:Business.txt with the standard dictionary and the Supplement Dictionary Program, Words.sdc.
3. In the Change Spelling Dictionary Menu, select Supplement Dictionary Program Name and Enter.	
4. At the prompt, type a:Words and Enter.	You are asking the system to place the words contained in the Supplement Dictionary Program a:Words.sdc in the supplement.
5. Enter again.	
6. In the Spelling Tasks Menu, choose Check Document and Enter.	
7. If b:Business.txt does not appear on the prompt line, type that document name and Enter.	
	Continued

Chapter 12 Spelling

PROCEDURES (Continued)

COMMENTS (Continued)

8. In the Check Document Menu, just Enter to accept the defaults and start the Spelling_Check.

At the end of the Spelling_Check, you will see the message "Spelling check complete. Words marked: 0." None of the names in the document were marked as misspellings because they were in the supplement dictionary program.

REVISING A SUPPLEMENT DICTIONARY PROGRAM

In this section, you will make revisions to the stored words in a supplement dictionary program by transferring them to a document and revising at that point. After this revision, you will add the revised words back to the system supplement and then replace the previously stored words in the Words.sdc supplement dictionary program.

EXERCISE 54

PROCEDURES

COMMENTS

1. From the Text Task Selection Menu, select Spelling Tasks and Enter.

2. At the prompt, insert the dictionary program diskette and Enter.

3. In the Spelling Tasks Menu, select Change Spelling Dictionary and Enter.

You are turning the words in the supplement into a document so that you can revise them.

4. In the Change Spelling Dictionary Menu, choose Supplement Dictionary Program Name.

This is the name of the document you wish to use. You cannot revise in Spelling Tasks.

5. At the prompt, type a:Words.sdc and Enter twice.

6. In the Spelling Tasks Menu, select Convert Supplement to Document.

Continued

PROCEDURES (Continued)	COMMENTS (Continued)
7. In response to the prompt, type b:update.txt and Enter.	You will see the message "Supplement words written to (B:UPDATE.TXT)" on the screen.
8. Select Return to Task Selection and Enter.	
9. Remove the Dictionary Program diskette and insert Volume 2.	Now you can make the changes to the document that will be used as your supplement.
10. In the Text Task Selection Menu, select Revise Document and Enter.	
11. At the prompt, type b:update (if the document name does not appear on the prompt line) and Enter.	
12. In the typing area, delete palmiped and add the names Fran and Jones.	These are the revisions.
13. Press End Task.	
14. Print b:update.txt.	
15. In the Text Task Selection Menu, select Spelling Tasks and Enter.	
16. At the prompt, remove Vol. 2 and insert the Dictionary Program disk. Press Enter.	
17. In the Spelling Tasks Menu, select Change Spelling Dictionary and Enter.	
18. Select Supplement Dictionary Program Name.	
19. At the prompt, type a:Words and Enter twice.	

Continued

Chapter 12 Spelling 197

PROCEDURES (Continued)	COMMENTS (Continued)
20. Choose Clear Supplement and Enter.	This is to make sure that no words are stored except those you want. The prompt "Supplement cleared" appears on the screen.
21. Select Add Words to Supplement and Enter twice.	
22. Choose Store Supplement on Disk and Enter.	The list of words you just revised is now stored in place of the old, unrevised list.

CHAPTER SUMMARY

A. You can spell check individual words using Spell Word.

B. You can spell check individual pages using Spell Page.

C. You may spell check in either prompted or automatic mode.

D. The words in the system supplement may be converted to a document.

E. The Supplement Dictionary Program may be revised at any time the word processing operator wishes.

F. A document containing supplemental words may be created, renamed, and loaded into the supplement. This type of "personalized dictionary" is handy for documents which contain proper names or uncommon terms.

G. When composing a document of supplemental words, be sure to use syllable hyphens. These tell the system where to hyphenate the words when they fall at the ends of lines.

H. The Supplement Dictionary Program may be loaded into the system supplement. After this has been done, both the regular dictionary program and the supplement will be used when spell checking. It may also be made into a document again for revision.

I. You may add words to a supplement through the prompted mode spell check.

J. Do not add the extension .sdc yourself.

Chapter 13

COLUMNS OF TEXT

When you complete this chapter, you will be able to:

1. Set up text columns.

2. Type in the text columns.

3. Revise columns of text.

4. Create a set-up document containing only the text format codes.

5. Change text column format.

6. Set up and type aligned paragraphs.

7. Revise aligned paragraphs.

8. Use Line Adjust in text columns including aligned paragraphs.

SETTING UP AND TYPING TEXT COLUMNS

If you have ever wished that the columns you use when typing tables could be set automatically to save time and prevent errors in calculation, you will like DisplayWrite 3's ability to set up columns for you. Even if you decide to add or delete columns after the table has been typed, the program will adjust the table setting automatically so that the columns will still be properly spaced on the page.

DisplayWrite 3 automatically inserts the codes necessary to create text columns, such as Begin Table, End Table, and Format Changes. This is done with the use of Column Layout.

When you are typing the text that goes into the columns, the program allows you to type one column at a time. When you have typed all of the columns, your work will be spaced evenly across the screen. For your convenience, in addition to Exercise 55, condensed instructions for creating a text column are included at the end of this chapter. For now, do the following exercise to learn how to set up text columns. Be very careful to follow the instructions, as any small error will cause problems for you.

EXERCISE 55

PROCEDURES	COMMENTS
1. In the Text Task Selection Menu, choose Create Document and name the document b:Columns.	
2. Go to the typing area.	
3. In the typing area, hold down the Control key and press F4. This key combination will be called Ctrl-Column for the rest of this chapter.	The word "Layout" will appear on the screen.
4. Press Enter to display a screen of instructions.	At this point, only read the instructions on the screen.
5. Press Line Adjust (F5).	You will tell the system that you want to make a column of text. A flush left tab will appear where the line will begin.

Continued

PROCEDURES (Continued)	COMMENTS (Continued)
6. Type the letter a 25 times.	Twenty-five "a´s" appear on the screen. (Note: When you are defining the length of a column initially, you will always see "a´s" on the screen regardless of which key you press.)
7. Press Ctrl-Column.	This will insert a space between the columns. You will see it tells the system that you have set up the first column.
8. Press Line Adjust.	Again, this is to tell the system that you are going to type text into this column.
9. Type 25 a´s.	
10. Press Command (F6) and Enter.	Do NOT press Ctrl-Column this time. You will see a prompt line across the bottom of the screen. The default is Adjust. When you press Enter, you are selecting Adjust. This means that you have set up the columns and would like to adjust them between the margins now. After you strike Enter, the columns will spread out between the right and left margins.
11. Press Continue (F10) twice.	After striking Continue the first time, you will see an End Table code on the screen. After you have struck Continue a second time, you will be returned to the regular typing area.

You have now set up the columns. Of course, you will want to fill these columns with text.

Assume, for a moment, that you are responsible for writing a monthly newsletter. You would probably use a two-column format similar to the one you just set up. In the next exercise, you will do part of such a newsletter and use the columns you have set up. You will fill the columns with text by isolating them first.

Chapter 13   Columns of Text

EXERCISE 56

PROCEDURES	COMMENTS
1. If you are still in the typing area of b:Columns, remain there.	
2. If you are in the Text Task Selection Menu, go to the typing area of b:Columns.	
3. In the typing area, turn on the Display codes (F6 and D, Enter). Look for the Begin Table code.	The Begin Table Code looks like this ⊨ . If it is followed by a return, it will look like this ⊨⌐ .
4. With the arrow keys, place the cursor under the Begin Table code.	The status line will show the words Begin Table when the cursor is under the Begin Table code.
5. Press Ctrl-Column.	
6. Type the letter R.	You have chosen Revise from the prompt line. You are now in the separate typing area for the first column. This is called isolating a column.
7. Type the following few lines without using the return key except after the title and between the paragraphs.	Text will wrap automatically just as it does in full screen documents. Remember, the column is only 25 characters wide, and your text will look different from the following paragraphs.

Zoo News

This month at the zoo, we implemented our new reduced-amount feeding program. It has saved $1,300 so far.

We plan to use this money to hire a new zookeeper to replace the one who disappeared last week near the lion compound.

8. Press Continue.	This takes you out of the left column typing area, and the cursor returns to the top of the table.

Continued

PROCEDURES (Continued)	COMMENTS (Continued)
9. On the same line as the Begin Table code, use the right arrow key to position the cursor under the tab setting for the next column.	If you have set the columns up correctly, there will be only one tab setting to the right.
10. When you are under the tab setting, press Ctrl-Column.	This is Control--F4.
11. Type R.	You will be in the right column typing area.
12. In the column typing area, type the following text that will comprise your second column.	Only return after the title.

Lonely Lilly Finds Love

Famous resident Lilly the Chimp, star of the ever-popular "Life Is a Jungle" afternoon television series, may have found love at last. The budding romance began when Lilly, having imbibed some "old grape juice," fell off her limb and into the arms of handsome Harry the Gorilla. The inseparable pair are now a familiar sight on a number of vines around the zoo.

13. Press Continue.	You will now see both columns of b:Columns on the screen.
14. Press End Task.	
15. Print a copy of b:Columns.	

CREATING A SET-UP DOCUMENT

You may have occasion to set up a text table several times in a document or in different documents. If you create a document which contains only the text column format, you can copy it into the document without having to go through the steps to set up a text column table each time you wish to write text in columns. In the following exercise, you will create a document containing text column format codes. In the next exercise, you will copy these codes into another document.

Chapter 13 Columns of Text

EXERCISE 57

PROCEDURES	COMMENTS
1. In the Text Task Selection Menu, choose Create Document and Enter.	
2. Name the document b:Setup and Enter.	This will be the document with the column format codes only.
3. Go to the typing area.	
4. Press Ctrl-Column.	You are going to set up a column format here.
5. Press Enter.	
6. Press Line Adjust.	This means that you want text in the columns, and you want the column 20 characters wide.
7. Type a 20 times.	
8. Press Ctrl-Column.	You have defined the first column.
9. Press Line Adjust.	This designates a text column.
10. Type a 20 times.	The column will be 20 characters wide.
11. Press Command (F6).	
12. Press Enter to accept the default.	This adjusts your columns between the margins.
13. Press Continue (F10) twice.	
14. Press End Task.	You have just created and saved a document containing only a text column table format.

ALIGNING PARAGRAPHS

When your paragraphs have to start on the same lines and in columns, you can take advantage of a special technique to create them. When text appears on the page in this fashion, you are creating aligned paragraphs.

When you set up text columns, you are really creating a table with words instead of numbers. Therefore, this technique uses separate tables for each pair of paragraphs. In Figure 13.1 four text tables (text column formats) were used.

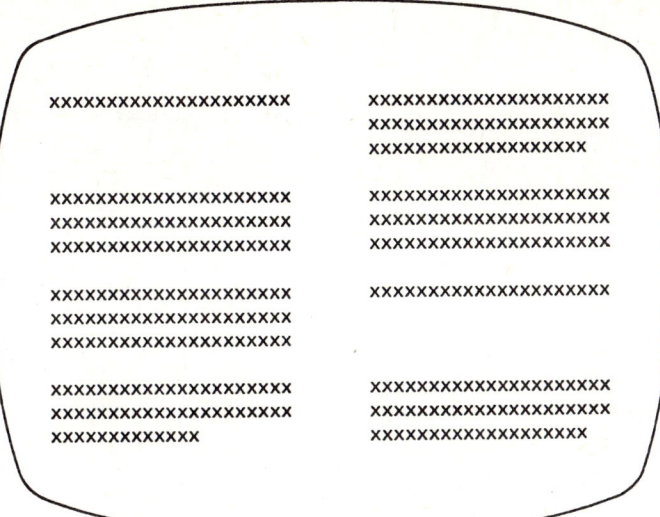

Figure 13.1 Aligned Paragraphs

In this exercise, you will create a document containing aligned paragraphs. You will use Get (explained fully in a later chapter) to copy the format codes necessary to set up the table from b:Setup.

EXERCISE 58

PROCEDURES	COMMENTS
1. In the Text Task Selection Menu, select Create Document and name it b:Aligned.	
2. Go to the typing area.	
3. Press Command (F6) and Enter.	This will bring the Get Menu up to the screen, because Get is the default choice on the prompt line.
4. In the Get Menu, type a and Enter.	
5. Type b:Setup and Enter twice.	The Table Format codes will be brought into your document.
6. Back in the typing area, place your cursor under the Begin Table code and press Ctrl-Column.	The text columns are now ready to be filled with words.
7. Type R for Revise.	You can now type the left column of the first section.

Continued

PROCEDURES (Continued)   COMMENTS (Continued)

Question

What types of printers are available on the market today that can be used with a microcomputer?

8. Press Continue (F10).   This takes you out of the
                                           column typing area and back on
                                           the same line as the Begin
                                           Table code.

9. On the same line as the
    Begin Table code, using
    the right arrow key,
    move the cursor so that
    it is beneath the table
    setting for the right
    column.

10. Press Ctrl-Column.   Remember, this is Control--F4.

11. Press R for Revise.

12. Type the following text
    in the separate column
    typing area where you
    are now.

Answer

Among the printers available are laser, ink jet, thermal, dot matrix, daisy wheel, and erosion. These printers can be used for correspondence, reports, and spreadsheets. Daisy wheel printers are not suited to printing graphics.

13. Press Continue.   Continue is F10.

14. Press End.   You will now be at a position
                                           below the table of text.

15. Return twice.   You are returning so that you
                                           will have some space between
                                           paragraphs.

16. To type the second col-
    umn, press the Command
    key.

17. Press Enter to accept
    the default which is Get.

18. In the Get Menu, type a
    and Enter.

19. Type b:Setup and Enter.

                              Continued

206   Chapter 13 Columns of Text

| PROCEDURES (Continued) | COMMENTS (Continued) |

20. Enter again.

This will copy the document b:Setup into your document which contains only the codes necessary to set up your text columns.

21. Place the cursor under the Begin Table code.

(If you cannot find it, turn Display codes on.)

22. Press Ctrl-Column.

23. Type R for Revise.

24. Type the following text in this column:

How should secretaries be prepared to work in business and industry?

25. Press return and Continue.

26. Place the cursor under the tab setting for the right-hand column.

27. Press Ctrl-Column and choose Revise from the prompt line.

28. Type the following text in the right column:

Lois Kisner, a manpower consultant, states that a secretary should be able to take shorthand at a minimum of 80 words per minute and type at the speed of 60 words per minute. The ability to file alphabetically and numerically is needed also. The secretary should be able to word process on a dedicated word processor as well as on at least one word processing software package using a microcomputer.

29. Press Continue.

30. Press End.

31. Return twice.

Use your knowledge of the procedure for setting up text columns to set up and type these last sets of aligned paragraphs. Feel free to refer back to the procedures you have just covered. When you reach the end of a page, press Continue to leave the column typing area, and press End to go back to the end of the page. Press Page End. At the top of the next page, get the set-up document again, and continue typing in columns.

Continued

PROCEDURES (Continued)	COMMENTS (Continued)
What reference materials should a secretary have on the desk?	Jeanne Gonzalez, an authority on the subject, feels that a secretary should have an office procedures book and at least a formatting reference manual. Also close at hand should be an instruction book for the word processor being used.
32. Press Page End (Ctrl--E) to start page 2.	
What kinds of letters are written by secretaries and administrative assistants?	Cathy Greenwell, administrative assistant, states that she is requested to compose rough drafts of press releases, routine information letters, and an occasional status report.
What are some considerations when constructing an organization chart?	Bill Lind, a corporate planner, constructs organization charts by placing all positions of equal authority on the same level. He states that boxes on the chart are of identical size regardless of the status of the individual holding the position.
What factors should be kept in mind when working abroad?	Sandra Ross, a foreign service secretary in Baghdad, believes that it is important to adjust to the language of time. "Americans," she says, "are used to an accelerated pace. The rest of the world does not work at the same speed that we do." Ross also states that you should be prepared to be kept waiting for appointments; however, when you do see the executive, you will be given as much time as necessary to transact business.
33. You have finished typing the aligned paragraphs; press Continue (F10) to return to the regular typing area (if you have not already done so).	

Continued

PROCEDURES (Continued)	COMMENTS (Continued)
34. Press End Task.	
35. Print the document.	You will now do some revising in the columns.

REVISING COLUMNS OF TEXT

Many of the same editing techniques you are familiar with in text operate in the same manner in columns of text. In Exercise 59, you will create some aligned text tables. After printing them, you will make some minor revisions and print them again.

EXERCISE 59

From your knowledge of text columns, set up a document named b:Setup2 with a left text column of 30 spaces and a right text column of 25 spaces. You may wish to refer to the procedure for setting up columns of text you used to create b:Setup. Remember, though, that the number of characters in each column is different from b:Setup2.

Create a new document named b:Advice. The document will contain aligned paragraphs. You will use Get to copy the format codes necessary to set up the table from b:Setup2. Type the question in the left column and the answer in the right column. You may wish to refer to b:Aligned.

Question
What are some of the duties you would perform to plan a trip for a busy executive?

Answer
Find out the availability of planes around the times when the executive wants to travel. Call the airlines or a travel agent, or even bring up the airline guide on your microcomputer, via modem, to see which flights still have seating space. Find out which class the executive prefers. Make a list of the people to be seen, where they are, and what has to be taken on the trip to be used in the meetings. Get the phone numbers of the companies and the hotels where the traveler will be on the trip. You should arrange for rental cars or taxis.

Question
What are some items to pack in the executive's briefcase?

Answer
You should pack correspondence relative to the companies he or she is visiting. Any personal details (names of spouses or children), whether or not the person being visited plays golf, and so on may be noted. Ask the executive what information is needed for each meeting.

> Question
> What are some clothing considerations when traveling across the country?
>
> Answer
> Sara Warren, Patty LaRosa, and Suzanne Scarry, seasoned travel agents, suggest very warm clothing as well as hats if the executive is visiting Chicago in the winter. They suggest lighter clothing when traveling in the Deep South. In Southern California, heavy clothing would be too warm.

Print b:Advice and save it for use with Exercise 60. After you have printed b:Advice, follow the steps to revise:

EXERCISE 60

PROCEDURES	COMMENTS
1. In the Text Task Selection Menu choose Revise Document.	
2. Type b:Advice and Enter.	
3. Go to the typing area.	
4. Place the cursor under the Begin Table code for the left-hand column of the first set of aligned paragraphs and press Ctrl--F4.	
5. Type R for Revise.	
6. Replace "executive" with "manager."	
7. After making the revision, press Continue to leave the column typing area.	
8. Place the cursor under the tab for the right-hand column of text in the second set of aligned paragraphs and press Ctrl--F4.	
9. Type R for Revise.	

Continued

PROCEDURES (Continued)	COMMENTS (Continued)
10. In the column typing area, change "golf" to "tennis."	
11. Press Continue to leave the column typing area.	

On your own, change the following words on the page: change "via" to "by way of," "briefcase" to "attache," and "correspondence" to "letters." Print a copy of the revised version of this exercise.

CHANGING TEXT COLUMN FORMAT

It is possible in DisplayWrite 3 to make the columns of text wider or narrower. You can adjust the new column widths between the margins also without doing complicated mathematical calculations. In Exercise 61, you will change the widths of two columns and adjust them.

EXERCISE 61

PROCEDURES	COMMENTS
1. In the Text Task Selection Menu, choose Revise Document.	
2. At the prompt, type b:Aligned.	
3. Go to the typing area of b:Aligned.	
4. Using the arrow keys, place the cursor under the Begin Table code at the beginning of the last text table. Press Continue (F10).	The layout appears with the cursor under the first "a."
5. Use the right arrow to move the cursor to the first "a" in the left column. Be sure that you are to the right of the underline that represents text in a column.	
6. Press a four times.	You have added four characters to the width of the left column.

Continued

Chapter 13 Columns of Text

PROCEDURES (Continued)

7. Press Command (F6) and Enter.

8. Press Enter twice.

9. In the typing area, notice how the tabs have shifted somewhat to accommodate the new width of the left column.

10. Press End Task.

11. Print b:Aligned.

COMMENTS (Continued)

You are adjusting the area between the columns.

You will return to the typing area.

LINE ADJUST

When you are revising in a column of text, sometimes you will insert many words. If the words extend past the right margin of the column, this situation is remedied by simply moving the cursor down with the down arrow. However, you may wish to use the Line Adjust key to allow for the hyphenation of some words.

In the following exercise, you will add some words to one of the documents you have typed, and then use the Line Adjust key to distribute the text evenly throughout the column.

EXERCISE 62

PROCEDURES

1. If you are not already there, go to the typing area of b:Aligned.

2. Using the arrow keys and your knowledge of column revision, go to the paragraph that contains the words "What kinds of letters are written by secretaries and administrative assistants?"

3. Use your knowledge of column revision to isolate this column.

COMMENTS

Continued

Chapter 13   Columns of Text

PROCEDURES (Continued)	COMMENTS (Continued)
4. Change the question so that it reads "What types of business letters are written by secretaries and administrative assistants?"	Delete the word "kinds" and type the word "types." Also insert the word "business."
5. Move the cursor up so that it is under the word "What." Press Line Adjust (F5) and adjust the lines. When you are asked to make a hyphenation decision, you may either press Enter to place the word on the next line or move the cursor to the point of hyphenation and Enter to divide and hyphenate the word.	You may want to use a dictionary or word division book to determine hyphen placement.
6. When you have finished line adjusting, press Continue (F10) and End Task.	

QUICK REFERENCE FOR CREATING COLUMNS OF TEXT

(This sample is for two columns of text)

1. While holding down Control, press F4.

2. Press Enter when you see the word "Layout" in the lower left-hand corner of the screen.

3. Press F5 (Line Adjust).

4. Determine how many characters you want in the first column of text and strike any key that many times.

5. Press Control--F4. This is to separate the columns.

6. Press F5 (Line Adjust).

7. Determine how many characters you want in the second column of text and strike any key that many times.

8. Press F6. A prompt line will appear across the bottom of the screen. The default will be "Adjust."

9. Enter to accept the default choice.

10. Press F10 (Continue).

11. Press F10 again to get back into the typing area.

12. Position the cursor under the Begin Table code with the arrow keys. The code is usually two lines up and one space to the right. If you have a difficult time finding it, turn on the Display codes.

13. While holding down Control, press F4.

14. Type R to choose Revise from the prompt line.

15. Type the text in the first column.

16. Press F10 (Continue) when you are finished with the first column.

17. Make sure that the cursor is on the same line as the Begin Table code. If you have just finished Step 16 and have not done anything else, the cursor will already be on the right line. Use the right arrow key to position the cursor under the table for the second column. When you are under that tab, hold down Control and press F4.

18. Type **R** to indicate Revise, which appears on the prompt line.

19. Type the text in the second column.

20. Press F10 when you are finished.

CHAPTER SUMMARY

A. Aligned paragraphs are different from simple text columns in that in each pair, the paragraphs start on the same line.

B. You would use aligned paragraphs in a situation such as placing questions in the left column and the corresponding answers in the right column.

C. Be sure to use Command (F6) to adjust the columns after widening or narrowing one of the columns.

D. Use Continue (F10) to exit the column typing area.

E. When you wish to revise an aligned paragraph that is in the left column, place the cursor under the Begin Table code, hold down the Ctrl key, and strike F4. Choose Revise from the prompt line choices. If you wish to revise a column other than a left column, place the cursor underneath the tab for that column. Hold down Ctrl and strike F4. Choose Revise from the prompt line choices.

Chapter 14
NUMERIC TABLES

When you complete this chapter, you will be able to:

1. Create numeric tables.

2. Isolate columns in numeric tables for revision.

3. Add numbers to columns in numeric tables.

4. Delete numbers from columns in numeric tables.

5. Add columns to numeric tables.

6. Move columns in numeric tables.

7. Copy columns in numeric tables.

8. Revise column formats in numeric tables.

NUMERIC TABLES

After mastering tables containing columns of text, you are ready to start setting up tables containing numbers. Much of the knowledge accumulated while learning about text columns will help you when preparing documents with numeric tables.

In addition to familiar items such as Begin and End Table codes, you will be introduced to various ways of using tab settings. Moving and copying columns are both features of DisplayWrite 3.

When you are working with columns of numbers, four types of tabs may be chosen. They are the center tab, flush left tab, flush right tab, and decimal tab. You may even use a combination of these kinds of tabs within the same table. All you need to do is tell the system, during Column Layout, what types of tabs you want and where you want them. If you wish to review the various tab settings available on DisplayWrite 3, they are illustrated in brief following this paragraph. There is additional information in the reference manual that accompanied your DisplayWrite 3 program diskettes.

A Quick Review of Tabs

A center tab automatically centers material that is typed at that tab stop.   xxxxx.xxxxx

A flush left tab aligns material at the left of the tab.   .xxxxxxxxxx

A flush right tab aligns numbers at the right.   xxxxxxxxxx.

A decimal aligned (dec.) tab aligns numbers by their decimal points.

```
       x.xxxx
      xx.xx
      xx.xx
    xxxx.x
```

CREATING NUMERIC TABLES

Decimal points are often used in numeric tables to denote dollar amounts. Therefore, decimal tabs will be used in the first exercise. The period key is used to type a decimal point. You will notice a difference from text column typing in that the typist tabs from one column to the next when initially creating the table. This should not cause a problem, though, since numeric tables are normally typed this way on a typewriter.

Let us do a simple numeric table to begin with, just to get a feel for this type of table creation. The table you will set up follows this paragraph. Notice that three numbers are before the decimal point and two after it. You will see why when you set up the columns. When creating numeric tables, it is important to count the spaces that will be used by the longest number in each column as well as to know where the decimal points are located in these numbers. Four columns are

used in this table. After you have examined this table, go to
Exercise 63 to begin the steps for creating it on your own.

253.56	908.73	109.34	325.67
393.80	153.00	325.64	194.57
333.88	555.55	190.00	675.43
543.89	943.70	167.39	786.58
767.90	344.67	175.36	195.43

EXERCISE 63

PROCEDURES	COMMENTS
1. In the Text Task Selection Menu, choose Create Document and name it b:numeric.tbl.	
2. Go to the typing area.	You may turn on the Display codes or leave them off.
3. Press Ctrl-Column.	Just as in creating text tables, the word "Layout" displays on the screen.
4. Press Enter.	You are now in the Column Layout area.
5. Type the letter a three times.	You are telling the system that the longest number you will be typing has three numbers before the decimal point.
6. Press the period key.	Pressing the period key designates where you plan to type a decimal point and that you want numbers in the column aligned by these decimal points.
7. Type the letter a two times.	You have told the system that you will be typing two numbers after the decimal point.
8. Press Ctrl-Column.	This separates the first column from the second.
9. Type the letter a three times.	You are starting to give the directions for the second column of numbers. Continue following the steps.
10. Type a period.	

Continued

Chapter 14 Numeric Tables

PROCEDURES (Continued)	COMMENTS (Continued)
11. Type the letter a two times.	
12. Press Ctrl-Column.	You are separating the second column from the third.
13. Type the letter a three times.	
14. Type a period.	
15. Press the letter a two times.	
16. Press Ctrl-Column.	This separates the third column from the fourth.
17. Press the letter a three times.	
18. Type a period.	
19. Press the letter a two times.	
20. Press Command (F6).	Do not press Ctrl-Column after the last column.
21. Press Enter to accept the default.	The columns adjust between the margins.
22. Press Enter.	The status line will read "End Table."

At this point, you are ready to begin putting the numbers in the table. This is done much like you would type a table with a typewriter, tabbing from column to column and returning after each line. However, after typing the last number in the fourth column, do not return; press Continue. Take time to be careful at this point. Since you are just beginning numeric tables, a mistake now may cause you to have to start over.

23. Type 253.56.		
24. Tab to the second column.		
25. Type 908.73.		
26. Tab to the third column.		
27. Type 109.34.	Be sure to use the number 1 instead of the "L" key.

Continued

Chapter 14 Numeric Tables

PROCEDURES (Continued)	COMMENTS (Continued)
28. Tab to the fourth column.	
29. Type 325.67.	
30. Press return.	You are now starting the second row of numbers.
31. Follow this pattern of typing numbers until you reach the last number (195.43).	After the last number in the table has been typed, do not press return.
32. After typing the last number (195.43), press Continue (F10) to be returned to the regular typing area.	
33. Press End Task.	
34. Print a copy of this document.	

ISOLATING COLUMNS AND ADDING NUMBERS IN NUMERIC COLUMNS

As in text tables, the column which is to be revised must be isolated. Then the changes are made. After revision, the column again is placed with the other columns in the table. Let us work through this procedure in the next exercise as we isolate the first column and add a number to it.

EXERCISE 64

PROCEDURES	COMMENTS
1. In the Text Task Selection Menu, choose Revise Document.	
2. Type b:numeric.tbl.	
3. Go to the typing area.	
	Continued

Chapter 14 Numeric Tables

PROCEDURES (Continued)

4. Turn on the Display codes (F6 and D).

   This will help you find the Begin Table code. The first number in the table should appear to be out of alignment. Turning on the Display codes causes this. It will realign when the codes are turned off.

5. Using the arrow keys, place the cursor under the "2" in 253.56.

   The cursor must be on the same line as the Begin Table code. The cursor could be placed under any character in this number (253.56), but for the sake of simplicity, we will always choose the first character when isolating a column.

6. To isolate the column, press Ctrl-Column.

7. Type R for Revise.

   The column will appear isolated on the screen.

8. Using the down arrow key, place the cursor at the left margin of the line where 333.88 appears. In this example, the left margin will be the first "3" itself.

   Note: Adding material between two numbers or at the beginning of a column is similar to inserting text in a paragraph. Simply place the cursor at the left margin where you want the new material to begin and the old material will move over to accommodate it. In numeric columns, you would, therefore, type a number at the left margin where you want to make the insertion. The numbers following the insertion will, of course, remain after it. When you are adding a number at the end of a column, press End. Press carrier return if the cursor is not on a new line. Then type the new number.

9. Press the tab key.

   You are tabbing so that your number will align with the decimal tab.

10. Type 581.11.

    Do not use the letter "L" for a numeric "1."

11. Press the carrier return key.

Continued

COMMENTS (Continued)

PROCEDURES (Continued)   COMMENTS (Continued)

12. Press Continue.

13. Press End Task and print
    a copy of the table.

Your first column should now have six numbers in it. The number
"581.11" should be the third number from the top.

```
253.56
393.80
581.11
333.88
543.89
767.90
```

DELETING A NUMBER FROM A COLUMN

Let us assume that you want to remove the first number in the first
column (253.56). In Exercise 65 you will delete a number from a
numeric table.

EXERCISE 65

PROCEDURES   COMMENTS

1. If you are in the Text
   Task Selection Menu,
   select Revise Document
   and go to the typing
   area of b:numeric.tbl.

2. In the typing area,   You are isolating a column
   place the cursor under   from which you will delete a
   the "2" in the first row   number. Using the right arrow
   of numbers in the first   key, move the cursor to the
   column (253.56) and   right two spaces so that the
   press Ctrl-Column.   "2" will not be "under" any
                                       codes.

3. Press R for Revise.

4. Press Block (F4) and   You can select Delete by
   select Delete from the   either typing the letter "D"
   prompt line at the bot-   or using the right arrow key
   tom of the screen.   to highlight the word Delete
                                       and pressing Enter.

Continued

Chapter 14 Numeric Tables

PROCEDURES (Continued)

5. Using the right arrow key, highlight all of the numbers in this row of the column and the carrier return after it.

6. Press Enter.

7. Press Continue (F10).

8. Press End Task and print a copy of this table.

COMMENTS (Continued)

If you wanted to replace this number with another, you would highlight only the numbers and not the tab or carrier return after them.

In addition to adding and deleting numbers, you can also add an entire column in tables. This is the next operation we will explore.

ADDING AN ENTIRE COLUMN TO A NUMERIC TABLE

Adding an entire column to a numeric table involves two major steps. The first is the addition itself, and the second is realigning the columns on the page afterward. In this exercise, you will create a numeric table and insert a column between the second and third columns. The table you will be creating follows this paragraph. Look at it carefully before starting. Do not be concerned with column headings for now. You will learn about those later.

Quarterly Sales Figures

North	44,389.67	29,364.77	79,576.01
East	55,980.22	19,004.32	68,735.98
South	79,040.98	23,476.90	43,209.43
West	68,035.12	22,708.59	67,486.31

EXERCISE 66

PROCEDURES

1. In the Text Task Selection Menu, choose Create Document and name it b:Figures.

2. Go to the typing area.

3. In the typing area, center the title, Quarterly Sales Figures.

4. Return three times.

COMMENTS

This is not part of the table. You will start the table below the title.

Continued

PROCEDURES (Continued)		COMMENTS (Continued)
5.	Press Ctrl-Column and Enter.	
6.	In the Layout screen, press Line Adjust (F5).	The first column will be text.
7.	Type **a** five times.	There are five characters in the longest word in the first column of the table.
8.	Press Ctrl-Column.	This separates the columns.
9.	Type **a** six times.	The table you are about to type will have six characters to the left of the decimal point, one being a comma. If you were using a dollar sign, you would count it as a character also.
10.	Press period.	The period represents the decimal point.
11.	Type **a** two times.	Your table will also have two characters to the right of the decimal point.
12.	Press Ctrl-Column.	This separates the columns.
13.	Type **a** six times.	
14.	Press period.	
15.	Type **a** two times.	
16.	Press Ctrl-Column.	
17.	Type **a** six times.	
18.	Press period.	
19.	Type **a** two times.	
20.	Press Command and Enter.	You have now aligned the columns between the margins.
21.	Enter again.	
22.	Type the table remembering to press Continue, rather than Enter, after the last number.	

Continued

PROCEDURES (Continued)		COMMENTS (Continued)
23.	After you have finished typing the table, using the arrow keys, position the cursor under the first number in the third column of the table.	The cursor is where you want the new column to be inserted in your table. It should be under the number "2" in 29,364.77. You must be on the same line as the Begin Table code.
24.	Press Ctrl-Column.	A menu appears across the bottom of the screen.
25.	Type I to select Insert from the menu.	The Layout Instructions screen will appear. You should be able to see your original layout at the top of the screen. You will be inserting a new column here.
26.	Using the right arrow key, move the cursor to the end of the third set of "a´s." The cursor will be on the space after the last "a" in the set.	
27.	Press Ctrl-Column.	
28.	Type six "o´s," one period, and two more "o´s."	The "o´s" represent spaces where you will type numbers to the left of the decimal point. The period designates where you want the decimal point. The last two "o´s" represent spaces where the two numbers to the right of the decimal point will be typed.
29.	Press the Command key and Enter to accept the default.	The default is Adjust. The columns will spread out between the margins so that they are equally spaced.
30.	Press Continue once.	You are now in the column typing area. An empty column is now inserted in the table.

Note: For the sake of simplicity, you struck the "o" key for new characters to be added to a table. Any number or letter key would have the same effect; that is, it would represent a space to type a number in our example.

You are now ready to insert the numbers in the column you have just inserted.

Continued

PROCEDURES (Continued)	COMMENTS (Continued)
31. The cursor will be in the correct place to start typing. Do not move it yet.	An empty column that you can fill with numbers is on the screen.
32. Type the following numbers in the new column, returning after each number: 96,831.00 11,734.00 48,097.00 19,842.00	
33. Press Continue.	You are back in the regular typing area.
34. Print a copy of the table. It should look like Figure 14.1.	

Quarterly Sales Figures

North	44,389.67	96,831.00	29,364.77	79,576.01
East	55,980.22	11,734.00	19,004.32	68,735.98
South	79,040.98	48,097.00	23,476.90	43,209.43
West	68,035.12	19,842.00	22,708.59	67,486.31

Figure 14.1 Exercise 66 Printout

DELETING AN ENTIRE COLUMN FROM A NUMERIC TABLE

Deletion of entire columns is also possible with DisplayWrite 3. After the column is removed from the table, you will want to readjust the remaining columns so that they are spaced evenly between the margins. The next exercise will give you practice in deleting columns. If you had been asked to take the first column out of the table, you could follow the procedures in Exercise 67 to delete it.

EXERCISE 67

PROCEDURES	COMMENTS
1. Go to the typing area of b:Figures.	
2. Place the cursor beneath the first "4" in 44,389.67.	This is the first number in the first column.

Continued

PROCEDURES (Continued)	COMMENTS (Continued)
3. Press Ctrl-Column.	
4. Press "D" for Delete.	The entire column is highlighted.
5. Press Enter.	Now that the column is deleted, you will need to readjust the remaining columns.
6. Position the cursor under the Begin Table code.	If you cannot locate the Begin Table code, you may wish to turn on the Display codes.
7. Press the Continue key.	
8. Press the Command key and Enter to accept the default to adjust.	
9. Press Continue again.	This will return you to the typing area. The columns will be adjusted so that they are arranged evenly between the margins.

MOVING A COLUMN IN A NUMERIC TABLE

Occasionally you will have to move columns around on the page. This can be accomplished with DisplayWrite 3 without destroying the work you have already done. You will type the following table and move two columns within that table. For now, we will concentrate on the table and leave out the column headings.

                        Stocks

International Slag	22.725	22.500	22.375
MRA	58.875	57.875	78.000
Webber Glass	31.625	31.000	31.500
Gonzalez, Inc.	89.000	88.125	88.250

                      EXERCISE 68

PROCEDURES	COMMENTS
1. In the Text Task Selection Menu, choose Create Document and name it b:Stocks.	
Continued	

PROCEDURES (Continued)	COMMENTS (Continued)
2. Go to the typing area and type the main heading, Stocks.	
3. Press return three times.	
4. Using your knowledge of creating tables, type the previous table.	
5. When you are finished typing the table, press Continue. Instead of pressing End Task to save the table on the diskette, use the arrow keys to place the cursor above the table.	

Now that the table is complete, let us assume that the data are correct, but that they are listed in the wrong columns. You will have to switch the positions of the second and third columns.

6. Position the cursor under the first character in the third column.	This character is the first "2" in 22.500.
7. Press Ctrl-Column.	
8. Press Enter to accept the default, Move. The column is highlighted.	
9. Using the arrow keys, place the cursor under the first character in the second column.	This character is the first "2" in 22.725.
10. Press Enter.	The column has been moved.
11. Print a copy of the table. It should look like Figure 14.2.	After printing it, you may wish to practice moving the columns in this table.

Note: A column can be moved only to another area that is already set up as a table. In the exercise you have just completed, you moved a column within an area that was set up to be a table. You would not have been able, for example, to move one of the columns to the top of the page because no table exists there.

Chapter 14 Numeric Tables

```
                        Stocks

    International Slag         22.500      22.725      22.375
    MRA                        57.875      58.875      78.000
    Webber Glass               31.000      31.625      31.500
    Gonzalez, Inc.             88.125      89.000      88.250
```

Figure 14.2   Exercise 68 Printout

COPYING COLUMNS IN A NUMERIC TABLE

If you need another column in a table and that column will contain numbers that are identical to those in another column in the table, it is possible to copy the column that already exists and save yourself several keystrokes. You will type the following numeric table and copy a column within it. You will be using flush right tabs for whole numbers. The procedures and comments will tell you how to set up a column of right aligned numbers. You will center the single-spaced heading and leave a blank line for the column headings. Then set up the table. The last thing you will do is add the column headings.

```
              Gross Profit by Month
               (to nearest thousand)


    Greenville             32           54           80
    San Mateo              29            5           31
    San Francisco          88           56           72
    San Diego              45           46           42
```

EXERCISE 69

PROCEDURES

1. In the Text Task Selection Menu, choose Create Document and name it b:Profit.

2. Go to the typing area.

3. Type the two centered heading lines.

4. Return four times.

5. Press Ctrl-Column.

COMMENTS

These lines are single-spaced.

You are leaving enough room for the column headings to be typed later.

Continued

PROCEDURES (Continued)	COMMENTS (Continued)
6. Press Enter.	You are in the Layout screen.
7. Press Line Adjust.	The first column is composed of text.
8. Type the letter a 13 times.	There are 13 characters in the longest item in this column, San Francisco.
9. Press Ctrl-Column.	Note: There will be sufficient room for the column heads in this exercise. If, however, you were working with very long column heads and narrow numeric columns, you would want to leave enough spaces in the columns that the headings would fit across the top.
10. Type the letter a two times.	
	You do not have to allow for extra spaces in this exercise.
11. Press End.	Pressing End tells the system that this column is to be right aligned.
12. Press Ctrl-Column.	
13. Type the letter a two times.	
14. Press End.	
15. Press Ctrl-Column.	
16. Type the letter a two times.	
17. Press End.	
18. Press Command and Enter to accept the default.	
19. Press Continue.	Be sure to end by pressing Continue.
20. Using your knowledge of columns, type the numeric table.	After you have typed the table, you are going to copy a column.

Continued

Chapter 14 Numeric Tables

PROCEDURES (Continued)	COMMENTS (Continued)
21. Place the cursor under the "5" in 54.	This is the first character in the column you are going to copy. Note: The cursor must always be underneath the first character of the column you want to move or copy.
22. Press Ctrl-Column and type C for Copy.	The entire column is highlighted.
23. Using the right arrow key, move the cursor to the right until it is directly under the right margin.	Remember that the right margin graphic looks like this: >>. When moving or copying columns to the right of the last column in the table, always move the cursor to or past the right margin graphic.
24. Press Enter.	The column was copied to the right of the last column in the table.
25. Press Ctrl-Column.	
26. Press L for Layout and Enter.	You will be able to see your original layout instructions at the top of the screen.
27. Press Command and Enter.	You have adjusted the columns between the margins.
28. Press Continue.	The columns all fit on the screen.
29. Using your knowledge of typing, go back to the blank line you left for the column heads and type them on that line. The headings for the columns are City, May, June, July, and Aug.	
30. After adding the column headings, print a copy of the table. It should look like Figure 14.3.	

REVISING COLUMN FORMAT IN NUMERIC TABLES

As you already know, you can change margins when text editing. If you were to change the size to 11- by 8 1/2-inch paper by inserting the sheet into the printer sideways, you would naturally change the margins to accommodate the new width. A change in document format does not change the format of any of the tables within the document. The table formats must be changed by you.

Gross Profit by Month
(to nearest thousand)

City	May	June	July	Aug.
Greenville	32	54	80	54
San Mateo	29	5	31	5
San Francisco	88	56	72	56
San Diego	45	46	42	46

Figure 14.3   Exercise 69 Printout

In the following exercise, you will type a table to be printed on 8 1/2- by 11-inch paper. Then you will change the format of the document as though you had decided to print it on paper turned sideways. You will need to change the format of the table also so that it will spread out across the page of 11- by 8 1/2-inch paper.

You will be setting up and typing a table. It contains five types of columns. The first column is set up for text. The second is set up with a right flush tab. The third column is set up with a left flush tab. The fourth column is set up with a dec. (decimal) tab, and the last column is set up with a center tab.

In Exercise 70, you will perform the steps necessary to set up all of these types of columns. When you have finished with the layout, you will type the table and print a copy for reference. After printing the reference copy, you will change the page format so that you can print on paper turned sideways. Then you will revise the column format to spread the table across this new, wider page.

Following is the table you will be typing. Examine it before starting to set it up.

Employee Directory

Employee	Anniversary	Number	Salary	Department
Ivalou Morser	10-5-79	M283	1,500.94	Manufacturing
Dessie Wray	5-14-82	W476	1,600.80	Accounting
Lawrence Dady	3-1-84	D89	1,300.78	Shipping
Jan Schurz	12-30-57	S418	1,450.63	Administration
Henry Glenn	10-10-57	I3	1,703.46	Import

Chapter 14   Numeric Tables

EXERCISE 70

PROCEDURES	COMMENTS
1. In the Text Task Selection Menu, choose Create Document and name it b:Wide.tbl.	
2. In the Create or Revise Document Menu, select Change Document Format.	
3. In the Format Change Menu, choose Change Margins and Tabs.	
4. In the Margins and Tabs Menu, move the left margin to 10 and leave the right margin on 75.	You are still using 8 1/2- by 11-inch paper.
5. Return to the typing area and return six times.	You are now ready to set up the table.
6. Press Ctrl-Column and Enter.	
7. Press Line Adjust (F5).	This is a text column.
8. Type the letter a 13 times.	
9. Press Ctrl-Column.	
10. Type the letter a 9 times.	
11. Press End.	This is a right-aligned column.
12. Press Ctrl-Column.	
13. Press tab.	This is a left-aligned column.
14. Type the letter a four times.	
15. Press Ctrl-Column.	
16. Type the letter a five times.	
17. Type a period.	This is a decimal-aligned column.

Continued

PROCEDURES (Continued)	COMMENTS (Continued)
18. Type the letter a two times.	
19. Press Ctrl-Column.	You are separating columns.
20. Type the letter a 14 times.	
21. Press center (Control--X).	This is a center tab column.
22. Press Command and Enter.	You are adjusting the columns between the margins.
23. Press Continue.	
24. Type the table.	Type the main heading and return four times. This leaves a blank line for column headings.
25. After you have typed the last line of the table, instead of returning, press Continue to leave the column typing area.	
26. Press End Task and print a copy of the table.	You will now change the format of the document so that it can be printed on 11- by 8 1/2-inch paper.
27. In the Text Task Selection Menu, choose Revise Document and go to the typing area of b:Wide.tbl.	
28. Press Home.	
29. Press the Format key (F7).	Look at the choices.
30. In the Page Format Change Menu, choose Change Page Format and Enter.	This is the choice for 11- by 8 1/2-inch paper.
31. In the Page Format Menu, press d and Enter.	
32. Press 4 and Enter.	
33. Press c and Enter.	You have selected page length.
34. Type 51 and Enter.	The last line is now 51.

Continued

Chapter 14 Numeric Tables

PROCEDURES (Continued)	COMMENTS (Continued)
35. Enter again.	
36. Press **b** and Enter.	You are changing the margins.
37. In the Margins and Tabs Menu, move the right margin to 100.	This new margin will fit on 11- by 8 1/2-inch paper.
38. Press Enter twice.	You are back in the typing area.
39. Position the cursor under the Line Format Change code that is located just to the left of the Begin Table code.	You will now change the format for the table so that it can spread out between new document margins.
40. Press Continue (F10).	
41. In the Line Format Change Menu, choose Change Margins and Tabs and Enter.	This is how you change the format for the table.
42. In the Margins and Tabs Menu, move the right margin to 100 and Enter twice.	The margins for the document and the table now match.
43. In the typing area, position the cursor under the Begin Table code and press Continue.	You are accessing the Layout Instructions so that you can change them.
44. Press Command and Enter.	You are adjusting the table to fit the new margins.
45. Press Continue.	This takes you back to the document.

After you have finished the table itself, center and type the main heading. An easy way to place the column headings is to first fill the blank line you initially left for column headings with blank spaces. Strike the insert key so that you are in the replace mode. Type the headings over the columns.

46. Print a copy of the new, wide format employee directory.

47. Be sure that you put your paper in sideways with the long side up.

CHAPTER SUMMARY

A. To set up a center tab column in the column layout screen, type enough "a´s" to equal the longest item in the column and press center.

B. To set up a right flush tab column in the column layout screen, type enough "a´s" to equal the longest item and then press End.

C. To set up a left flush tab column in the column layout screen, type enough "a´s" to equal the number of characters in the longest item in the column.

D. To set up a decimal-aligned tab column in the column layout screen, type enough "a´s" to equal the number of characters to the left of the decimal point of the longest item in the column. Press period. Type enough "a´s" to equal the number of characters to the right of the decimal point.

E. To set up a text column in the column layout screen, press Line Adjust and type enough "a´s" to equal the number of characters you want in the column.

F. To revise a column format in the typing area, position the cursor under the Format Change code and press Continue. Go to the Margins and Tabs Menu and change the margins.

G. When adding or moving columns, keep in mind that they can only be moved into areas that are already set up to be columns. They cannot be moved outside of column areas.

Chapter 15

REFERENCE AREAS

When you complete this chapter, you will be able to:

1. Set up reference areas.

2. Create a table using the reference areas.

3. Revise in the reference areas.

4. Use the screen movement keys to cause a particular line to appear at the top of the screen.

5. Use the screen movement keys to cause a particular line to appear at the bottom of the screen.

6. Use the screen movement keys to cause a particular character to appear at the left edge of the screen.

7. Use the screen movement keys to cause a particular character to appear at the right edge of the screen.

8. Use the screen movement keys to move up or down the length of the screen.

INTRODUCTION

You already know one method of creating aligned paragraphs. However, creating multiple tables may seem to be a rather cumbersome task to some people. You have an alternative through the use of reference areas. A reference area is a column that appears on the screen next to the isolated column that you are creating or revising. Although you cannot revise a column while it is in the reference area, you can see the text and how it aligns with the isolated column. This allows you to know when to place extra carrier returns in one or the other of the columns so that your paragraphs align. This alternative is the use of the Side Reference Area. If you are creating a multi-column table, you can refer to the left column as you type or revise the other columns.

You may also create a reference area above your columns which will generally contain the column headings. This is called the Top Reference Area. You should keep in mind that the columns must have been created using Column Layout rather than just tabs. Also, the Column Reference Area can only be set up after the columns have been defined. Both Top and Side Reference areas can be created and used with the same document.

SETTING UP A TABLE CONTAINING COLUMNS AND USING REFERENCE AREAS

To create a table using reference areas, first you must go into Column Layout and set up the table. You will set up a text table of three columns. The first column will be seven spaces wide, and the second and third columns each will be twenty spaces wide.

EXERCISE 71

PROCEDURES	COMMENTS
1. Create a document and name it b:Tours.	
2. Set the margins at 10 and 75.	
3. Go to the typing area.	
4. Press Ctrl-Column (F4) and Enter.	The Column Layout screen appears.
5. Press F5 to indicate a text column.	
6. Type a 7 times.	
7. Press Ctrl-Column to separate the columns.	
	Continued

Chapter 15 Reference Areas

PROCEDURES (Continued)	COMMENTS (Continued)
8. Press F5 to tell the system that the second column is a text column.	
9. Type a 20 times.	
10. Press Ctrl-Column again.	
11. Press F5 to designate the third column as a text column.	
12. Type a 20 times.	
13. Press Command (F6).	The prompt line choices appear.
14. Accept the default of Adjust by pressing Enter.	The "a´s" adjust between the margins.
15. Press Command again.	
16. From the prompt line, select Setup_reference_area by striking the "S" key.	The Reference Area Setup Menu appears on the screen.
17. In the Reference Area Setup Menu, select "a" and Enter.	
18. Type the number 1 and Enter.	The number "1" means that you want a Side Reference Area. You will set up a Top Reference Area later.
19. Press Enter again.	
20. Press Continue (F10) two times.	
21. Press Command (F6) and "D."	This will turn on the Display codes.

CREATING A TABLE USING A REFERENCE AREA

Now that you have set up the columns and Side Reference Area, it is time to fill in the columns with text. Start with the middle column.

EXERCISE 72

PROCEDURES	COMMENTS
1. Making sure that you are on the same line as the Begin Table code, place the cursor under the tab for the second column (middle column) and press Ctrl-Column.	Be sure that you watch where the cursor is on the scale line rather than in the typing area.
2. Type **R** for Revise.	Your screen will show a vertical line between the first and second columns. Do not concern yourself with the text in the third column yet.
3. On the first line, type **Names** and return twice.	
4. Type the following names in the column.	

Names		Destinations
Enrique Ode		Sea World
John Cahill		Laguna Beach
Alice Cahill		Disneyland
Faye Thompson		Anaheim Stadium
Annette Rosenow		Dodger Stadium
Doug Rosenow		
Jan Stoltz		
Jack Ransom		
Candy Cashman		
Tom Thompson		
Gary Thompson		
Dan Thompson		
Gene Brown		
Fredia Brown		
Alan Reed		
Cheryl Ware		
Alta Dady		
Oswaldo Arana		
Kye Daniels		
Lela Dady		
Barbara Jensen		
Joyce Morton		

5. When you have finished typing the column of names, press Continue (F10).

Continued

Chapter 15   Reference Areas

PROCEDURES (Continued)	COMMENTS (Continued)
6. Move the cursor to the position under the tab for the third column.	The second tab is where the third column starts. It is farthest to the right.
7. Press Ctrl-Column and type R for Revise.	The second column disappears and you can now see the first and third columns.
8. Type the title Destinations and return twice.	
9. Type the text giving the names of the destinations in that column.	
10. When you finish with the third column, press Continue.	
11. Move the cursor to a position underneath the Begin Table code.	
12. Press Ctrl-Column and choose R for Revise.	You can see the other columns on the screen now, but you can type only in the column that is isolated.
13. Type Tour # on the first line and return twice.	
14. Type Tour 1 and return.	
15. Press Continue.	
16. Press End Task.	
17. Print b:Tours. It should look like Figure 15.1.	

Let us assume that another group has been formed. You will now need to revise the document to show a second tour.

18. In the Text Task Selection Menu, choose Revise Document. At the prompt, type b:Tours and Enter.

19. Go to the typing area of b:Tours and turn on the Display codes.

Continued

Tour#	Names	Destinations
Tour 1	Enrique Ode	Sea World
	John Cahill	Laguna Beach
	Alice Cahill	Disneyland
	Faye Thompson	Anaheim Stadium
	Annette Rosenow	Dodger Stadium
	Doug Rosenow	
	Jan Stoltz	
	Jack Ransom	
	Candy Cashman	
	Tom Thompson	
	Gary Thompson	
	Dan Thompson	
	Gene Brown	
	Fredia Brown	
	Alan Reed	
	Cheryl Ware	
	Alta Dady	
	Oswaldo Arana	
	Kye Daniels	
	Lela Dady	
	Barbara Jensen	
	Joyce Morton	

Figure 15.1   Exercise 72 Printout

PROCEDURES (Continued)

20. Place the cursor under the Begin Table code and press Ctrl-Column.

21. Press **R** for Revise.

22. Press End to get past the text already in the column.

23. Return enough times in the first column so that the cursor is two lines below the last name in the middle column.

    COMMENTS (Continued)

    Look at the reference area to see how far down to go.

24. Type **Tour 2** and return.

25. Press Continue to return to the regular typing area.

26. Place the cursor under the first character in the second column (middle column) and press Ctrl-Column.

    Be sure that you are on the same line as the Begin Table code. You should be under the "N" in Names.

Continued

Chapter 15   Reference Areas

PROCEDURES (Continued)	COMMENTS (Continued)
27. Type R for Revise.	
28. Move the cursor to the point where it is on the same line with the words "Tour 2" in the first column.	
29. Type the following list of names. Leann Heckathorn Paul Hulsman Debbie Glenn Judy Pertierra Ray Pertierra Kristen Pertierra Kimberly Pertierra Dick McKnight Bill Emerson Jeff Morser Randy Morser Nancy Morser Larry Morser George Morser Jack Wray Olga Fusco Wilma Mulholland Ken Mulholland Mark Mulholland Julie Mulholland Denise Mulholland Laura Mulholland	
30. When you have finished typing the list of names of people going on the second tour, press Continue.	
31. Position the cursor under the "D" in Destinations. Press Ctrl-Column.	
32. Type R for Revise. Move past the existing text by pressing End.	
33. Return enough times so that the cursor is on the same line as the words "Tour 2" in the first column.	Refer to the Column Reference Area.

Continued

242 Chapter 15 Reference Areas

PROCEDURES (Continued)	COMMENTS (Continued)
34. Type the third column information for Tour 2. The destinations are as follows: The Forum, Palm Springs, John Wayne Airport, Angel's Flight, and Marineland.	
35. When you finish typing the third column, press Continue.	
36. Press End Task.	
37. Print a copy of b:Tours. It should look like Figure 15.2.	

SETTING UP A TOP REFERENCE AREA

Now you will place the column headings in the Top Reference Area so that they can be seen by you at all times. It is not necessary to be close to the top of a column.

EXERCISE 73

PROCEDURES	COMMENTS
1. In the Text Task Selection Menu, choose Revise Document.	
2. At the prompt, type b:Tours.	
3. Go to the typing area.	
4. Turn on the Display codes.	
5. Place the cursor under the Begin Table code and press Ctrl-Column.	
6. Type S for Setup_reference_area. Type b to select Top Reference Area and Enter.	

Continued

Chapter 15 Reference Areas

Tour#	Names	Destinations
Tour 1	Enrique Ode	Sea World
	John Cahill	Laguna Beach
	Alice Cahill	Disneyland
	Faye Thompson	Anaheim Stadium
	Annette Rosenow	Dodger Stadium
	Doug Rosenow	
	Jan Stoltz	
	Jack Ransom	
	Candy Cashman	
	Tom Thompson	
	Gary Thompson	
	Dan Thompson	
	Gene Brown	
	Fredia Brown	
	Alan Reed	
	Cheryl Ware	
	Alta Dady	
	Oswaldo Arana	
	Kye Daniels	
	Lela Dady	
	Barbara Jensen	
	Joyce Morton	
Tour 2	Leann Heckathorn	The Forum
	Paul Hulsman	Palm Springs
	Debbie Glenn	John Wayne Airport
	Judy Pertierra	Angel's Flight
	Ray Pertierra	Marineland
	Kristen Pertierra	
	Kimberly Pertierra	
	Dick McKnight	
	Bill Emerson	
	Jeff Morser	
	Randy Morser	
	Nancy Morser	
	Larry Morser	
	George Morser	
	Jack Wray	
	Olga Fusco	
	Wilma Mulholland	
	Ken Mulholland	
	Mark Mulholland	
	Julie Mulholland	
	Denise Mulholland	
	Laura Mulholland	

Figure 15.2   Exercise 72 Printout

PROCEDURES (Continued)	COMMENTS (Continued)
7. Type 2 and Enter.	You have told the system that you want two lines in the Top Reference Area.
8. Press Enter to return to the typing area.	
9. Press Esc when you are back in the typing area.	This eliminates the prompt line.
10. In order to see how a Top Reference Area works, place the cursor on the same line as the Begin Table code and underneath the first character in the second column.	This character is the "N" in Names.
11. Press Ctrl-Column.	
12. Type R for Revise.	You should see both vertical and horizontal bars.
13. Hold down the down arrow key until you come to the end of the column.	The title did not disappear.
14. Print what you have on the monitor by holding down the shift and pressing PrtSc.	You performed the print screen operation so that you would have something to hand to your instructor to show that you know how to set up a Top Reference Area.
15. Press Continue.	

REVISING WITHIN THE REFERENCE AREAS

Now that you have set up reference areas and created a table using them, let us revise within the reference areas. The first revision will be in a column heading which is located in a Top Reference Area. Since you cannot access the Top Reference Area, you must "collapse" it by setting the number of lines in the Top Reference Area to "0" before revision.

EXERCISE 74

PROCEDURES	COMMENTS
1. If you are in the typing area of b:Tours, remain there. If you are in the Text Task Selection Menu, go to the typing area of b:Tours.	
2. In the typing area, turn on the Display codes.	
3. Place the cursor under the Begin Table code and press Ctrl-Column.	
4. Type S to select Setup _reference_area.	
5. In the Reference Area Setup Menu, type b and Enter.	
6. Type O and Enter.	You have removed the Top Reference Area and can now access it to make revisions.
7. Enter again to return to the typing area.	
8. Press Esc.	This will eliminate the prompt line at the bottom of the screen.
9. Place the cursor under the "D" in Destinations so that you can revise the third column and press Ctrl-Column.	
10. Type R to choose Revise.	
11. In the third column, change the word "Destinations" to "Stops."	
12. When you finish, press Continue to return to the regular typing area.	
13. To restore the Top Reference Area, place the cursor under the Begin Table code and press Ctrl-Column.	

Continued

```
PROCEDURES (Continued)                  COMMENTS (Continued)

14.    Type s.

15.    Type b and Enter.

16.    Type 2 and Enter.

17.    Enter again to return to
       the typing area.

18.    In the typing area,
       press Esc to remove the
       prompt line choices.
```

To practice revising in a reference area other than the top, let us change the words in the left column. This should be very simple for you to do since the operation is nothing more than revising in a text column.

EXERCISE 75

```
PROCEDURES                              COMMENTS

 1.    Position the cursor un-
       der the Begin Table
       code.

 2.    Press Ctrl-Column and
       choose Revise.

 3.    Change the word "Tour"
       to "Trip" at both places
       in the column.  Do not
       change the title,
       though.

 4.    Press Continue when you
       are finished.

 5.    Press End Task.

 6.    Print b:Tours.
```

Once you have created tables without using reference areas, as you have done in previous chapters, you will find that it is easy to set up the reference areas even after the tables have been completed. You merely place the cursor under the Begin Table code for the first column or the tabs for other columns, and press Ctrl-Column. After that, set up reference areas as you did in this chapter.

If you wish to use a column other than the left column as a reference area, move the column in question to the left while you are working

Chapter 15   Reference Areas

with the document. You can move it back to its original position just before printing.

SCREEN MOVEMENT KEYS

The second half of this chapter deals with screen movement keys. In order to move across large areas of text, first we will have to change the format of b:Tours to widen it. The next step will be to copy the middle column three times. After that, there will be room enough to practice screen movement.

EXERCISE 76

PROCEDURES	COMMENTS
1. In the Text Task Selection Menu, choose Revise Document.	
2. At the prompt, type b:Tours and Enter.	
3. In the Create or Revise Menu, select Change Document Format and Enter.	
4. In the Document or Alternate Format Menu, choose Change Margins and Tabs and Enter.	You must make the necessary changes to accommodate the wider table.
5. In the Margins and Tabs Menu, change the margins to 5 and 109 and Enter.	
6. In the Document or Alternate Format Menu, choose Change Page Format and Enter.	
7. In the Page Format Menu, choose Paper or Envelope Size and Enter.	
8. At the prompt, type 4 and Enter.	This is the choice for 11- by 8 1/2-inch paper.
9. Now select Last Typing Line and Enter.	
10. At the prompt, type 45.	The last typing line on the page should now be one inch above the bottom of the paper.

Continued

PROCEDURES (Continued)	COMMENTS (Continued)
11. Enter until you are in the typing area.	
12. In the typing area, the cursor should be positioned under the Line Format Change code just to the left of the Begin Table code. If it is not, move it there.	
13. Press Continue.	
14. In the Format Change Menu, choose Change Margins and Tabs and Enter.	You will see a prompt that says "A table follows. Tabs should not be changed." You will not be changing the tabs yourself. The system will do it for you.
15. Change the margins to 5 and 109.	
16. Enter enough times to return to the typing area.	
17. Place the cursor under the Begin Table code and press Ctrl-Column.	
18. Press D for Delete and Enter.	
19. Place the cursor under the first character in the third column and press Ctrl-Column.	
20. Press D for Delete.	
21. Position the cursor under the Begin Table code and press Ctrl-Column.	You will now copy the column of names so that it occurs four times on the page.
22. Select Copy and wait for the column to highlight.	
23. Move the cursor to the right margin and Enter.	

Continued

PROCEDURES (Continued)	COMMENTS (Continued)
24. To make another copy of the column, place the cursor under the first character in the second column (the one on the right margin) and press Ctrl-Column.	
25. Press C for Copy, and when the column is highlighted, move the cursor to the first character in the first column and press Enter.	You will now see three identical columns.
26. Position the cursor under the first character in the middle column and press Ctrl-Column.	
27. Type C for Copy.	
28. After the column has highlighted, move the cursor to the left margin on the same line and press Enter.	You now have four identical columns. The columns of characters should adjust within the margins.

PLACING CHARACTERS AT THE RIGHT OR LEFT EDGE OF THE SCREEN

Now that b:Tours is a very wide table, you can place certain characters in the text columns at the right or left edge of the screen. This type of movement can be used in situations where you wish to screen print only certain columns of a table. It is faster than copying the document and then deleting those columns that you do not wish to print.

EXERCISE 77

PROCEDURES	COMMENTS
1. Place the cursor under the "L" in Leann in the fourth column and press Ctrl-PgUp.	
2. Print the screen.	

Continued

Chapter 15   Reference Areas

PROCEDURES (Continued)	COMMENTS (Continued)
3. Place the cursor under the "C" in Candy in the second column and press Ctrl-PgDn. The "C" is moved to the left margin of the screen. Look at the scale line to see where the arrow is located. 4. Print the screen.	

MOVING AN ENTIRE SCREEN WIDTH TO THE RIGHT OR LEFT

When you have a wide document on the screen, it is easy to move the entire screen width to the right or left to view parts of the document which are close to the right or left margins. Now you will learn to move the entire screen width rapidly.

EXERCISE 78

PROCEDURES	COMMENTS
1. If you are in the Text Task Selection Menu, choose Revise Document and go to the typing area of b:Tours.	
2. Position the cursor under the "E" in the first name in the first column.	
3. Press Ctrl-PgDn.	You have moved an entire screen width to the right.
4. Print your screen.	
5. Position the cursor underneath the "B" in Barbara Jensen in the fourth column.	
6. Press Ctrl-PgUp.	You have moved back the entire width of the screen.

MOVING THE LENGTH OF THE SCREEN

To get to the very top or bottom of the screen, you need to press only one key: either PgUp or PgDn. If the cursor is on the first line of

Chapter 15   Reference Areas

the screen, and you press PgDn, the next page length plus the last line from the previous screen will appear on the screen. The cursor will be on that line. When you have a very wide table, it is a good idea to take advantage of the horizontal screen movement keys.

EXERCISE 79

PROCEDURES

1. Place the cursor under the "L" in Leann Heckathorn.

2. Press the PgDn key.

3. Print your screen.

4. Position the cursor under the "L" in Leann and press the PgUp key. Print the screen.

COMMENTS

You have just moved the line containing Leann Heckathorn to the top of the screen.

The line containing Leann Heckathorn will appear as the last line on the screen.

Note: The first few lines of a document cannot be moved to the bottom of the screen because you cannot go past the top of your document.

CHAPTER SUMMARY

A. Reference areas can be used to set up columns.

B. You can revise in both the Side and Top Reference Areas.

C. Using the screen movement keys can cause particular lines to appear at either the top or bottom of the screen.

D. You can use the screen movement keys to place particular characters at either the left or right edge of the screen.

E. The screen movement keys can be used to move the length of the screen up or down.

F. The screen movement keys are most useful with wide tables and full pages.

Chapter 16
MATH

When you complete this chapter, you will be able to:

1. Use Column Add to add a column of numbers.

2. Use Row Add to add a row of numbers.

3. Use math functions to perform mathematical calculations within a document.

4. Use DisplayWrite 3 to calculate averages.

5. Establish a constant and use it in mathematical calculations.

INTRODUCTION

DisplayWrite 3 can perform mathematical calculations for you. It can add, subtract, multiply, divide, find averages, and use constants to perform calculations.

You will find the math functions to be helpful when you are creating a table of numbers with totals. The math functions can calculate the totals for you or check to see if the existing totals are correct. The math functions of DisplayWrite 3 are not limited to just tables of numbers. They can also perform mathematical calculations with numbers imbedded in the text.

The following rules apply to all math functions:

--The numeric key pad can be used to type numbers. You must first press the Num Lock key.
--A number cannot exceed 15 digits; this includes the totals.
--Use the numeral one (1), not a lowercase "l" when typing numbers.
--Use one of the following ways to indicate negative numbers:
  --The left-most digit or decimal point is preceded by a required hyphen or a required hyphen followed by a space.
  --The right-most digit or decimal is immediately followed by a required hyphen.
  --The number is enclosed in parentheses, brackets, or less than/greater than symbols. The closing symbol must immediately follow the right-most digit or decimal point.

ADDING COLUMNS AND ROWS

Column Add and Row Add give you the capability of adding numbers that have been aligned at a decimal tab. Column Add allows you to add a vertical column of numbers. Row Add allows you to add a horizontal row of numbers.

Column Add and Row Add can be used only to add numbers that are aligned at a decimal tab. Column Add and Row Add can be used to compile totals to insert in a document, as well as to verify existing totals.

Keep the following points in mind as you use Column Add and Row Add:

--A column or row of numbers must be aligned at a decimal tab.
--A decimal point does not need to be added to the end of a whole number.
--Negative numbers will be subtracted from the total.

STEPS FOR ADDING COLUMNS

1. All of your numbers should be aligned at a decimal tab.

2. Make sure Display codes is turned off.

3. Place the cursor under the first number in the column to be added, as shown in Figure 16.1.

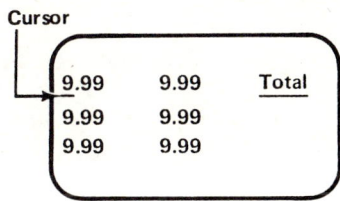

Figure 16.1   First Number To Be Added

4. Press Cmd (F6) and select Math. When the prompt appears, select Block_add (see Figure 16.2).

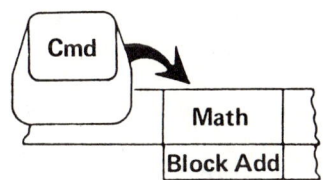

Figure 16.2   Block_add

5. Move the cursor down to the last number in the column.

6. Press Continue (F10). The numbers are added and the total is displayed on the prompt line.

7. If you wish to have the total inserted on the page, place the cursor where you want the total to appear and press Continue.

8. Press Esc to clear the total. Now you are ready to add a second column.

9. Repeat Steps 3-7 for any additional columns you may need to add.

10. When you have added all of the columns, press Esc twice to end the Column Add function.

If you need to add only a portion of a column, place the cursor on the first number to be added, move the cursor to the last number to be added, and press Continue. The number that the cursor is placed under will be highlighted, and a total will be displayed in the prompt.

STEPS FOR ADDING ROWS

1. Make sure the numbers in your table are aligned at a decimal tab.

2. Turn Display codes off.

3. Place the cursor under the first number in the row to be added.

4. Press Cmd and select Math. When the prompt appears, select Block_add.

5. Move the cursor across the row to the last number to be added.

Chapter 16   Math

6. Press Continue. The numbers are added and the total is displayed on the prompt line.

7. If you wish to have the total inserted on your page, place the cursor where you want the total to appear and press Continue.

8. Press Esc to clear the total. You are now ready to add a second row.

9. When you have added the rows, press Esc twice to end the Row Add function.

If you wish to add only a portion of a row, place the cursor on the first number in the row to be added, move the cursor to the last number to be added, and press Continue. The numbers designated by the cursor will be highlighted and a total will be displayed in the prompt.

EXERCISE 80

In Exercise 80, you will be recalling the document Income.tbl to the screen. You will be using the DisplayWrite 3 math functions to add the columns and rows in Income.tbl.

PROCEDURES	COMMENTS
1. Place the cursor under the first number to be added.	Place the cursor under the first "2" in 2,248.30.
2. Press Cmd (F6).	The prompt line choices display.
3. Select Math.	The prompt line choices display.
4. Select Block_add.	
5. Move the cursor down to the last number in the column.	The entire column should be highlighted.
6. Press Continue (F10).	The total is displayed in the prompt line.
7. Move the cursor down two lines.	This is where you want the total to be inserted.
8. Press Continue.	The total has been inserted in the table.
9. Press Esc to clear the total.	

Continued

PROCEDURES (Continued)	COMMENTS (Continued)
10. Repeat Steps 1-9 to add the second column.	Now that you have added the columns successfully, you will add the rows going across.
11. Place the cursor under the first number in the row.	The cursor should be under the first "2" in 2,248.30
12. Press Cmd.	The prompt line choices display.
13. Select Math.	The prompt line choices display.
14. Select Block_add.	
15. Move the cursor across the row to the last number to be added.	
16. Press Continue.	The total displays in the prompt line.
17. Place the cursor on the decimal tab in the Y-T-D column.	The totals will appear in the Y-T-D column.
18. Press Continue.	The total has been inserted in the table.
19. Press Esc to clear the total.	
20. Repeat Steps 11-19 to add all of the rows.	
21. When you have completed adding the rows, press Esc twice to end the Row Add function.	
22. Insert an underscore under the number 8,731.04 in the Y-T-D column.	
23. Press End task.	
24. Print the table.	

STEPS FOR USING MATH FUNCTIONS

Math functions allow you to add, subtract, multiply, and divide. With math functions, you can check calculations in a table, compute numbers

Chapter 16 Math

in text, or insert totals in a document. When using math functions, numbers may be in text or columns. Decimal alignment of numbers is not required.

Math functions are used to add, subtract, multiply, or divide numbers within a document. You also can add, subtract, multiply, or divide by a constant number not contained in the document. A constant is a number entered and held in the system for repeated use.

1. Place the cursor under the first number that is to be calculated. The cursor must be under the decimal tab or on any digit to the left of the decimal tab.

2. Press Cmd (F6).

3. Select Math.

4. Select Add.

5. The number is highlighted and entered in the total at the bottom of the screen. Whenever you use math functions to do any calculations, always select Add to enter the first number into the total.

6. Place the cursor under the next number to be calculated. This number can be anywhere in the document.

7. Press Cmd and select Math. A command will appear asking you to select the desired sign function (Add, Subtract, Multiply, or Divide).

8. The number will be highlighted, and the new total appears at the bottom of the screen.

9. To insert the total into your text, place the cursor where you want the total to be inserted and press Continue.

10. Press Esc to clear the total. You may continue to use the sign functions with other sets of numbers.

11. To end the task, press Esc twice and then press End Task (F2).

STEPS FOR CALCULATING AVERAGES

Through the Math Requests Menu, DisplayWrite 3 gives you the capability of quickly calculating the average of any number of entries you have added. Ordinarily, to find an average you would need to add the entries and then divide by the total number of entries. With DisplayWrite 3, you need not do all of this. The average is calculated for you in one step. The software also allows you to insert the average in the appropriate place in your document.

1. Your document should be displayed on the screen. Use the appropriate commands to perform your mathematical calculations in your

document. When you obtain your total, leave it on the screen.
Do NOT cancel your total.

2. Press Cmd.

3. Select Math and then select Request. The Math Requests Menu will appear. Look under Item "e." You will notice that the average has been calculated for you.

4. Set Copy Average into Total to "Yes" in the Math Requests Menu.

5. Press Enter to return to the typing area. The average appears as the total at the bottom of the screen.

6. Place the cursor at the location where you want the average to be inserted.

7. Press Continue. The average is placed in your document.

8. Press Esc to clear the total. If you wish to calculate another average, you must clear the total, add the new figures, and return to the Math Requests Menu. The total and the item count clear after you press Esc.

9. Press Esc again to leave the math function.

EXERCISE 81

In Exercise 81, you will be typing a short document which contains figures. You will use the math functions to add the figures and insert the total into the text. Then, through the Math Requests Menu, you will find the average and have the average inserted into the text.

PROCEDURES	COMMENTS
1. Create a new document and name it b:Exerci81.	
2. Type the following paragraphs: During the 1980 Census, the following population figures were established: Hampton 3,243; Larkin 1,196; Willow 6,311; and Alpine 3,926. The population total for the county is . The average city population (population total divided by number of cities) is .	
3. Place the cursor under the first "3" in 3,243.	
4. Press Cmd (F6).	The prompt line choices display.

Continued

Chapter 16   Math

PROCEDURES (Continued)	COMMENTS (Continued)
5. Select Math.	The prompt line choices display.
6. Select Add.	
7. Place the cursor under the first "1" in 1,196.	
8. Repeat Steps 4-6.	
9. Place the cursor under the "6" in 6,311.	
10. Repeat Steps 4-6.	
11. Place the cursor under the "3" in 3,926.	
12. Repeat Steps 4-6.	
13. Place the cursor on the . following the word "is."	Your screen should look like this: for the county is .
14. Press Continue (F10).	The total is inserted in the text.
15. Press Cmd (F6).	The prompt line choices display.
16. Select Math.	The prompt line choices display.
17. Select Request.	The Math Requests Menu displays.
18. Type e and press Enter.	This is to select Copy Average into Total.
19. Type 1 and press Enter twice.	The average appears as the total at the bottom of the screen.
20. Place the cursor under the . following the words "of cities) is ."	Your screen should look like this: of cities) is .
21. Press Continue.	The average is inserted in the text.
22. Press Esc twice.	This is to leave the math function.
23. Press End Task.	

Continued

PROCEDURES (Continued)

24. Print the document.

COMMENTS (Continued)

CONSTANTS

A constant is a number that is entered into the system and is held in the system for repeated use in mathematical calculations. The constant number does not need to appear anywhere in your document. Constants can be positive or negative numbers. You can also use a constant to figure a percentage by typing a constant number followed by a percent sign.

Here is an example of how you might use a constant. You have a series of numbers which you need to multiply by 12 in order to obtain yearly figures. You would enter 12 as a constant into the system and ask the system to multiply each of the figures by the constant. This would save you from having to key in 12 each time you perform the multiplication.

STEPS FOR ESTABLISHING A CONSTANT

1. Press Cmd and select Math.

2. Select Constant. The Constant prompt appears.

3. Type the number you would like to use as the constant. Press Enter. The total and the item count appear at the bottom of the screen.

STEPS FOR USING A CONSTANT

1. Move the cursor under the number with which you wish to use the constant.

2. Press Cmd and select Math; then select Add. The number should be highlighted and added to the total at the bottom of the screen.

3. Press Cmd and select Math; then select Constant. The constant you have established appears at the bottom of the screen. If the constant is not correct, press Esc and type a new constant.

4. Press Cmd and select Math. Then select the desired sign function (Add, Subtract, Multiply, or Divide).

5. The new total will appear at the bottom of the screen.

6. To insert the total in your text, place the cursor where you want the total to appear and press Continue. If you want the total to accumulate, repeat Steps 1-5.

7. To clear the total, press Esc. The total and the item count will return to 0.

Chapter 16 Math

8. To end the document, press Esc until the total and the item count disappear. Then press End Task.

EXERCISE 82

Exercise 82 will give you the chance to establish a constant and then use the constant in mathematical calculations. You will need to recall the prerecorded exercise b:Payroll.tbl to the screen to perform this exercise.

PROCEDURES	COMMENTS
1. Recall the document b:Payroll.tbl to the screen.	The table should be displayed on the screen.
2. Press Cmd (F6) and select Math.	
3. Select Constant.	The Constant prompt appears.
4. Type 12 and press Enter.	The 12 will be the constant.
5. Place the cursor under the "1" in $1,422.	
6. Press Cmd and select Math.	
7. Select Add.	The $1,422 is highlighted and added to the total.
8. Press Cmd and select Math.	
9. Select Constant.	The 12 appears at the bottom of the screen.
10. Press Cmd.	
11. Select Math.	
12. Select Multiply.	The total appears at the bottom.
13. Place the cursor in the "Total for the Year" column.	This is where you will insert the total.
14. Press Continue (F10).	The total appears in the text.
15. Press Esc.	This clears the total.
16. Place the cursor under the "9" in 980.	

Continued

PROCEDURES (Continued)	COMMENTS (Continued)
17. Repeat Steps 6-15.	
18. Place the cursor under the "2" in 2,365.	
19. Repeat Steps 6-15.	
20. Place the cursor under the first "1" in 1,910.	
21. Repeat Steps 6-15.	
22. Press Esc twice.	This is to clear the Total prompt.
23. Press F2.	This is to end the task.
24. Print the document.	

CHAPTER SUMMARY

A. Using the Column Add or Row Add

  1. Make sure all of the numbers are aligned at a decimal tab.
  2. Display codes should be turned off.
  3. Place the cursor under the first number in the column or row to be added.
  4. Press Cmd (F6) and select Math. When the prompt appears, select Block_add.
  5. Move the cursor to the last number to be added in the column or row.
  6. Press Continue (F10).
  7. To place the total in the document, place the cursor where you want the total to appear and press Continue.
  8. Press Esc to clear the total. Repeat Steps 3-7 for additional rows or columns to be added.
  9. When you have completed adding all of the rows and columns, press Esc twice to end the Column Add function.

B. Using Math Functions

  1. Place the cursor under the first number to be calculated.
  2. Press Cmd and select Math; then select Add.
  3. Place the cursor under the next number to be calculated.
  4. Press Cmd and select Math.
  5. Select the desired sign function.
  6. To insert the total into your text, press Continue.

C. Finding An Average

  1. The total for your mathematical calculations should display on the screen.

Chapter 16 Math 263

2. Press Cmd.
3. Select Math and then select Request.
4. The average should be calculated for you under Item "e" in the Math Requests Menu.

D. Establishing and Using a Constant

1. Press Cmd and select Math.
2. Select Constant.
3. Type the number you would like to use as the constant and press Enter.
4. Move the cursor under the number with which you wish to use the constant.
5. Press Cmd and select Math; then select Add.
6. Press Cmd and select Math; then select Constant.
7. Press Cmd and select Math; then select the desired sign function.
8. The new total will appear at the bottom of the screen.

Chapter 17
FOOTNOTES

When you complete this chapter, you will be able to:

1. Create a document containing footnotes.

2. Revise footnotes in a document.

3. Insert additional footnotes in a document.

4. Describe a footnote library.

INTRODUCTION

DisplayWrite 3 eliminates the cumbersome task of placing footnotes at the bottom of corresponding pages. With DisplayWrite 3, adding, deleting, and revising footnotes is a simple task. As Figure 17.1 illustrates, the system will number each footnote, calculate the amount of space needed at the bottom of each footnoted page, insert a separator line between the body text and the footnote text, and place the footnote correctly on each page. If you revise a footnoted document, the system will renumber and reposition the footnotes for you.

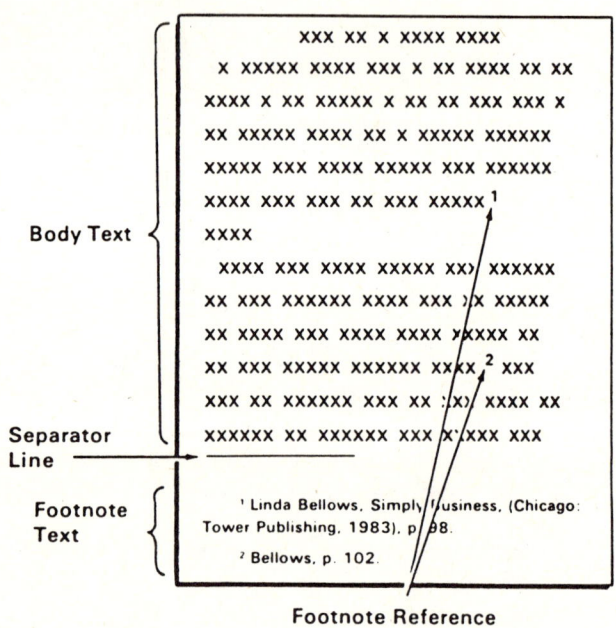

Figure 17.1 Footnotes

The following is a brief explanation of the terminology that will be used to refer to various parts of a footnoted document.

Body Text: The text portion of the document that is to be footnoted.

Footnote Reference: This is usually a number printed above the normal line of typing, in the body text, to indicate a footnote. This number serves as a cross-reference because it is also at the beginning of the footnote. The footnote reference contains leading characters and trailing characters. Leading characters are characters or codes that precede the footnote reference in the body text. You can have up to eight leading characters. The system's default leading character is a Half Index Up code. Trailing characters are any characters that follow the footnote reference in the body text. The default is a Half Index Down code.

Separator Line: The line that separates the body text from the footnote.

Footnote Text: The text that appears below the separator line at the bottom of the page. The footnote also contains leading characters in front of the footnote reference and trailing characters after the footnote reference. The default leading characters in footnote text are a Tab and Half Index Up code. The default trailing character is a Half Index Down code.

CREATING AND REVISING A FOOTNOTED DOCUMENT

The body text of a footnoted document is created the same way you create any other document until you reach the place for a footnote reference. At this point, you will indicate to the system that you need to add footnotes. Once this is done, formatting codes will be placed into the body text and into the footnote. The codes inserted into the body text are shown in Figure 17.2.

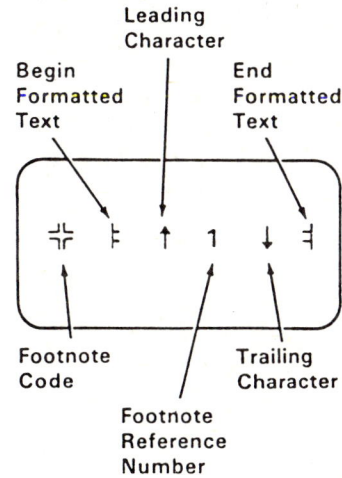

Figure 17.2 Footnote Codes

The system then will bring up a blank page with the system page number 9000 on which to type the footnote (see Figure 17.3). The footnotes will not appear at the bottom of their corresponding pages until after you complete the document and paginate the document using Automatic Pagination.

If you need to revise or delete a footnote, this must be done on the footnote text stored at the end of the document and not the footnote text at the bottom of the page. Changes made to footnote text at the bottoms of the pages are only temporary and will be deleted the next time the document is paginated or merged.

STEPS FOR CREATING A FOOTNOTED DOCUMENT

1. Type the body text until you reach the point for a footnote reference.

2. Press Instr (F8) and select Footnote. The Footnote Menu will display.

3. Check to see that Create/Revise Footnote Text is set to "Yes." Press Enter to go to the Footnote typing area. Your status line should show a page number of 9000 or greater, as shown in Figure 17.4.

Chapter 17 Footnotes

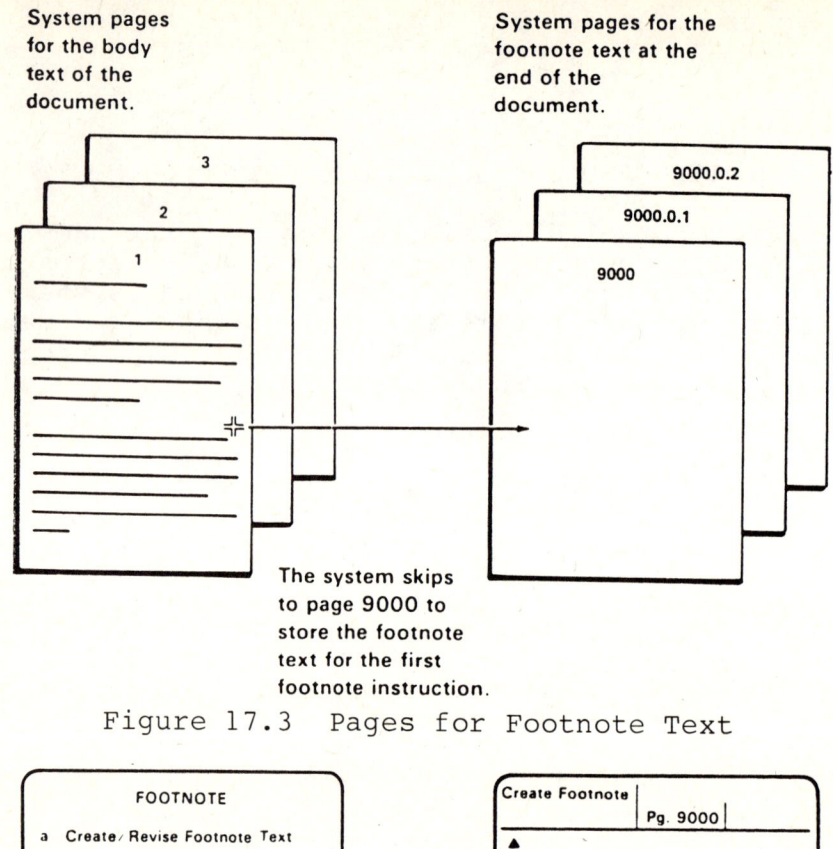

Figure 17.3   Pages for Footnote Text

Figure 17.4   Create Footnote

4. Type the footnote text. Do not type the footnote number or any leading or trailing characters. Do not end the footnote text with a carrier return. The system will insert the appropriate footnote number, leading and trailing characters, and the ending carrier return for you during pagination.

5. Press Continue (F10) to return to the typing area and continue typing the body text. The footnote text is stored at the end of your document. A footnote reference and the formatting codes have been placed in the body text. The formatting codes are not visible unless you turn on Display codes.

6. Repeat Steps 1-5 for each additional footnote reference to be included in your body text.

7. When you have completed typing the body text, paginate the document.

STEPS FOR REVISING EXISTING FOOTNOTE TEXT

1. Place the cursor under the Footnote code (see Figure 17.5) in the body text.

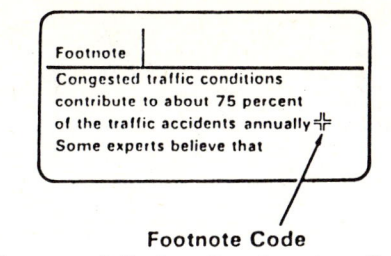

Footnote Code
Figure 17.5   Footnote Code

2. Press Continue (F10). This takes you to the Footnote Menu.

3. Press Enter. This takes you to the footnote typing area. Accessing the footnote in this manner takes you directly to the correct footnote text.

4. Revise the footnote text using normal revision procedures.

5. Press Continue (F10) to return to the typing area. The revised footnote will not display at the bottom of the page until after you paginate the document.

6. After you have made all of your revisions, paginate your document to incorporate the revised footnotes.

Note: If you are moving body text, move the text and the footnote reference in the body text. Do not move the footnote text at the bottom of the page. Paginating the document will renumber and reposition the footnotes.

STEPS FOR ADDING A FOOTNOTE

1. In the body text, place the cursor at the desired position for the new footnote.

2. Follow the steps for creating a new footnote. The new footnote reference may not be numbered sequentially.

3. Paginate the document. The new footnote will be included and all of the footnotes will be renumbered.

Note: To add body text at the end of a footnoted page, position your cursor on the Begin Formatted Text code after the last line of body text as shown in Figure 17.6. Type the new text. Paginate the document to adjust the page endings and footnotes, as necessary. If you attempt to add text or make revisions to text with your cursor after the Begin Formatted Text code, the message "These text changes will be removed by Pagination or Merge" displays. The revisions you have made are temporary and will be deleted the next time you paginate or merge the document.

Chapter 17   Footnotes

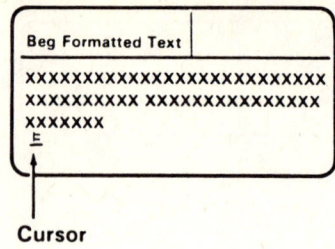

Figure 17.6 Begin Formatted Text

STEPS FOR DELETING A FOOTNOTE

1. Position the cursor under the Footnote code in the body text.

2. Delete the Footnote code. The footnote formatting codes and the footnote at the bottom of the page are not deleted and footnotes are not renumbered until the document is paginated.

3. After all revisions have been made to the document, paginate the document to remove the deleted footnote and renumber the remaining footnotes. The footnote text will remain stored at the end of your document.

EXERCISE 83

In Exercise 83, you will be creating a document which contains two footnotes.

PROCEDURES	COMMENTS
1. In the Text Task Selection Menu, choose Create Document and press Enter.	
2. Name the document b:Footnote.	
3. Press Enter twice to reach the typing area.	
4. Type the text on page 272 until you reach the ⬡1⬡ sign.	Your line endings may differ from the example.
5. Press F8 and type F to select Footnote.	A Footnote Menu appears.
6. Check to be sure a in Create/Revise Footnote Text is set to "Yes." Press Enter.	

Continued

PROCEDURES (Continued)

COMMENTS (Continued)

7. Type the first footnote. Do not type the footnote number or the tab. Do not end the footnote text with a carriage return.

Notice that you have a blank page on the screen. Each footnote will have its own blank page.

Type: **Ruth Painter Randall**, <u>Mary Lincoln, Biography of a Marriage</u>. Boston: Little, Brown & Co., 1953.

8. Press Continue (F10).

Notice you have returned to the body of the text. The number 1 has been inserted in the text.

9. Continue typing text until you reach ⟨2⟩.

10. Press F8 and type **F** for Footnote.

The Footnote Menu appears.

11. Press Enter.

A blank page appears.

12. Press F8.

Ibid needs to be enclosed in Begin and End Underscore instructions. Do not use Ctrl-U to underscore Ibid. If you do, the footnote reference number will also be underscored.

13. Choose Begin.

14. Choose Underscore.

15. Type **Ibid**.

16. Press F8.

17. Choose End.

18. Choose Underscore.

19. Type **., p. 22**.

20. Press Continue.

The number 2 is inserted into the text that has been returned to the screen.

21. Finish typing the document.

22. Press F2.

This will end the document.

23. Paginate the document.

Continued

Chapter 17 Footnotes

PROCEDURES (Continued)	COMMENTS (Continued)
24. Print the document. It should like look like Figure 17.7.	

MARY LINCOLN

Mary Lincoln was quite exceptional in regard to her educational background. She began her education at the Academy of Dr. John Ward who, quite ahead of his time, believed in co-education and conducted a school for over a hundred boys and girls from the best families.(1)

At the age of fourteen she entered Madame Mentelle's select boarding school where she spent four years. During this time she learned to speak French and was thought of as a person who "saw her own point of view so strongly, it shut out the viewpoint of the other person."(2) This is clearly not a sign of a submissive woman.

During Mary's childhood she often listened to the conversations of Senator Crittenden and Henry Clay who were visitors in the Todd home. This, along with her father's encouragement to express herself and pursue an <u>academic</u> education, contributed to Mary's interest in politics and her tendency to be outspoken.

EXERCISE 84

In Exercise 84, you will be recalling the document b:Footnote to the screen to insert an additional footnote.

PROCEDURES	COMMENTS
1. In the Text Task Selection Menu, type b for Revise Document.	
2. The document name is b:Footnote.	
3. Press Enter until the document appears on the screen.	
4. Using your down arrow key, place your cursor in the space following the sentence "... visitors in the Todd home."	You will be inserting another footnote.

Continued

MARY LINCOLN

   Mary Lincoln was quite exceptional in regard to her educational background. She began her education at the Academy of Dr. John Ward who, quite ahead of his time, believed in co-education and conducted a school for over a hundred boys and girls from the best families.[1]

   At the age of fourteen she entered Madame Mentelle's select boarding school where she spent four years. During this time she learned to speak French and was thought of as a person who "saw her own point of view so strongly, it shut out the viewpoint of the other person."[2] This is clearly not a sign of a submissive woman.

   During Mary's childhood she often listened to the conversations of Senator Crittenden and Henry Clay who were visitors in the Todd home. This, along with her father's encouragement to express herself and pursue an academic education, contributed to Mary's interest in politics and her tendency to be outspoken.

----

   [1] Ruth Painter Randall, *Mary Lincoln, Biography of a Marriage*. Boston: Little, Brown & Co., 1953.

   [2] *Ibid.*, p. 22.

   Figure 17.7   Exercise 83 Printout

PROCEDURES (Continued)	COMMENTS (Continued)
5. Press F8.	The prompt line choices display.
6. Type F to select Footnote.	The Footnote Menu displays.
7. Press Enter.	
8. Type the footnote: Ibid., p. 24.	Remember to use the Begin and End Underscore to underline the word "Ibid."
9. Press Continue.	
10. Press End Task.	
11. Paginate the document.	Paginating your document will arrange your footnotes in the proper order.
12. Print the document. It should look like Figure 17.8	

EXERCISE 85

Exercise 85 will require that you recall the document b:Footnote to the screen to revise a footnote.

PROCEDURES	COMMENTS
1. In the Text Task Selection Menu, choose Revise Document.	
2. Recall b:Footnote to the screen.	Your text is on the screen.
3. Using the down arrow key, place the cursor under the first Footnote code in the body text.	Your screen should look like this: Families.
4. Press Continue.	This takes you to the Footnote Menu.
5. Press Enter.	
6. At the end of the footnote, delete the final period. Type , p. 18.	This will be added to the end of the footnote.

Continued

274   Chapter 17   Footnotes

MARY LINCOLN

Mary Lincoln was quite exceptional in regard to her educational background. She began her education at the Academy of Dr. John Ward who, quite ahead of his time, believed in co-education and conducted a school for over a hundred boys and girls from the best families.[1]

At the age of fourteen she entered Madame Mentelle's select boarding school where she spent four years. During this time she learned to speak French and was thought of as a person who "saw her own point of view so strongly, it shut out the viewpoint of the other person."[2] This is clearly not a sign of a submissive woman.

During Mary's childhood she often listened to the conversations of Senator Crittenden and Henry Clay who were visitors in the Todd home.[3] This, along with her father's encouragement to express herself and pursue an academic education, contributed to Mary's interest in politics and her tendency to be outspoken.

---

[1] Ruth Painter Randall, *Mary Lincoln, Biography of a Marriage*. Boston: Little, Brown & Co., 1953.

[2] *Ibid.*, p. 22.

[3] *Ibid.*, p. 24.

Figure 17.8   Exercise 84 Printout

PROCEDURES (Continued)	COMMENTS (Continued)
7. Press F10 to return to the typing area.	
8. Press F2.	This will end the document.
9. Paginate the document.	You must paginate after each revision.
10. Print a copy of the document. Your printout should look like Figure 17.9.	

MODIFYING THE APPEARANCE OF FOOTNOTES

The system uses the default settings for footnote reference number, separator line, footnote lines per page, and other items contained in the document format or alternate format. If the default settings do not meet your needs, you can change these settings through the Document or Alternate Format Menu.

STEPS FOR RESETTING THE FOOTNOTE NUMBER

1. In the body text, place the cursor at the point for a footnote reference.

   If creating a footnote, press Instr (F8) and select Footnote.

   If revising an existing footnote, press Continue (F10) with your cursor under the appropriate Footnote code. The Footnote Menu will display as shown in Figure 17.10.

2. Select Reset Footnote Number or Character.

3. Type the number or character of your choice to reset the footnote sequencing. If you reset the footnote number with a numeric character, the footnotes that follow in the document will be numbered sequentially beginning with the number you select. If you reset the footnote number with a graphic character, such as an asterisk, the system will use the graphic character for the current footnote only.

4. Press Enter to go to the footnote typing area. Type or revise the footnote, as necessary.

5. Press Continue (F10) to return to the typing area.

6. After you have made all of your changes, paginate the document to sequence the footnotes correctly.

MARY LINCOLN

Mary Lincoln was quite exceptional in regard to her educational background. She began her education at the Academy of Dr. John Ward who, quite ahead of his time, believed in co-education and conducted a school for over a hundred boys and girls from the best families.[1]

At the age of fourteen she entered Madame Mentelle's select boarding school where she spent four years. During this time she learned to speak French and was thought of as a person who "saw her own point of view so strongly, it shut out the viewpoint of the other person."[2] This is clearly not a sign of a submissive woman.

During Mary's childhood she often listened to the conversations of Senator Crittenden and Henry Clay who were visitors in the Todd home.[3] This, along with her father's encouragement to express herself and pursue an academic education, contributed to Mary's interest in politics and her tendency to be outspoken.

---

[1] Ruth Painter Randall, *Mary Lincoln, Biography of a Marriage*. Boston: Little, Brown & Co., 1953, p. 18.

[2] *Ibid.*, p. 22.

[3] *Ibid.*, p. 24.

Figure 17.9 Exercise 85 Printout

```
Create Document    |B:TEST.TXT                           |
Page End           |Ins  |   |Pg. 1     |Ln. 7  |Ext 340-B|Pitch 10  |100
                              FOOTNOTE

                              YOUR          POSSIBLE
        ID   ITEM              CHOICE        CHOICES

        a    Create/Revise        1          1 = Yes    2 = No
             Footnote Text

        b    Reset Footnote Number
             or Character

        c    Document Name

        d    System Page Number
```

Figure 17.10 Footnote Menu

STEPS FOR CHANGING THE FOOTNOTE FORMAT FOR THE CURRENT DOCUMENT

1. From the Create or Revise Document Menu, select Change Document Format. The Document or Alternate Format Menu will display. If you are using an alternate format, be sure to change the footnote format for both the document format and the alternate format.

2. Select Change Footnote Format. The Footnote Format Menu will display.

3. Make the necessary changes in the Footnote Format Menu or select Change Footnote Text Options to go to the Footnote Text Options Menu. If you need additional information on the items in the footnoting menus, refer to pages 22-14 and 22-15 of your IBM DisplayWrite 3 Reference Manual.

4. After you have made all of your changes, paginate the document to implement the changed format.

STORING FOOTNOTES FOR REPEATED USE

You made find that you use the same footnotes in many different documents. DisplayWrite 3 has a footnote library which allows you to store footnotes in a separate document and recall these footnotes for repeated use.

You create and store footnotes in a footnote library in the same way that you create footnotes in a document. However, the footnotes will be stored in the footnote library. The footnotes will not be stored at the end of the document you are creating (see Figure 17.11).

Revisions made to footnotes stored in the footnote library should be made in the footnote typing area, as shown in Figure 17.12. Always make revisions to the footnotes stored in the footnote library. Do not make revisions to the footnotes that appear at the bottoms of the pages in the footnoted document.

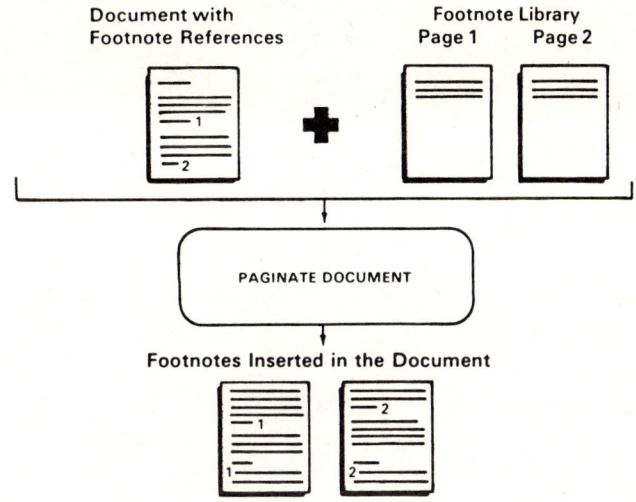

Figure 17.11   Stored Footnotes

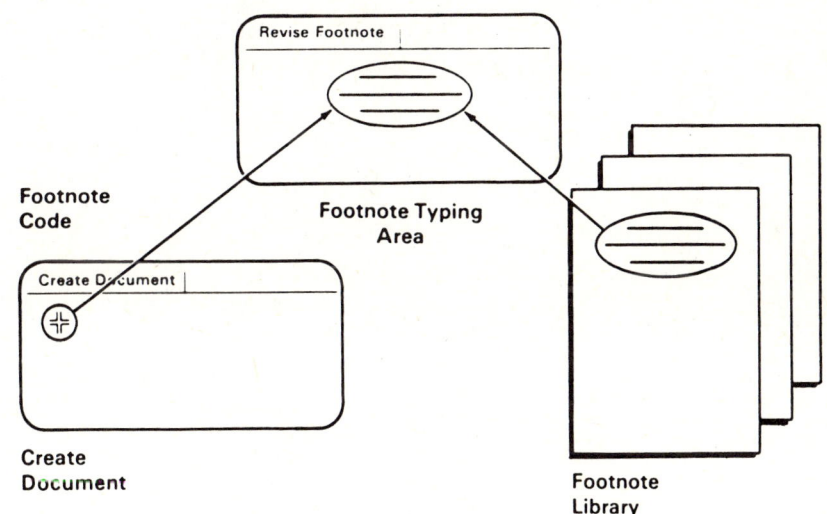

Figure 17.12   Footnote Library

In order to recall a footnote, you will need to know the system page number where the footnote is stored. Therefore, it is a good idea to print out a copy of your footnote library (as shown in Figure 17.13) to use as a reference when you incorporate the footnotes into other documents. You will need to handwrite the corresponding system page number for each footnote since the system does not print the page numbers.

Each footnote stored in the footnote library must remain on a page by itself in order to be used again in other documents. To prevent paginating the footnote library accidentally, set Preserve Page

Chapter 17   Footnotes

Numbers to "Yes" in the Create or Revise Document Menu of the footnote library.

```
1   XX XXXXX X
    XX X XXXXX

2   XX XXXX XX
    XXX XXXXX

3   X XX XXXXX
    XXX XXXX X

4   X XXX XXXX

5   XX XXXX XX
    XX XXX XXX
```

Figure 17.13   Footnote Library Printout

When you print out your footnote library to be used as a reference, you will want several footnotes placed on a page for easy reference. To do this, make a copy of the footnote library and set Preserve Page Numbers to "No" in the Create or Revise Document Menu of the copy. Paginate the copy. This will place several footnotes on a page. Print the copy, and then delete the duplicated footnote library from your disk.

STEPS FOR STORING FOOTNOTES IN A FOOTNOTE LIBRARY

1. Type the body text until you reach the point for a footnote reference.

2. Press Instr (F8) and select Footnote. The Footnote Menu will display.

3. Select Document Name. Type the name of the document in which you want to store the footnotes. Do **not** select a system page number. The system will store the footnote on the first empty page of the footnote library, beginning with the first system page number. Each footnote is stored on a page by itself.

4. Press Enter. This takes you to the footnote typing area. Type the footnote text.

5. Press Continue (F10) to return to the typing area. Continue typing the body text.

6. Repeat Steps 1 through 5 for each footnote reference.

7. When you have completed typing the body text, paginate the document. Pagination places the footnotes at the bottoms of the corresponding pages. The footnotes are stored, though, in the document you named in Step 3.

STEPS FOR USING FOOTNOTES STORED IN A FOOTNOTE LIBRARY

1. Type the body text until you reach the point for a footnote reference.

2. Press Instr (F8) and select Footnote. The Footnote Menu will display.

3. Set Create/Revise Footnote Text to "No." You will be using an existing footnote, not creating a new one.

4. Specify the document name and the system page number in which your footnote is stored. (Use your printed reference copy with the handwritten numbers to identify the correct system page number.)

5. Press Enter to return to the typing area. Continue typing the body text.

6. Repeat Steps 1-5 until you have included all footnote references.

7. When you have completed typing the body text, paginate the document. Pagination will place the footnotes at the bottoms of the corresponding pages in the footnoted document.

STEPS FOR REVISING FOOTNOTES STORED IN A FOOTNOTE LIBRARY

1. From the Text Task Selection Menu, select Create Document and go to the typing area. You will not be typing any body text. The purpose of this document is to provide a means for quickly accessing the appropriate footnote text in the footnote library.

2. Press Instr (F8) and select Footnote. The Footnote Menu will display.

3. Type the document name and the system page number that contains the footnote to be revised. Use your printed reference copy of your footnote library as a guide to identify the correct system page number.

4. Press Enter to go to the footnote typing area.

5. Revise the footnote text using normal revision procedures.

6. Press Continue (F10) to return to the typing area. A Footnote code, footnote reference number, and formatting codes are placed in the document. Only the footnote reference number is visible unless you turn on Display codes.

7. Repeat Steps 2 through 6 for each footnote you need to revise.

8. After you have made all your revisions to the footnote library, delete the document that you created in Step 1.

CHAPTER SUMMARY

STEPS FOR CREATING A FOOTNOTED DOCUMENT

1. Type the body text until you reach the point for a footnote reference.
2. Press Instr (F8) and select Footnote.

3. Check to see that Create/Revise Footnote Text is set to "Yes." Press Enter to go to the footnote typing area.
4. Type the footnote text.
5. When you complete the footnote text, press Continue (F10) to return to the typing area and continue typing the body text.
6. Paginate the document.

STEPS FOR REVISING EXISTING FOOTNOTE TEXT

1. Place the cursor under the Footnote code in the body text.
2. Press Continue (F10). This takes you to the Footnote Menu.
3. Press Enter. This takes you to the footnote typing area.
4. Revise the footnote text.
5. Press Continue (F10) to return to the typing area.
6. Paginate the document after you have made all of your revisions.

STEPS FOR ADDING A FOOTNOTE

1. In the body text, place the cursor at the desired position for the new footnote.
2. Follow the steps for creating a new footnote.
3. Paginate the document.

STEPS FOR STORING FOOTNOTES IN A FOOTNOTE LIBRARY

1. Type the body text until you reach the point for a footnote reference.
2. Press Instr (F8) and select Footnote.
3. Select Document Name, and type the name of the document in which you want to store the footnotes.
4. Press Enter. Type the footnote text.
5. Press Continue (F10) to return to the typing area.

STEPS TO USE FOOTNOTES STORED IN A FOOTNOTE LIBRARY

1. Type the body text until you reach the point for a footnote reference.
2. Press Instr (F8) and select Footnote.
3. Set Create/Revise Footnote Text to "No."
4. Specify the document name and the system page number in which the footnote is stored.
5. Press Enter to return to the typing area.

Chapter 18

AUTOMATIC OUTLINING AND CURSOR DRAW

When you complete this chapter, you will be able to:

1. Create and revise outlines automatically.
2. Change the outline characters.
3. Change the outline levels.
4. Identify leading and trailing characters.
5. Paginate outlines.
6. Draw a figure with cursor draw.
7. Erase a figure done in cursor draw.
8. Change the draw character.
9. Type text inside a box using cursor draw.
10. Delete and revise text inside a box.

INTRODUCTION TO OUTLINING

Much of the mechanical work is taken out of outlining when you use DisplayWrite 3. It leaves you free to concentrate on ideas and how you will prioritize them, rather than worry about indention levels.

The system will insert the outline characters automatically such as I, A, 1, a), (1), (a), and i) at the appropriate Outline levels. The system also inserts the necessary punctuation and indention codes so that your text will wrap at the appropriate Outline levels instead of returning back to the left margin.

The following is an example of an outline done with the Automatic Outline feature.

OFFICE LANDSCAPING

   I.   Office Landscaping
        A.   Small Businesses
        B.   Large Businesses
             1.   Executive Offices
                  a)   Coloring
                  b)   Lighting
                  c)   Fabrics
                  d)   Accessories
                       (1)   Ashtrays
                       (2)   Wastebaskets
                       (3)   Clocks
                             (a)   Old World Style
                             (b)   Contemporary
                                   i)   Lucite
                                   ii)   Gold Metal and Carved Wood Style Clocks
             2.   Middle Management Offices
                  a)   Coloring
                  b)   Lighting
             3.   Open Clerical Areas
                  a)   Coloring
                  b)   Lighting
                       (1)   Task Lighting
                       (2)   Ambient Lighting

"I." is an example of an Outline level. Other examples of Outline levels are "A." and "1." Notice that the sentences following the outline characters were indented. This is because of the indentions that the system inserted <u>before</u> the outline character.

Codes that come before the outline character (I, A, i, and so on) are called leading characters. The codes that are positioned after the outline character are called trailing characters because they "trail" the outline character. When you turn on your Display codes, the screen graphics which represent these codes can be seen easily. If you were to alter the leading or trailing characters, up to 16 characters or codes could be placed before and after the outline character. Figure 18.1 shows examples of leading and trailing characters.

Figure 18.1 Leading and Trailing Characters

Seven Outline levels are available to you that use the default outline characters shown in the example. Although there is an eighth level, it does not have a default outline character. Unless you change the type of character used, uppercase Roman numerals will always be used at the first level, capital letters at the second, Arabic numerals at the third, and so on as shown in the example. Although the defaults can be changed for unusual applications, we will deal only with the most common type of outline here because of its widespread use and the ease with which it can be learned.

You should keep in mind that a document containing an outline should be paginated using Automatic Pagination to sequence the outline correctly. Underscoring and bolding is also possible in the outline. In Exercise 86, you will construct an outline using the Automatic Outline feature of DisplayWrite 3.

EXERCISE 86

PROCEDURES	COMMENTS
1. Create a document named b:Outline and go to the typing area.	
2. Center and type the title **OFFICE LANDSCAPING** and return three times.	
3. Holding down the Control key, press the letter "O" (for Outline).	The cursor moves to the right and the Roman numeral "I" appears on the screen. If you went past the Outline Level you wanted, press Esc to begin again. Be sure you press Enter to accept the Outline Level or your typing will appear on the prompt line instead of in the outline.
4. Press Enter to accept this Outline Level.	
5. Type Office Landscaping and return.	
6. Holding down the Control key, press "O" twice to get to the second Outline Level and Enter to accept this level.	Refer to the outline.

Continued

Chapter 18 Automatic Outlining and Cursor Draw

PROCEDURES (Continued)	COMMENTS (Continued)
7. Type the words Small **Businesses** as shown in the outline and return. 8. Type the sample outline as shown on the Introduction page. 9. Paginate the document with Adjust Page Endings set to "Yes." 10. Print a copy of b:Outline.	

REVISING AN OUTLINE

Once you have created an outline, it can be revised very easily. Kinds of revisions that can be made are as follows: adding entries, revising text in entries, deleting text, and moving or copying text. In the next exercise, you will do all of these revisions to the outline you created in your document named b:Outline.

EXERCISE 87

PROCEDURES	COMMENTS
1. Recall your document b:Outline to the screen.	
2. Turn on the Display codes and position the cursor beneath the Outline Level code in front of "Executive."	
3. Press Outline (this is Control and the letter "O") three times and Enter. Type **Top Management Offices** and return.	
4. Move the cursor down a line with the down arrow so that it is on the Outline code in front of the line that reads a) Coloring.	The status line will tell you that you are on Outline Level 4.

Continued

286 Chapter 18 Automatic Outlining and Cursor Draw

PROCEDURES (Continued)	COMMENTS (Continued)
5. Strike F4 and then type C to indicate to the system that you wish to copy.	
6. Strike the down arrow three times. Holding down Ctrl, strike the right arrow and Enter.	The lines from a) Coloring to d) Accessories will highlight. Be sure the Outline Level on the next line is not highlighted.
7. Tap the up arrow key four times. Holding down Ctrl, strike the left arrow and Enter.	The cursor should be on the Outline code in front of "1. Executive Offices." Make sure you are on the left margin. Both Top Management and Executive Offices are numbered 1. When you repaginate the document, this will rectify itself.

Your outline should now have additional Levels 3 and 4 that look like this:

```
Top Management Offices
   a)   Coloring
   b)   Lighting
   c)   Fabrics
   d)   Accessories
```

You have added a new Level 3 by inserting Top Management Offices. Your new Level 4 was simply copied from another area of the existing outline.

EXERCISE 88

PROCEDURES	COMMENTS
1. Move the cursor to the word "Top" and delete it. Replace the word "Top" with the word "Senior."	You are editing text just as you would in documents that are not outlines.
2. Paginate this document and print it.	Look at your printed copy to see how the outline resequenced the numbering to accommodate the added material.

Chapter 18 Automatic Outlining and Cursor Draw

RESETTING OUTLINE CHARACTERS

If you have occasion to type multiple outlines in the same document, you will need to reset the outline characters. This is also true if you want to continue the same outline in other documents. When you reset the outline characters, pagination does not affect them. That is, it will not "unset" them.

In the next exercise, you will reset the outline. Assume that someone else is going to do Part II of the outline. This means that you will have to start your next section with III.

EXERCISE 89

PROCEDURES	COMMENTS
1. Recall b:Outline to the screen.	
2. If you are not two returns below the last line of typing, return twice.	
3. Start a new outline by pressing Outline. Do not press Enter. Instead, type III and Enter. Type **Building Locations** and return.	Outline is Ctrl--O. You will not Enter because you are not going to accept the outline character on the screen. You are going to type your own choice of outline character.

4. Continue typing the outline as shown.
 	
 III.   Building Locations
     A.   Rural Areas
     B.   Small Towns
     C.   Cities
         1.   Atlanta
         2.   Boston
         3.   Chicago
         4.   Dallas
         5.   Denver
         6.   Los Angeles
         7.   Minneapolis
         8. San Francisco	

5. Paginate b:Outline and then print it.	

INTRODUCTION TO CURSOR DRAW

Outlining is used to organize thoughts in reports, whether they are for business, school, or other purposes. When the organizing and composing is finished, though, sometimes a visual aid is helpful in explaining the material contained in text form. This is where the Cursor Draw feature of DisplayWrite 3 is useful.

You can, with an appropriate printer, draw lines that represent organization charts, graphs, and other items which can be used to clarify and dress up your report. In the rest of this chapter, you will learn how to draw using DisplayWrite 3. Cursor Draw will also allow you to draw line and bar graphs.

The following points need to be kept in mind when using Cursor Draw:

1. When using Cursor Draw, the system will be in the replace mode. If you are using Draw_with_cursor, the character the cursor is under will be replaced with the draw character; or it will be erased if you use Erase_with_cursor.
2. When you leave Cursor Draw, the system will return to the Insert/Replace mode that was previously set.
3. In order to draw or erase past the right margin, Adjust Line Endings in the Line Format Menu must be set to "No."
4. You cannot draw or erase to the left of the left margin.
5. You cannot draw or erase if the typestyle uses proportional spacing.
6. You cannot draw across pitch changes.
7. The Line Format Menu should be set for single-spacing and left-line alignment.

STEPS FOR DRAWING A FIGURE

1. In the typing area, place the cursor at the position where you want to begin drawing. Do not use the Center key or the Tab key to position the cursor. These keys cause the lines to misalign.
2. Press Ctrl--Cursor Draw (F5) and select Draw_with_cursor. "Draw with Lines" displays on the status line.
3. Use the Cursor Movement keys to draw the figure. While you are making your drawings, you can press Ctrl--Cursor Draw (F5) again to use Erase_with_cursor or Change_draw_character.
4. When you are finished making your drawings, press Continue (F10) to resume normal typing.

STEPS FOR ERASING A FIGURE

1. Place the cursor at the position where you want to begin erasing.
2. Press Ctrl--Cursor Draw (F5) and select Erase_with_cursor. "Cursor Erase" displays on the status line.
3. Use the Cursor Movement keys to move the cursor under the character or characters to be erased. While you are erasing, you can press Ctrl--Cursor Draw (F5) to use Draw_with_cursor or Change_draw_character, if needed.
4. When you are finished with the drawing, press Continue (F10) to return to normal typing.

STEPS FOR CHANGING THE DRAW CHARACTER

The default draw character is Lines (___); however, you can change the draw character to any graphic, alphabetic, or numeric character.

1. In the typing area, press Ctrl--Cursor Draw (F5) and select Change_draw_character.
2. Type the new draw character and press Enter.

STEPS FOR TYPING TEXT INSIDE A BOX

If you wish to have typed text inside a box drawing, you will need to type the text before drawing the box.

1. Press carrier return to place the cursor on the line where the text is to begin.
2. Press the space bar to place the cursor at the horizontal position where the text is to begin. Do not use the Center or Tab keys to position the cursor.
3. Type the text, and press carrier return to end the lines.
4. Repeat Steps 1 through 3 until all of the text is typed.

STEPS FOR DELETING OR REVISING TEXT INSIDE A BOX

1. Check to see that the system is in the Replace mode. "Repl" should be displayed on the status line.
2. Place the cursor under the text you want to delete or revise.
3. Type the spaces or characters over the characters you want to delete or revise.

EXERCISE 90

This exercise will take you through the steps of using Cursor Draw to draw a simple organization chart.

PROCEDURES	COMMENTS
1. Create a new document and name it b:Cursordr.	
2. Change the left margin to 10.	
3. In the typing area, insert three carrier returns.	
4. Press the space bar until the cursor is at position 38.	
5. Type PRESIDENT.	
6. Press carrier return five times.	
7. Press the space bar until the cursor is at position 16.	
Continued	

PROCEDURES (Continued)	COMMENTS (Continued)

8. Type **VICE**.

9. Press the space bar until the cursor is at position 41.

10. Type **VICE**.

11. Press the space bar until the cursor is at position 66.

12. Type **VICE**.

13. Press carrier return once.

14. Press the space bar until the cursor is at position 13.

15. Type **PRESIDENT**.

16. Press the space bar until the cursor is at position 38.

17. Type **PRESIDENT**.

18. Press the space bar until the cursor is at position 63.

19. Type **PRESIDENT**.

20. Press carrier return once.

21. Place the cursor on line 8. — Use the Cursor Movement keys.

22. Press the right arrow key until the cursor is at position 36.

23. Press Ctrl--F5. — The prompt line choices display.

24. Press Enter. — This will select Draw_with_cursor.

25. Press the right arrow key until the cursor is at position 48.

Continued

Chapter 18 Automatic Outlining and Cursor Draw

PROCEDURES (Continued)	COMMENTS (Continued)
26. Press the down arrow key three times.	
27. Press the left arrow key until the cursor is at position 36.	
28. Press the up arrow key three times.	This is to complete the box.
29. Press F10.	This is to end Cursor Draw.
30. Place the cursor on line 14 at position 11.	Use the Cursor Movement keys.
31. Press Ctrl--F5 and select Draw_with_cursor.	
32. Press the right arrow until the cursor is at 23.	
33. Press the down arrow three times.	
34. Press the left arrow until the cursor is at 11.	
35. Press the up arrow three times.	This is to complete the box.
36. Press F10.	
37. Make sure the cursor is on line 14, position 36.	Use the Cursor Movement keys.
38. Press Ctrl--F5 and select Draw_with_cursor.	
39. Press the right arrow until the cursor is at 48.	
40. Press the down arrow key three times.	
41. Press the left arrow key until the cursor reaches 36.	
42. Press the up arrow key three times.	

Continued

PROCEDURES (Continued)	COMMENTS (Continued)
43. Press F10.	This is to end Cursor Draw.
44. Draw the box around the last "VICE PRESIDENT."	
45. Press F10.	This is to end Cursor Draw.
46. Move the cursor to line 11, position 42.	Use the Cursor Movement keys.
47. Press Ctrl--F5 and select Draw_with_cursor.	
48. Press the down arrow key once.	
49. Press the left arrow until the cursor is at position 17.	
50. Press the down arrow twice.	
51. Press F10.	This is to end Cursor Draw.
52. Place the cursor on line 12, position 42.	Use the Cursor Movement keys.
53. Press Ctrl--F5 and select Draw_with_cursor.	
54. Press the right arrow until the cursor reaches position 67.	
55. Press the down arrow twice.	
56. Press F10.	
57. Move the cursor to line 12, position 42.	Use the Cursor Movement keys.
58. Press Ctrl--F5 and select Draw_with_cursor.	
59. Press the down arrow twice.	
60. Press F10.	
61. Press F2.	This is to end the task.

Continued

Chapter 18 Automatic Outlining and Cursor Draw

PROCEDURES (Continued)	COMMENTS (Continued)
62. Print the chart.	

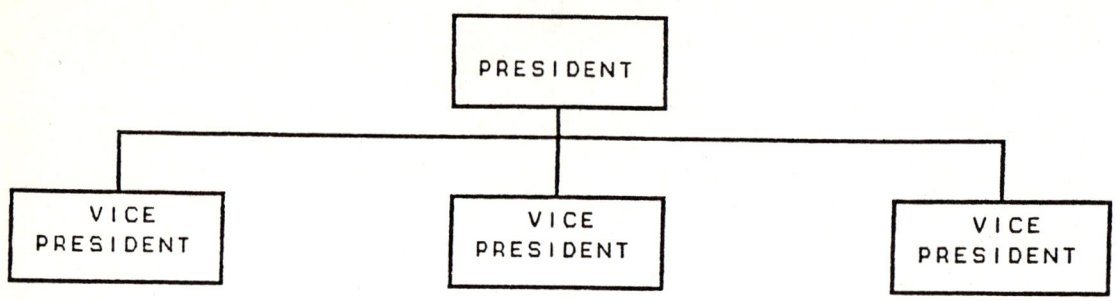

Figure 18.2   Exercise 90 Printout

CHAPTER SUMMARY

1. Outline characters are letters or numbers such as I, A, 1, and so on.

2. Seven Outline levels have default outline characters. The eighth does not.

3. Located before and after the outline characters are leading and trailing characters which consist of Formatting codes, an Outline Level code, and punctuation.

4. You can change the outline so that you may continue the same outline throughout two or more documents. You may also create more than one outline in the same document by changing the outline.

5. You can perform the same block operations that you can with text that is not in an outline.

6. Text editing, including inserting, can be done in outlines.

7. You should paginate a document containing an outline before printing.

8. You can use Cursor Draw to place line drawings such as graphs and organization charts in text.

9. Do not use proportional spacing with line drawing.

10. You can write text inside of figures such as organization charts.

11. You can change the Cursor Draw figure.

12. You also have the ability to erase any drawings you no longer want.

Chapter 19
KEYSTROKE

When you complete this chapter, you will be able to:

1. Capture and play back a Keystroke Program.

2. Create a Keystroke Program using the Pause function.

3. Use Programmable Function keys to store Keystroke Programs.

4. Save and recall a Keystroke Program on a magnetic disk.

KEYSTROKE PROGRAMMING

Keystroke programming allows you to store keystrokes in memory and play them back at a later time. If you are keying in a document that contains repetitive phrases, you can type the phrase once, have the phrase "captured" or stored in memory, and recall the phrase each time you need it. This would save you from having to rekey the phrase each time it appears in your document.

Keystroke programming can also be used to store keystrokes that take you to a particular task, such as Check Document in Spelling Tasks. Each time you need to verify the spelling of a document, you can use the Keystroke Program.

The Keystroke Program allows you to store a maximum of 500 keystrokes. The program can be stored in the memory of the computer or on a magnetic disk.

CAPTURING AND PLAYING BACK KEYSTROKE PROGRAMS

The Capture function is used to retain the Keystroke Program in the memory of the computer. The Keystroke Program will remain in memory and can be used repeatedly until you capture new keystrokes, recall another Keystroke Program, or exit DisplayWrite 3.

STEPS FOR CAPTURING KEYSTROKES

1. At the point where you want to begin capturing keystrokes, press Ctrl--Key Progrm (F6) and select Capture. "Capt" will display on the status line. Keystrokes that were previously in memory are removed.

2. Type the new keystrokes to be stored in memory. You can type approximately 500 keystrokes. If the keystroke capacity is exceeded, the system will beep once, "Capt" will blink on the status line, and the message "Maximum keystrokes captured. Last captured keystroke was (character)" will display.

3. When you have typed all of the keystrokes that you wish to have in the Keystroke Program, press Ctrl--Key Progrm (F6) and select End_capture. This ends the Capture function. "Capt" will no longer display on the status line. Your Keystroke Program is now stored in memory.

STEPS FOR AUTOMATICALLY PLAYING BACK KEYSTROKES

1. Place the cursor at the point where you want to use the Keystroke Program.

2. Press Ctrl--Key Progrm (F6). Select Auto_playback. "Play" displays on the status line as the keystrokes play back from memory. When all of the keystrokes have been played, "Play" will no longer display on the status line. Do not try to type or initiate a new task until playback is complete.

STEPS TO PLAY BACK AND DELETE KEYSTROKES ONE AT A TIME

1. Place the cursor at the point where you want to use the Keystroke Program.

2. Press Ctrl--Key Progrm (F6) and select Playback_singly. "Play" will display on the status line. The system will also highlight on the status line the first keystroke to be played back.

3. Determine whether you wish to play back or delete the displayed keystroke.
   --To play back the displayed keystroke, press Continue (F10).
   --To delete the displayed keystroke, press Del. Then, follow the prompt to press Continue (F10) to delete the keystroke, or press Esc to cancel the Delete function.

4. Repeat Step 3 until all keystrokes have been played. The prompt line choices, End_play and Capture, display when all keystrokes have been played back. If the keystroke capacity has been reached, the Capture function will not display.

5. Determine if you wish to end playback or add keystrokes to the end of the Keystroke Program.
   --To end the playback session, select End_play or press Esc.
   --To add keystrokes to the end of the Keystroke Program, follow the directions in the next section.

STEPS TO ADD KEYSTROKES TO A KEYSTROKE PROGRAM

1. While in Auto_playback or Playback_singly, press Ctrl--Key Progrm (F6) at the point in the keystroke sequence where you want to add keystrokes.

2. Select Capture. "Capt" displays on the status line. Capture will not be available if the keystroke capacity has been reached.

3. Type the keystrokes to be captured.

4. Press Ctrl--Key Progrm (F6) and select End_capture. "Play" displays on the status line and the prompt line choices will appear at the bottom of the screen.

5. Determine whether you want to play back the remaining keystrokes, end playback, or add keystrokes.
   --To play back the remaining keystrokes, select Auto_playback or Playback_singly.
   --To end playback, select End_play. The keystrokes that are not played back remain in the Keystroke Program.
   --To add keystrokes, select Capture and repeat Steps 3 through 5.

STEPS TO CHANGE PLAYBACK MODE

1. During Auto_playback or Playback_singly, press Ctrl--Key Progrm (F6) at the point in the Keystroke Program where you want to change playback modes.

2. Determine whether you want to continue playback in Auto_playback or Playback_singly.
   --To have the remaining keystrokes played back automatically, select Auto_playback.
   --To monitor and delete keystrokes, select Playback_singly.

STEPS FOR EXITING PLAYBACK BEFORE ALL KEYSTROKES ARE PLAYED

1. During Auto_playback or Playback_singly, press Key Progrm (F6) at the point in the keystroke sequence where you want to exit playback.

2. Select End_play.

EXERCISE 91

In this exercise, you will be capturing a chemical equation in a keystroke program and then playing back the equation each time it is repeated in the document. You will find that capturing the equation in the Keystroke Program will save you considerable time, as well as make the typing task much easier.

PROCEDURES	COMMENTS
1. Create a new document and name it b:Exerci91.	You will be typing the problem that follows these procedures and comments.
2. Center and type the title. Return three times.	Stop when you reach ③.
3. Press Ctrl--Key Progrm (F6).	You will be capturing the equation for repeated use.
4. Type C.	This selects Capture.
5. Press the space bar until the cursor is at position 45.	
6. Press Ctrl--X.	This is to center the equation.
7. Type until you reach ⑧. Continue with Procedure 8.	The first line of the equation is captured in memory.
8. Press the carrier return.	
9. Position the cursor at 45 and press Ctrl--X.	This is to center the second line of the equation.

Continued

PROCEDURES (Continued)	COMMENTS (Continued)
10. Type until you reach ⟨11⟩.	The second line of the equation is captured in memory.
11. Press the carrier return twice.	
12. Press Ctrl--Key Progrm (F6).	The prompt line choices display.
13. Select End_capture.	
14. Type until you reach ⟨15⟩.	
15. Press carrier return twice.	
16. Press Ctrl--Key Progrm (F6).	The prompt line choices display.
17. Select Auto_playback.	The equations will appear centered on the screen.
18. Continue typing the rest of the document. Repeat Steps 16 and 17 to play back the equations.	
19. Print your document.	

FUEL-HEATING VALUE

⟨3⟩ $CH_4 + 2O_2 = CO_2 + 2H_2O + HEAT$ ⟨8⟩
$2C_6H_6 + 15O_2 = 12CO_2 + 6H_2O + HEAT$ ⟨11⟩

When a hydrocarbon is burned, two things happen: A chemical reaction takes place and heat is generated. Typically, the chemical reaction is a transformation of the hydrocarbon and oxygen into water and carbon dioxide.

The amount of heat given off by each of the reactions ⟨15⟩

$$CH_4 + 2O_2 = CO_2 + 2H_2O + HEAT$$
$$2C_6H_6 + 15O_2 = 12CO_2 + 6H_2O + HEAT$$

is unique to each type of hydrocarbon. The standard measure for heat is the British Thermal Unit (BTU).

Continued

Chapter 19 Keystroke

The CH_4 in the equation

$$CH_4+2O_2=CO_2+2H_2O+HEAT$$
$$2C_6H_6+15O_2=12CO_2+6H_2O+HEAT$$

represents the hydrocarbon Methane.

The C_6H_6 in the equation

$$CH_4+2O_2=CO_2+2H_2O+HEAT$$
$$2C_6H_6+15O_2=12CO_2+6H_2O+HEAT$$

represents the hydrocarbon Benzene.

USING PAUSE

The Pause function allows you to suspend Capture temporarily so that you can type variable information. Variable information is information that changes each time you use the program.

For example, you may wish to create a Keystroke Program that will delete documents for you. You will create the Keystroke Program as you delete the first document. When you reach the point where the system prompts you for the document name, you will use Pause to suspend Capture. While the system is in the Pause mode, no keystrokes will be recorded in the program. Then type the name of the first document. Use Continue Capture to resume capturing the remainder of the keystrokes.

You now have a document deletion program that can be used with any document you wish to delete (see Figure 19.1). Later, when you play back the program to delete a document, Pause will suspend playback so that you can type the document name.

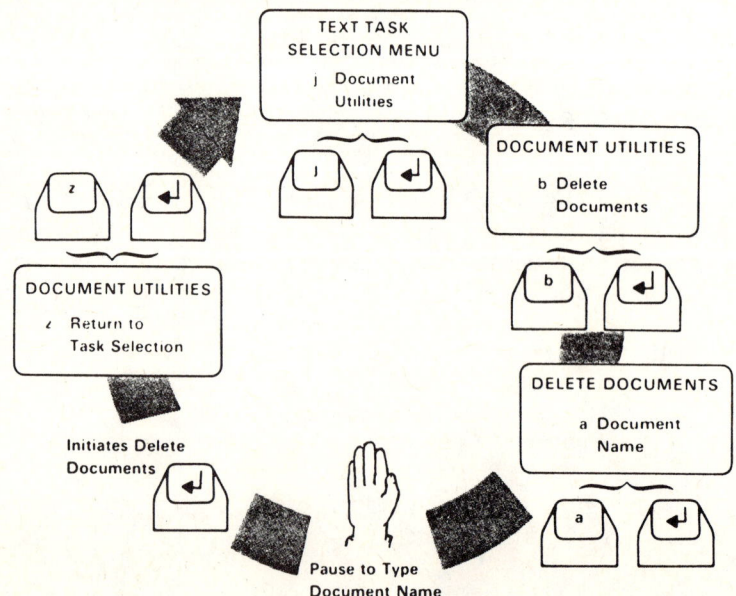

Figure 19.1 Delete Program

STEPS FOR USING PAUSE WHILE CAPTURING KEYSTROKES

1. Press Ctrl--Key Progrm (F6) and select Capture. "Capt" will display on the status line. Keystrokes that were previously in memory are removed.

2. Type the keystrokes to be kept in memory.

3. When you reach the point where the variable information is to be inserted, press Ctrl--Key Progrm (F6) and select Pause. The pause has been captured, and "Capt" displays highlighted on the status line. Capture is temporarily suspended. Keystrokes that are typed at this time will be processed by the system, but not included in the Keystroke Program.

4. Type the variable information.

5. Press Ctrl--Key Progrm (F6). The prompt line choices will display.

6. Determine whether you want to add more keystrokes or end Capture.
   --To capture more keystrokes, select Continue_capture. Repeat Steps 2 through 5 until all keystrokes have been entered. Then select End_capture.
   --To end the keystroke capturing, select End_capture.

STEPS FOR PLAYING BACK KEYSTROKE PROGRAMS CONTAINING PAUSES

1. Press Ctrl--Key Progrm (F6) and select Auto_playback or Playback_singly. If you select Playback_singly, press Continue (F10) to play back each keystroke. When "Pause" displays on the status line, press Continue (F10) to begin the pause.

   When the system reaches the pause state during playback, "Play" will display highlighted on the status line and the message "Playback stopped to allow typing; press KEY PROGRAM to continue" will display.

2. Type the variable information.

3. Press Ctrl--Key Progrm (F6) and select Auto_playback or Playback_singly to continue playback.

   If there are no more pauses and you are in Auto_playback, the remaining keystrokes are played back automatically until playback is complete.

   If there are no more pauses and you are in Playback_singly, continue to play back the Keystroke Program, and then select End_play when playback is complete.

   If there are more pauses, repeat Steps 2 and 3.

Chapter 19 Keystroke

EXERCISE 92

In Exercise 92, you will be creating a Keystroke Program that will allow you to delete documents automatically from your disk. A pause will be inserted into the program to suspend capture temporarily and allow you to type variable information.

PROCEDURES	COMMENTS
1. The Text Task Selection Menu should be displayed on the screen.	
2. Press Ctrl--Key Progrm (F6).	The prompt line choices display.
3. Select Capture.	All keystrokes from this point will be captured in memory.
4. Type j and insert the DisplayWrite 3, Volume 1 disk.	This is to select Document Utilities.
5. Press Enter.	The Document Utilities Menu displays.
6. Type b.	This is to select Delete Documents.
7. Press Enter.	The Delete Documents Menu displays.
8. Type a and press Enter.	This is to enter the document name.
9. Press Ctrl--Key Progrm (F6).	The prompt line choices display.
10. Select Pause.	This temporarily suspends Capture so you can type variable information.
11. Type b:Exercil4.txt and press Enter.	This is the name of the document you wish to delete.
12. Press Ctrl--Key Progrm (F6).	The prompt line choices display.
13. Select Continue_capture.	The keystrokes again will be captured in memory.
14. Press Enter.	This initiates Delete Documents.

Continued

Chapter 19 Keystroke

15. The Document Utilities Menu displays.	The prompt "(B:EXERCI14.TXT) deleted" displays.
16. Type **z**.	This returns you to the Text Task Selection Menu.
17. Press Enter.	
18. Leave the Text Task Selection Menu on your screen and continue reading. You will continue with this exercise in Exercise 93.	Do not press F2 or shut off the computer at this time.

DEFINING PROGRAMMABLE FUNCTION KEYS

A Keystroke Program that has been captured in memory can be linked to a function key. This is known as using a Programmable Function key. Using Programmable Function keys provides short cuts to recalling and playing back Keystroke Programs.

Once a Keystroke Program has been captured in the memory of the computer, press Shift or Alt plus a function key (F1 through F10). The system will assign a document name to your program that corresponds to the Programmable Function key. Each time that you need to play back the Keystroke Program, all you need to do is press the Shift or Alt plus the function key.

By combining the ten function keys with Shift or Alt, you can define up to 20 Programmable Function keys. Illustration 19.2 shows three examples of Keystroke Programs assigned to a Programmable Function key.

You will want to use Programmable Function keys to store programs that you use frequently. For example, if you frequently total a column of numbers, you can create the Keystroke Program and store it using a Programmable Function key. Each time you need to use the program, you press the Programmable Function key, and your columns are added for you.

1. Capture a Keystroke Program or recall an existing program. The Keystroke Program now resides in the memory of the computer.

2. Press Ctrl--Key Progrm (F6) and select Save. A prompt will appear asking for the document name.

3. Press Shift or Alt plus a function key (F1 through F10). The system will provide a document name that corresponds to the Programmable Function key. The Keystroke Program currently in memory is stored in the document named by the system.

4. To use the Programmable Function key, place the cursor at the point where you want to play back the Keystroke Program. Press

Chapter 19 Keystroke

the Programmable Function key and the Keystroke Program will begin playing back automatically.

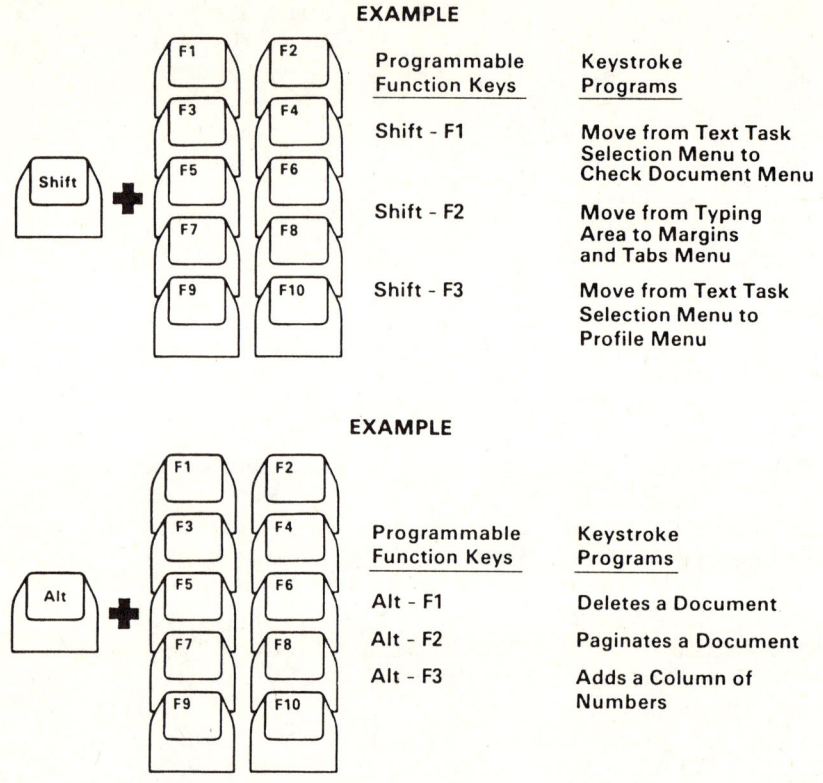

Figure 19.2   Keystroke Programs

EXERCISE 93

Exercise 93 is the continuation of Exercise 92. You will take the Keystroke Program created in Exercise 92 and store the program with a Programmable Function key.

PROCEDURES	COMMENTS
1. The Text Task Selection Menu should be displayed on the screen.	"CAPT" should be displayed on the status line since this is the continuation of Exercise 92.
2. Press Ctrl--Key Progrm (F6).	
3. Select End_capture.	
4. Press Ctrl--Key Progrm (F6).	
5. Select Save.	The prompt appears asking for the program name.

Continued

PROCEDURES (Continued)	COMMENTS (Continued)
6. Press Alt and F1.	The system provides a document name that corresponds to the Programmable Function key, AF01.KEY.
7. The Text Task Selection Menu should be displayed on the screen.	
8. Press Alt and F1.	This activates the delete program.
9. When the program pauses for you to enter in the document name to be deleted, type b:Payroll.tbl.	
10. Press Enter.	
11. Press Ctrl--Key Progrm (F6).	
12. Select Auto_playback.	
13. Leave this exercise on the screen and continue reading.	

SAVING AND RECALLING KEYSTROKE PROGRAMS

The Keystroke Program which you have created currently resides in the memory of the computer. You may wish to have the program stored on a disk for later use. The Save feature will transfer the Keystroke Program from the memory of the computer onto your disk.

The Recall feature will transfer the stored program from your disk back into the memory of the computer. After you have used Recall to place the program back into memory, then you can use Playback to play out the program.

STEPS FOR SAVING A KEYSTROKE PROGRAM

1. Capture the Keystroke Program. (See STEPS FOR CAPTURING KEYSTROKES.)

2. Press Ctrl--Key Progrm (F6) and select Save. The prompt "Type name of captured keystroke program; press ENTER" displays.

3. Type in a name for the keystroke program which is currently in memory, and press Enter. The system will assign a default extension of .KEY to the program name unless you specify another extension.

You can replace an existing Keystroke Program (or other document) with the current Keystroke Program by giving the current Keystroke Program the same name as the existing program you wish to replace. The prompt "Press CONTINUE to replace or press ESC" displays. Press Continue (F10) if you wish to replace the existing Keystroke Program or document, or press Esc and type a new name. After the keystrokes have been saved, the message "Saved keystrokes stored in (...)" displays.

STEPS FOR RECALLING SAVED KEYSTROKE PROGRAMS

1. Press Ctrl--Key Progrm (F6) and select Recall. The prompt "Type name of saved keystrokes; press ENTER" will display.

2. Type the name of the Keystroke Program you wish to recall, and press Enter. The message "Saved keystrokes recalled from (...)" will display when recall is completed. The Keystroke Program is now available for playback.

EXERCISE 94

The Keystroke Program for deleting a document is presently stored in the Programmable Function Key Alt--F1. We will now save the program on your disk so that you can recall the program for future use.

PROCEDURES	COMMENTS
1. The Text Task Selection Menu should be displayed on your screen.	
2. Press Ctrl--Key Progrm (F6).	
3. Select Save.	The prompt appears asking for the name of the Captured Keystroke Program.
4. Type b:AF01.KEY and press Enter (you will need to type the number 0, not the letter O).	The message "B:AF01.KEY already exists" appears on the screen.
5. Follow the prompt to press Continue to replace the document.	The message "Saved keystrokes stored in (B:AF01.KEY)." appears on the screen.

CHAPTER SUMMARY

A. STEPS FOR CAPTURING KEYSTROKES

1. At the point where you want to begin capturing keystrokes, press Ctrl--Key Progrm (F6) and select Capture.
2. Type the new keystrokes to be stored in memory.

3. When you are finished typing the Keystroke Program, press Ctrl--Key Progrm (F6) and select End_capture.

B. STEPS FOR AUTOMATICALLY PLAYING BACK KEYSTROKES

1. Place the cursor at the point where you want to use the Keystroke Program.
2. Press Ctrl--Key Progrm (F6). Select Auto_playback.

C. STEPS FOR USING PAUSE WHILE CAPTURING KEYSTROKES

1. Press Ctrl--Key Progrm (F6) and select Capture.
2. Type the keystrokes to be kept in memory.
3. When you reach the point where the variable information is to be inserted, press Ctrl--Key Progrm (F6) and select Pause.
4. Type the variable information.
5. Press Ctrl--Key Progrm (F6). Select either Continue_capture or End_capture.

D. STEPS FOR PLAYING BACK KEYSTROKE PROGRAMS CONTAINING PAUSES

1. Press Ctrl--Key Progrm (F6) and select Auto_playback or Playback_singly.
2. When the system reaches the pause state, type the variable information.
3. Press Ctrl--Key Progrm (F6) and select Auto_playback or Playback_singly to continue playback.

E. STEPS FOR DEFINING A PROGRAMMABLE FUNCTION KEY

1. Capture a Keystroke Program or recall an existing program.
2. Press Ctrl--Key Progrm (F6) and select Save.
3. Press Shift or Alt plus a function key (F1 through F10).
4. To use the Programmable Function key, place the cursor at the point where you want to play back the Keystroke Program. Press the Programmable Function key and the Keystroke Program will begin playing back automatically.

F. STEPS FOR SAVING A KEYSTROKE PROGRAM

1. Capture the Keystroke Program.
2. Press Ctrl--Key Progrm (F6) and select Save.
3. Type in a name for the Keystroke Program which is currently in memory, and press Enter.

G. STEPS FOR RECALLING SAVED KEYSTROKE PROGRAMS

1. Press Ctrl--Key Progrm (F6) and select Recall.
2. Type the name of the Keystroke Program you wish to recall and press Enter.

Chapter 20

USING GET FOR REPETITIVE DOCUMENTS

When you complete this chapter, you will be able to:

1. Use Get to produce repetitive documents.

2. Use Stop codes effectively in your documents.

3. Create and use a paragraph library.

INTRODUCTION

On the job and in your personal life, there will be times when you can prevent retyping by getting text that you have already saved on a disk. In a legal office, for example, many paragraphs in certain types of documents are the same from case to case. The verbiage that does not change can be used repetitively in document after document. An annual Christmas letter may contain parts that can be sent to both sides of your family and other parts that only pertain to one side or the other.

The DisplayWrite 3 program can be given a Get command that enables you to put previously saved sentences, paragraphs, and whole documents into your current documents without retyping them. (For information about getting a DOS print file, refer to the DisplayWrite 3 Manual that came with the program diskettes. Your instructor probably has access to one.)

In the following exercise, you will create a two-page document. Later in this lesson, you will use Get to retrieve the second page for use with another document you will be creating.

Exercise 95 gives the steps necessary for creating the first document.

EXERCISE 95

PROCEDURES	COMMENTS
1. In the Text Task Selection Menu, choose Create Document, and name it b:page2.get.	
2. In the Create or Revise Document Menu, choose Change Document Format and Enter.	
3. In the Document or Alternate Format Menu, choose Change Margins and Tabs and Enter.	
4. Change your margins to 20 and 70 in the Margins and Tabs Menu.	
5. Go to the typing area.	
6. In the typing area, type the following letter. Do _not_ press End Task when you finish typing the first page.	

Continued

January 1, 19--

Dr. Lloyd Hamady
Northside Medical Center
323 North Brea Boulevard
Brea, CA 92623-4579

Dear Dr. Hamady:

Enclosed is a copy of the announcement we discussed last week. Would you please post it at your office and on the bulletin board at the hospital.

I appreciate your and Dr. Tristan's support of this year's fund-raiser.

Sincerely,

Fred Laham
Chairman

xxx

(Do not press End Task when you finish this page.)

PROCEDURES (Continued)	COMMENTS (Continued)
7. When you finish typing the letter, press Page End (Control--E).	
8. Return 16 times and type the "Have a Heart Dinner" announcement on page 2 of the letter.	
	Have a Heart Dinner
	To Benefit the Heart Society

	Where: Grand Hall
	              1033 Poplar Street
	              Brea, California

	When: Valentine's Day, February 14, 19-- 6:30 p.m.
	Contribution: $15.00 for each dinner ticket
	To make your reservation, contact Muneer Yasin at (714) 555-1010 before February 1, 19--.
	Continued

PROCEDURES (Continued)	COMMENTS (Continued)
9. Press End Task (F2) to return to the Text Task Selection Menu. 10. Print a copy of this document.	

You are now ready to start saving yourself time and work by using Get. The following memo will be two pages in length but you will have to type only the first page of it. This is because you will use Get to retrieve the second page from the document you just finished.

EXERCISE 96

PROCEDURES	COMMENTS
1. In the Text Task Selection Menu, select Create Document and name it b:cover. 2. Change your margins to 20 and 70, and go to the typing area. 3. In the typing area, type the following memo. Do <u>not</u> press End Task when you finish. M E M O R A N D U M To: Elizabeth Lamason From: Fred Laham Date: January 2, 19-- Subject: Have a Heart Dinner Attached is the announcement we are sending out advertising the dinner on Valentine´s Day. Will you be there? I look forward to seeing you. urs Attachment Do not press End Task here. Continued	

Chapter 20 Using GET for Repetitive Documents

Now you will get the announcement from the second page of the previous document so that you will not have to retype it.

PROCEDURES (Continued)	COMMENTS (Continued)
4. Press Page End (Control--E).	You are now on the second page of your document.
5. Press the Command key (F6) and Enter.	Get is the default in the menu which appears across the bottom of your screen. Therefore, it is not necessary to do anything to make a selection other than press Enter.
6. In the Get Menu, type a and Enter.	
7. At the prompt, type b:page2.get and Enter.	You are now telling the system which document you wish to get.
8. Type b and Enter.	
9. Type 2 and Enter.	This indicates which page you want to get. A copy of page 2 of b:page2.get is put into your document.
10. Enter again.	
11. Press End Task.	
12. Print a copy of b:cover.	Your document will be two pages in length. The first page will be the cover memo, and the second page will be the announcement.

PARAGRAPH LIBRARIES

Paragraphs, as well as pages, can be stored for use in constructing documents. These stored paragraphs are called a library of paragraphs. In the next exercise, you will create a document consisting of several paragraphs. After each paragraph, you will see a ▲. When you see it, put in a Page End.

With each paragraph on a separate page, you will be able to get only those individual paragraphs you want. Follow the procedures to create a library of paragraphs.

EXERCISE 97

PROCEDURES	COMMENTS
1. In the Text Task Selection Menu, choose Create Document and Enter.	
2. At the prompt, name the document b:society and Enter.	
3. In the Create or Revise Document Menu, set Preserve Page Numbers to "Yes" and go to the typing area.	This keeps the paragraphs on separate pages so that you can request them by page number. You will not be paginating the document.
4. In the typing area, turn on the Display codes (F6 and D) and press return eight times.	The eight carrier returns leave enough room to type a date line later on.
5. Type the following paragraphs. End each paragraph with two carrier returns and a Page End instruction. (You will see the ▲). Do not press Page End after the last paragraph.	Remember, each paragraph represents a page. These two carrier returns ensure that the paragraphs will be properly spaced on the finished documents.

Paragraphs for the Library

Do not type the paragraph numbers; they are for your reference.

(1) Dear :
     ▲
(2) Thank you for your donation to the Heart Society. It is
     very much appreciated.
     ▲
(3) Because of the generosity of yourself, and people like you,
     heart disease has decreased in the United States in past
     years.
     ▲
(4) Our campaign would not have been a success without you. We
     have exceeded last year's record, and our chapter is one of
     the top chapters in the state.
     ▲
(5) All of us are fighting heart disease. We sincerely hope
     that our work will further the efforts of research.
     Hopefully, in the near future, this killer will be
     eliminated.
     ▲

Continued

Chapter 20 Using GET for Repetitive Documents

(6) Thank you for the giving of your time during our recent campaign.
▲
(7) Thank you again for your check.
▲
(8) Sincerely,

    Fred Laham

PROCEDURES (Continued)	COMMENTS (Continued)
6. Press End Task.	
7. Print b:society and number the pages by hand for your reference.	

USING THE PARAGRAPH LIBRARY TO CONSTRUCT A DOCUMENT

Now that you have a few paragraphs in your library, you will be able to use some of them to create documents. The next exercise entails writing two form letters, both of which will be constructed from paragraphs in your library.

The first will be a form letter used to thank contributors. The second will be a form letter to thank volunteers for their time in a recent campaign.

EXERCISE 98

PROCEDURES	COMMENTS
1. In the Text Task Selection Menu, select Create Document and Enter.	
2. At the prompt, name the document b:contribu.tor and Enter.	This is the letter to people who donated money to the drive.
3. In the typing area, press Get (F6 and Enter).	
4. In the Get Menu, press a and Enter.	
5. At the prompt, type b:society and Enter.	
	Continued

314   Chapter 20 Using GET for Repetitive Documents

PROCEDURES (Continued)	COMMENTS (Continued)
6. Type b and Enter. At the prompt, type the following numbers with a space between each number: 1 2 3 5 7 8 and Enter twice.	Be sure to place a space between each number or the system may try to get page 123,578. You will be taken back to the document.
7. Press End Task.	
8. Print a reference copy of this form letter.	This is the first form letter.
9. In the Text Task Selection Menu, select Create Document and name it b:voluntee.rs.	You are now creating the second document. It will be slightly different from the first.
10. In the typing area, press Command (F6) and Enter.	This is the letter to the people who volunteered their time to the drive.
11. In the Get Menu, give the appropriate instructions to get paragraphs 1 2 3 4 5 6 8 from b:society and Enter twice.	
12. When you are back in the typing area, press End Task.	
13. Print a reference copy of the second form letter.	

STOP CODES

When you are creating a document and want to insert words in it at certain places at a later time, you may use Stop codes to "mark" the locations where the inserted words will go. This is done by holding down the Control key and striking the 6. A Stop code is put in the document and can be found later when you are ready to insert words. A Stop code looks like this: ■

In the following exercise, you will revise a document you created using the paragraph library by placing Stop codes in it. You can then get a copy of it whenever you wish and insert an inside address and salutation to personalize the letter.

Chapter 20   Using GET for Repetitive Documents

EXERCISE 99

PROCEDURES	COMMENTS
1. In the Text Task Selection Menu, select Revise Document and Enter.	
2. At the prompt, type b:contribu.tor and go to the typing area.	This is the donation thank-you letter that you created using the paragraph library. You may or may not want to clear a default document name from the prompt line (press Escape).
3. In the typing area, turn on the Display codes and press Stop (Control and 6) two lines above the first line of the letter.	This is where you will be typing the inside addresses. You are marking the place for later use. If you are not in Insert mode, press Insert so that you are in it.
4. Use the arrow keys to move the cursor under the colon.	
5. Press Stop.	You are placing a "marker" in the text where the salutation will go.
6. Press End Task (F2).	

Your form letter may now be personalized easily by adding an inside address and salutation. Repeat the previous procedure to place Stop codes in b:voluntee.rs.

PRODUCING A PERSONALIZED DOCUMENT

This is the final step in producing a personalized document created from a paragraph library into which you have placed Stop codes. In this exercise, you will get a form letter with Stop codes in it and use them to add the information needed to personalize the document.

EXERCISE 100

PROCEDURES	COMMENTS
1. In the Text Task Selection Menu, select Create Document and Enter.	

Continued

Continued

PROCEDURES (Continued)   COMMENTS (Continued)

2. At the prompt, type
    b:Suong.Lee and Enter.

3. In the typing area,
    press F6 and press Enter
    to choose Get.

4. In the Get menu, type a   You will not need to specify a
    and Enter.   page if you want the entire
                                   document.

5. Type b:contribu.tor and
    Enter twice.

6. Press Next Variable   The cursor will go to the
    (Control--N).   first Stop code from the point
                                   at which you gave the Next
                                   Variable command. It will
                                   search for Stop codes only
                                   from the point of the
                                   command to the end of the
                                   document. It cannot
                                   search backward toward the
                                   beginning of the document.

7. At the Stop code, type
    the following inside
    address:

8. **Mrs. Suong Lee**   Type each line of the inside
    455 Beachwood Street   address on a different line.
    Newport Beach, CA   Type the ZIP Code on the same
    92660-1273   line as the city and state.

9. Do not return after the
    last line of the inside
    address.

10. Press Next Variable
    (Control--N).

11. After the word "Dear"   Do not add any spaces or
    type the words **Mrs. Lee**.   punctuation when you type the
                                   salutation. This has already
                                   been done.

12. Press End Task.

13. Print a copy of this
    document.

You have produced a personalized letter thanking a contributor. Now you will use your knowledge to write a letter thanking a volunteer who donated her time to the campaign.

Chapter 20   Using GET for Repetitive Documents   317

EXERCISE 101

PROCEDURES	COMMENTS
1. In the Text Task Selection Menu, select Create Document and Enter.	
2. Name the document **b:Harris**.	
3. In the typing area, press F6 and press Enter to choose Get.	
4. In the Get Menu, type **a** and Enter.	
5. Type **b:voluntee.rs** and Enter twice.	
6. Press Next Variable (Control--N).	
7. Type the following inside address:	
8. **Mrs. Marilyn Harris 703 Mustang Drive Rolling Hills, CA 90311-8625**	Return after each line of the inside address except the last so that it will not all be printed on one line.
9. Do <u>not</u> return after the last line of the inside address.	
10. Press Next Variable.	
11. At the Stop code, type **Mrs. Harris**.	
12. Press End Task.	
13. Print a copy of this document.	

CHAPTER SUMMARY

1. You can bring a "copy" of another document into a second document to avoid rekeying the text.

2. A library of paragraphs can be created and used whenever needed through the Get function.

3. Each paragraph in a "library" must be on a separate page.

4. Paragraphs may be "gotten" in any order.

5. You may Get up to 10 paragraphs at once.

6. Stop codes placed in either the library paragraphs or other text are used to personalize letters or other documents.

7. To move the cursor to a Stop code, use Next Variable.

Chapter 21
MERGING WITH NAMED VARIABLES

When you complete this chapter, you will be able to:

1. Create and print a reference copy of a shell document.

2. Create and print a reference copy of a fill-in document.

3. Merge the shell and fill-in documents to create merged documents.

MERGING TEXT WITH NAMED VARIABLES

When you have a mailing list containing many names and you wish to send the same letter to everyone on the list, it is handy to have a way of merging the addresses with the text. DisplayWrite 3 offers this feature. It is called merging with named variables. You can also insert variable information within the letters.

Three documents comprise merging text with named variables. Each of the three documents will have its own name. The first is called the shell document. This is the document which contains information that does not change. This is constant text. The second document is the list of variables. It is referred to as the fill-in document. This is because it is used to fill in the shell document with the variable information. The last document is called the merged document.

When you are finished typing the first two documents, you will request the system to merge the shell and fill-in documents from the Text Task Selection Menu. The system will create the third set of documents for you! Then you will print your merged documents (see Figure 21.1).

This is the letter you will type in Exercise 102. This letter is the shell document.

October 15, 19--

!!

Dear !!:

Your application for entrance at Southland University has been received.

We will need the transcript from !! by December 1, 19--.
Please request the transcript as soon as possible.

You have a tentative appointment with a counselor on !!
Please go to your division counselor's office on that day at 1:00 p.m.

Sincerely,

Miss Becky Harrison
Admissions Clerk

xxx

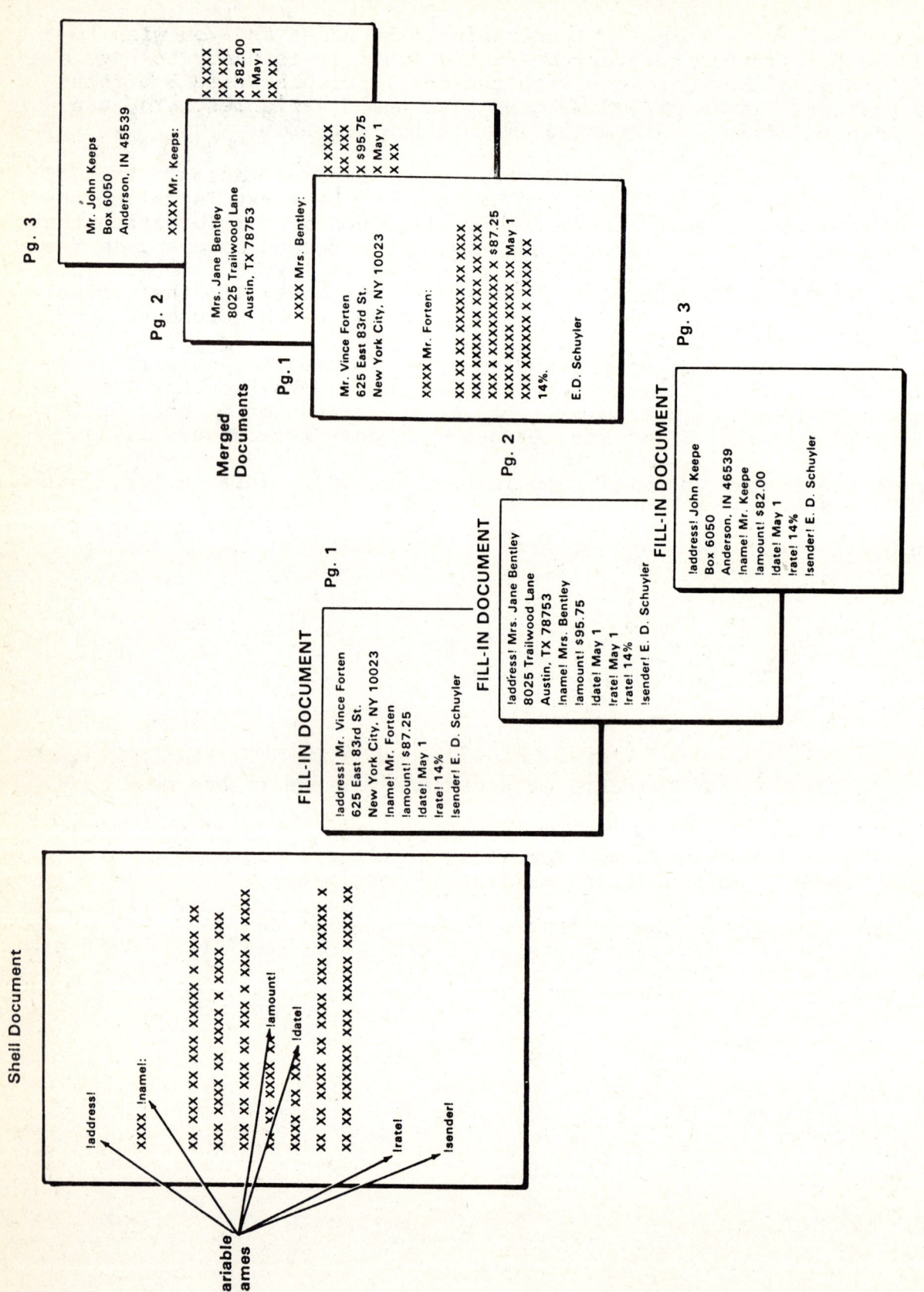

Figure 21.1 Merging Text with Named Variables

322 Chapter 21 Merging with Named Variables

EXERCISE 102

PROCEDURES	COMMENTS
1. From the Text Task Selection Menu, create a document named b:school.	This will be a letter from the admissions and records office at a university.
2. Set your left margin for 15 and your right margin for 70.	Be sure that the margins in the fill-in document match these margins.
3. Go to the typing area.	
4. When you are in the typing area, press F6 and choose Display codes.	You will be able to see the names of the variables with the codes on.
5. Type the letter until you come to the first !!.	You are now at the inside address. This is where you will place the first variable.
6. Press the Instruction key (F8). Choose Variable and Enter. Type the word **address** and Enter. Return twice. Continue typing to the next !!.	Do not put in carrier returns to allow for all of the lines that the inside address will use. You will put them in when you type the fill-in document. Be sure to type the word "Dear" and a space before the next !!.
7. Press F8 again and choose Variable. Type the word **salutation** and return twice.	This is where you will put the first names of the addressees in the fill-in document. A colon goes after the variable.
8. Continue typing until you reach the next !!.	
9. Leave a blank space and press the Instruction key (F8). Choose Variable and Enter. Type the word **college**. Enter.	Be sure always to insert all marks of punctuation and spaces that are necessary. Since words are separated by spaces, you are spacing before inserting a variable.
10. Type to the next !!, press the Instruction key and choose Variable. Type the word **date** and Enter.	A date will appear here when the merged document is produced.
11. Finish typing the letter and press End Task (F2).	

Continued

Chapter 21 Merging with Named Variables

PROCEDURES (Continued)	COMMENTS (Continued)
12. Print a copy for your reference.	

You are now ready to create the fill-in document. This will consist of the information that will be merged with the shell document. Follow the procedures to create this document.

EXERCISE 103

PROCEDURES	COMMENTS
1. Create a document and name it b:students.	
2. Set the Display codes to on (F6 and D).	
3. Press the Instruction key (F8) and choose Variable. Enter.	The name of the variable must match the name of the variable in the letter. The same variable name can be used several times in the letter; however, the spelling and capitalization must be consistent so that the system can identify it.
4. Type **address** and Enter.	
5. Type **Mr. Mark Hopkins** and Enter.	
6. Type **5700 Orangethorpe** and Enter.	
7. Type **La Palma, CA 90623-1910** and Enter.	
8. Press the Instruction key (F8) and choose Variable.	Variable is the default. You choose it by simply pressing Enter.
9. Type **salutation** and Enter.	
10. Type **Mark** and Enter.	
11. Press the Instruction key (F8) and choose Variable.	
12. Type **college** and Enter.	

Continued

PROCEDURES (Continued)	COMMENTS (Continued)
13. Type Rancho Santiago College and Enter.	
14. Press the Instruction key (F8) and choose Variable.	
15. Type date and Enter.	
16. Type November 1, 19-- and Enter. Press Page End (Control--E).	The Page End instruction ends the set of variables that is used in one merged document and begins the set that will be used in the next merged document.
17. Press the Instruction key (F8) and choose Variable.	You are now beginning the second set of variables.
18. Type address and Enter.	
19. Type Miss Holly Beck and Enter.	
20. Type 16017 Crenshaw and Enter.	
21. Type Torrance, CA 90506-0605 and Enter.	
22. Press the Instruction key (F8) and choose Variable.	
23. Type salutation and Enter.	
24. Type Holly and Enter.	
25. Press the Instruction key (F8) and choose Variable.	
26. Type college and Enter.	
27. Type El Camino College and Enter.	
28. Press the Instruction key (F8) and choose Variable.	

Continued

Chapter 21 Merging with Named Variables

PROCEDURES (Continued)   COMMENTS (Continued)

29. Type **date** and Enter.

30. Type October 5, 19-- and Enter.

31. Press Page End (Control--E).

Type two more sets of variables. The information and keystroke pattern are both on the next page. AFTER THE LAST SET OF VARIABLES IS TYPED, DO <u>NOT</u> PRESS PAGE END. DO NOT PAGINATE. You will press End Task (F2).

Note:

Pattern of keystrokes for entering variable information:

a. Press F8

b. Choose Variable by entering

c. Type variable name

d. Return

e. Type variable information and Enter

The last two sets of variables are:

Mr. Brian Heckathorn
3849 Juniper Street
Anaheim, CA 92651-6644
Brian
Cerritos College
October 19, 19--

Reminder: Be sure to press Page End between the sets of variables here.

Ms. Kelly Cummings
386 Main Street
Orange, CA 92638-1295
Kelly
Chapman College
November 19, 19--

Reminder: No Page End; press End Task here.

Finish the document by pressing End Task without a Page End instruction. You are ready to go on to merging the shell and fill-in documents.

MERGING DOCUMENTS

When you are producing merged documents, you have three options. They are as follows:

1. You may merge and store the merged documents on a disk to print later.

2. You may merge and print <u>without</u> storing the merged documents on a disk. This will save disk space. You still store the shell and fill-in documents.

3. You may merge, print, and store the merged document on a disk.

You will choose to merge, store, and print your documents. Follow the procedures to produce your merged documents.

EXERCISE 104

PROCEDURES	COMMENTS
1. From the Text Task Selection Menu, select Merge Documents Tasks and Enter.	You are going to merge two documents.
2. In the Merge Documents Tasks Menu, select Merge with Named Variables and Enter.	The variables you created are named. (They were address, salutation, college, and date.)
3. In the Merge with Named Variables Setup screen, select Shell Document Name and press Enter.	You are indicating to the system the name of the document you wish to use as the shell.
4. Type b:school and Enter.	
5. Select Fill-in Document Name and Enter.	You are indicating the name of the document which contains your variable information.
6. Type b:students and Enter.	
7. Select Merged Document Name and Enter. Type b:final and Enter.	Even if you do not print immediately, you must give the document a name.
8. Leave item "e" set on the default.	The system assumes that you wish to print the merged document. Your four sets of variables and the shell document will begin merging.
9. Press Enter.	

Continued

Chapter 21   Merging with Named Variables

PROCEDURES (Continued)	COMMENTS (Continued)
	A "merging" message will appear on the screen. After a short time, the merged documents will begin to print. Be sure your printer is on!

CHAPTER SUMMARY

A. The shell document is the document that contains the constant information.

B. The fill-in document contains the variables that change from document to document and allow you to personalize letters.

C. The merged document is the final product. It is created by the system for you. You may save the merged documents or just print them without saving.

Chapter 22

DOCUMENT ASSEMBLY

When you complete this chapter, you will be able to:

1. Create a paragraph library for use with Document Assembly.

2. Revise names of variables within the library.

3. Create a Document Assembly Fill-In Document.

4. Create a Document Assembly Shell.

5. Merge variables with selected paragraphs from the Document Assembly paragraph library.

DOCUMENT ASSEMBLY

This chapter incorporates many of the word processing skills that you have learned already. You will be creating a paragraph library and printing a reference copy of it. You will be working again with named variables as well as fill-in documents. You will be introduced to an operation called Include which is similar to Get. Because of your familiarity with DisplayWrite 3, the instructions will not go into as much detail as in the earlier chapters.

Document Assembly is useful for producing large volumes of correspondence in which many of the paragraphs are boilerplate; that is, they are used again and again in many documents. The difference between Document Assembly and Merging with Named Variables is that Document Assembly allows you to use a variety of paragraphs in any order when adding variable information. Merging with Named Variables allows you to merge variables with standard text but not change the order of paragraphs on the page.

You will be placing paragraphs from the paragraph library in a new document. If the paragraphs have variables in them, simply tell the system which words you want to appear in the finished product where the variables are now. This is done by means of a "link" or joining document, which is very short.

This allows you to customize each letter to a larger extent than Merging with Named Variables only. The advantage of using Document Assembly over Get is that it is designed to handle larger quantities of correspondence and is, therefore, a less time-consuming operation. Get is a useful tool for personalizing documents; however, it is intended to be used with small numbers of letters.

CREATING AND STORING A PARAGRAPH LIBRARY DOCUMENT

A paragraph library document (paragraph library) contains the text of your documents. Variables may also be present in some of the paragraphs. They may not contain variables at all. Some "paragraphs" contain only a variable. Most, however, will be a paragraph of text with one or more variables in them.

Your specified paragraphs can be assembled in any order (see Figure 22.1). Printing a reference copy of the library so that the originator can choose which paragraphs and variables are applicable is also something you will want to do on the job. You will also print a reference copy in this chapter.

CREATING THE DOCUMENT ASSEMBLY PARAGRAPH LIBRARY

Here you will create and store the paragraphs for your Document Assembly library. Each Document Assembly library is really one document consisting of many paragraphs which make up the library. You can have as many document libraries as you wish. The name of the document is the name of your library. You will see that there can be a variety of paragraph sizes in this document.

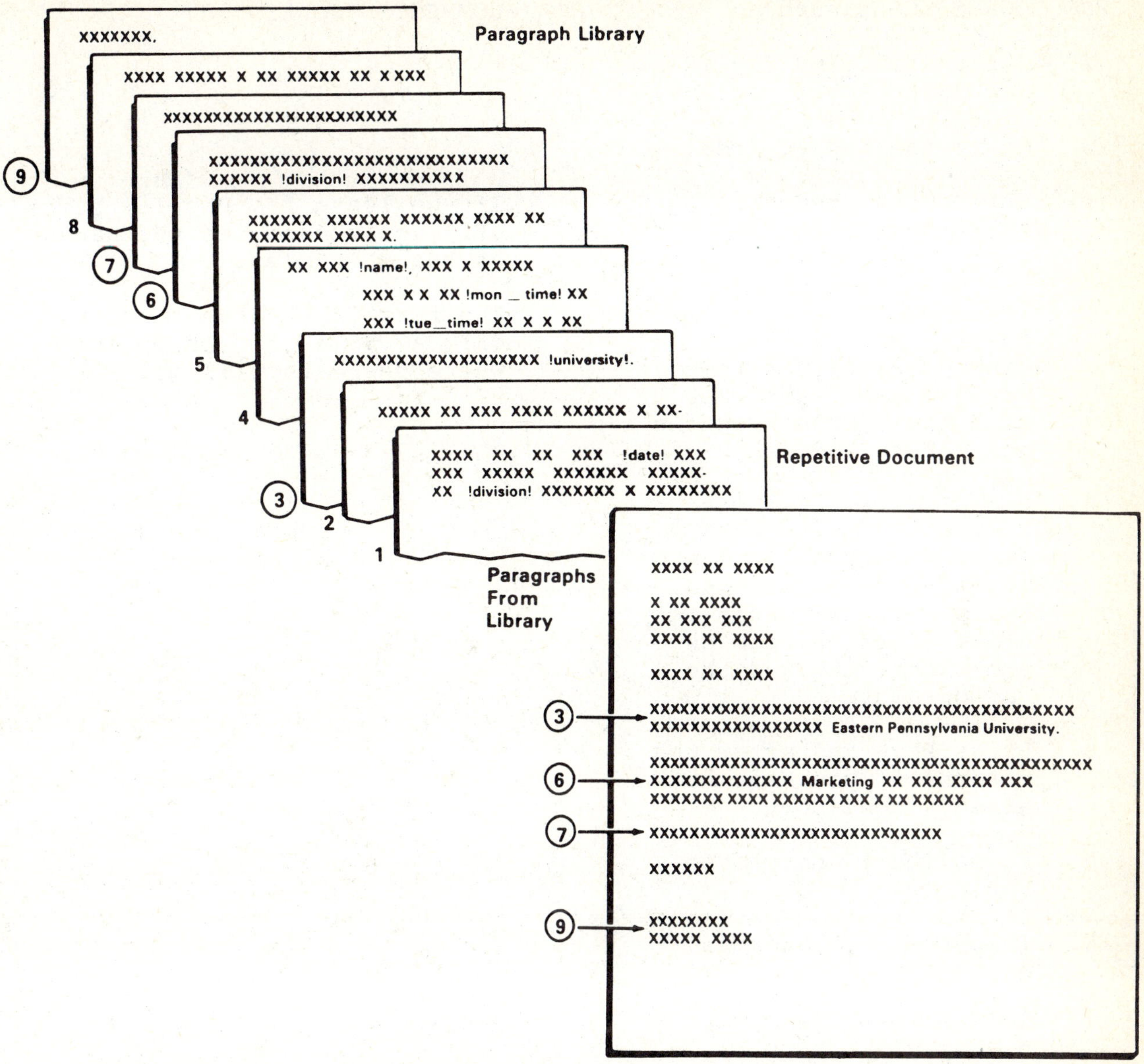

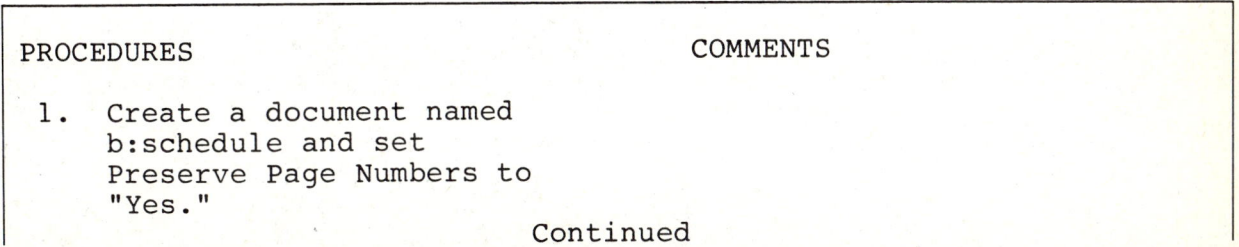

Figure 22.1 Paragraph Library and Repetitive Document

In this exercise, the first "paragraph" is a variable that will be used only for the inside address. The second "paragraph" consists of only one word, a variable to be used for the salutation, and a colon. The remaining paragraphs are more conventional.

EXERCISE 105

PROCEDURES	COMMENTS
1. Create a document named b:schedule and set Preserve Page Numbers to "Yes."	
Continued	

Chapter 22 Document Assembly

PROCEDURES (Continued)	COMMENTS (Continued)
2. Set the margins for 12 and 73.	
3. Go to the typing area.	
4. Set Display codes to "On."	If you leave the Display codes off, you cannot see the names of the variables.
5. Type the paragraphs at the end of this exercise, making sure that you end each paragraph with two carrier returns and a Page End.	The first "paragraph" contains only a variable. This is where the date will go.
6. Press Instr and choose Variable.	
7. Type the word date and Enter. Return seven times to allow room between the date and the inside address.	
8. Press Page End after the returns if you have not already done so.	
9. Press Instr and choose Variable.	
10. Type the word address and Enter.	
11. Return twice and press Page End.	You are now on page 3.
12. On the third page, type the word Dear, type a space, and insert a Variable named salutation. Then type a colon, return twice, and press Page End.	If you need to refresh your memory on named variables, refer back to Chapter 21.
13. You are now going to type a paragraph for your library without variables. After that, most of the remaining paragraphs will have variables in them.	You are now on page 4. Be sure to put two carrier returns and a Page End after the last sentence in each paragraph. This is so that the paragraphs will not run together but will be separated

Continued

PROCEDURES (Continued)

    Continue following this pattern until all of the paragraphs are typed.

COMMENTS (Continued)

by a blank line. The lines may appear beyond the right margin. Do not attempt to force them back within the margin. The lengths of the names of the variables are extending the lines. If the Display codes were not on, the lines would be shorter. Turn the Display codes off and on to see for yourself.

Paragraphs

As a continuing student at Fullerton College, you are required to meet with your counselor at least once a semester prior to registration for the following semester. As of yet, we have no record of your setting an appointment. Since you are scheduled to register two weeks from this date, please call for an appointment within the next few days.

The number of the counselor assigned to you is (insert variable named **phone**). Students majoring in (insert variable named **major**) should talk to (insert variable named **counselor**). You will need to prepare a tentative schedule of the classes you wish to take and bring it with you.

Your appointment is set for (insert variable named **time**) on (insert variable named **day**), (insert variable named **date**). If you cannot register in person, be sure you have someone register in your place.

The bookstore hours are from 8:00 a.m. to 9:00 p.m., Monday through Friday. You will want to check the book list for the titles of your books. General school supplies, as well as school sweaters and other articles of clothing bearing the college name, are available to students.

The library has notified us that you will need to settle an obligation with them prior to registration. The amount of your fine is (insert variable named **fine**).

You are eligible to receive financial aid. The maximum amount you may borrow is (insert variable named **aid**). The financial aid officer is in from 8:00 a.m. to 5:00 p.m., Monday through Friday. You may contact him by calling 555-8866 and asking for Dr. Clemmensen.

Football tickets to attend the Hornets' games are available beginning (insert variable named **Hornets**). The opening game against the Rancho Santiago College Dons is scheduled for (insert variable named **Dons**).

Again the Theater Department is presenting its fall play. This year the selection is (insert variable named **play**). The Music Department

Continued

Chapter 22 Document Assembly

also will give a concert featuring solos by (insert variable named pianist), (insert variable named drummer), and (insert variable named harpist).

Marching band tryouts will be held on (insert variable named band). They will be held in Music 304 at 4:00 p.m.

Cheerleader tryouts will be held at 9:00 a.m. on August 8 in the gym. When you arrive, you will want to give your name to present cheerleaders (insert variable named cheers).

A study tour to France will be conducted during the summer. For information on this opportunity to earn two units and expand your horizons, contact (insert variable named France).

Sincerely,   (The signature block is a separate
                                         paragraph.)

Dr. Charles Inacker

(Remember to press End Task instead of Page End here when you have finished the last paragraph.)

REVISING VARIABLE NAMES

If you wish, you may change the name of a variable because it contains a typing error or because you feel that another name would be more appropriate. In the exercise below, we will go back to the variables you named in b:Schedule and change one of them. The variable named "aid" will be changed to "money."

EXERCISE 106

PROCEDURES	COMMENTS
1. In the Text Task Selection Menu, choose Revise Document.	
2. At the prompt, type b:Schedule.	
3. In the typing area, go to the variable named "!aid!."	This is in paragraph 9.
4. Place the cursor underneath the first "!" of the variable.	
5. Press Continue.	
	Continued

PROCEDURES (Continued)	COMMENTS (Continued)
6. In the Variable Menu, select Variable Name.	
7. Type **money** and Enter.	Money is the new named variable.

PRINTING A REFERENCE COPY OF YOUR PARAGRAPH LIBRARY

Now you are ready to use Get to bring your paragraphs into a new document. Then you will have a reference copy of them.

EXERCISE 107

PROCEDURES	COMMENTS
1. Create a reference copy of these paragraphs by getting the entire document (name the new document b:pararef.cpy).	
2. Change the margins to 12 and 73.	
3. After you have gotten the document, in the Create or Revise Menu, make sure that Preserve Page Numbers is set to "No."	
4. Paginate the new document so that each page will fill with text.	You want to print as many paragraphs on each page as possible so that the paragraph choices can be seen easily.
5. Print the paragraph library reference copy.	Keep this copy with you because you will be using it.
6. Number the paragraphs by hand.	
7. Delete the document from your diskette so that you will not use it by mistake at some time in the future.	If you have forgotten how to delete, see the utilities chapter.

Chapter 22 Document Assembly

CREATING THE DOCUMENT ASSEMBLY FILL-IN

Instructions to include certain paragraphs from the paragraph library document, along with the variable information, come from Document Assembly Fill-In. Not <u>every</u> paragraph has a variable in it. Some consist of constant text only.

The Document Fill-In gives the order in which the paragraphs are to appear, and it can consist of one or more pages. This document contains the names of the variables. You are now about to create the fill-in document. When merged, each page of fill-in document constitutes one merged document. After merging the fill-in document and the shell, the paragraphs you want will be in the correct order and the information will be inserted in the places where you wanted it to be.

EXERCISE 108

PROCEDURES	COMMENTS
1. In the Text Task Selection Menu, choose Create Document and name it b:choices.	
2. Go to the typing area and set the Display codes to "On."	
3. Press Instr and choose Variable.	
4. In the typing area, type the word join and Enter.	This is the name of the variable that will join the fill-in document and the paragraph library.
5. Press Instr and choose Include.	
6. In the Include Instruction Menu, choose "a" and Enter.	
7. Type b:Schedule and Enter.	This document name is also referred to as your library name.
8. Type b and Enter. Type the paragraph numbers 1 2 3 4 5 15.	You are going to select paragraph (page) numbers now to include in your letter. Be sure to leave a space between each number. You may type a maximum of 10 paragraph
9. Press Enter twice.	

Continued

Chapter 22   Document Assembly

PROCEDURES (Continued)	COMMENTS (Continued)
	numbers for each inclusion instruction. Use your reference copy.
	Your screen should look like Figure 22.2.

```
Create Document   ]B:CHOICES.TXT                              ]
Page End          ]Ins 3   ]Pg. 1      ]Ln. 8   ]Ext 340-B]Pitch 10  ]100
.....2...._....3...._....4........5...._....6...._....7..../....8....*....9....
!join!
/Include,B:SCHEDULE.TXT,1,2,3,4,5,15/
```

Figure 22.2

So far, we have the instruction to join (or link) two documents, include text from b:Schedule, and use pages (paragraphs) 1, 2, 3, 4, 5, and 15 from that document.

10. Press Instr and choose Variable.
    Remember where "date" was in your reference copy?

11. Type date and Enter.
    Type each variable and the variable information on the same line; Enter after giving the variable information.

12. Type July 25, 19-- and Enter.

13. Press Instr and choose Variable.

14. Type the variable name address and Enter.

15. Type variable information which is
    Miss Joanna Warner
    333 Palisades Drive
    Anaheim, CA
    92626-5135
    and Enter.
    Make sure that you return after each line in the inside address.

    Your screen should look like Figure 22.3.

```
Create Document   ]B:CHOICES.TXT                              ]
Page End          ]Ins 3   ]Pg. 1      ]Ln. 12  ]Ext 340-B]Pitch 10  ]100
.....2...._....3...._....4........5...._....6...._....7..../....8....*....9....
!join!
/Include,B:SCHEDULE.TXT,1,2,3,4,5,15/!date!July 25, 19--
!address!Miss Joanna Warner
333 Palisades Drive
Anaheim, CA  92626-5135
```

Figure 22.3

Continued

Chapter 22 Document Assembly

PROCEDURES (Continued)	COMMENTS (Continued)
16. Press Instr and choose Variable.	
17. Name the variable. Type salutation and Enter.	
18. Type the variable information on the same line by typing Joanna and returning.	Your screen should look like Figure 22.4.

```
Create Document    3B:CHOICES.TXT                           3
Page End           3Ins 3   3Pg. 1    3Ln. 13  3Ext 340-B3Pitch 10  3100
.....2.....,....3.....,....4........5....,....6.....,....7..../....8....`....9....
!join!
/Include,B:SCHEDULE.TXT,1,2,3,4,5,15/!date!July 25, 19--
!address!Miss Joanna Warner
333 Palisades Drive
Anaheim, CA  92626-5135
!salutation!Joanna
```

Figure 22.4

19. Press Instr and choose Variable.

20. Type the variable name. Type phone and Enter.

21. Enter the variable information. Type 555-2244 and Enter.   Your screen should look like Figure 22.5.

```
Create Document    3B:CHOICES.TXT                           3
Page End           3Ins 3   3Pg. 1    3Ln. 14  3Ext 340-B3Pitch 10  3100
.....2.....,....3.....,....4........5....,....6.....,....7..../....8....`....9....
!join!
/Include,B:SCHEDULE.TXT,1,2,3,4,5,15/!date!July 25, 19--
!address!Miss Joanna Warner
333 Palisades Drive
Anaheim, CA  92626-5135
!salutation!Joanna
!phone!555-2244
```

Figure 22.5

22. Press Instr and choose Variable.

23. Name the variable. Type major and Enter.

24. Enter the variable information. Type English and Enter.   Your screen should look like Figure 22.6

Continued

```
Create Document    3B:CHOICES.TXT                              3
Page End           3Ins 3    3Pg. 1       3Ln. 15   3Ext 340-B3Pitch 10   3100
.....2.....,....3.....,....4........5.....,....6.....,....7..../....8....*....9....
!join!
/Include,B:SCHEDULE.TXT,1,2,3,4,5,15/!date!July 25, 19--
!address!Miss Joanna Warner
333 Palisades Drive
Anaheim, CA  92626-5135
!salutation!Joanna
!phone!555-2244
!major!English
```
Figure 22.6

PROCEDURES (Continued)   COMMENTS (Continued)

25. Press Instr and choose
    Variable.

26. Name the variable. Type
    counselor and Enter.

27. Enter the variable in-   Your screen should look like
    formation. Type Dr.   Figure 22.7.
    Ward and Enter.

```
Create Document    3B:CHOICES.TXT                              3
Page End           3Ins 3    3Pg. 1       3Ln. 16   3Ext 340-B3Pitch 10   3100
.....2.....,....3.....,....4........5.....,....6.....,....7..../....8....*....9....
!join!
/Include,B:SCHEDULE.TXT,1,2,3,4,5,15/!date!July 25, 19--
!address!Miss Joanna Warner
333 Palisades Drive
Anaheim, CA  92626-5135
!salutation!Joanna
!phone!555-2244
!major!English
!counselor!Dr. Ward
```
Figure 22.7

28. Since there is no varia-
    ble in the last para-
    graph, (a signature
    block) press End Task.

29. Do not paginate.   This, of course, is a document
                                    that should not be paginated.

Thus far we have told the system to join documents, include text, and use pages (paragraphs) 1, 2, 3, 4, 5, and 15 from b:Schedule.txt. Then we gave the names of the variables within those paragraphs which consist of date, address, salutation, phone, major, and counselor. There are two paragraphs which do not contain variables. They are numbers 4 and 15. You have placed each named variable and its corresponding variable information on a line separate from the rest of the lines. You have pressed return after each line in the inside address because you do not want the entire address to print on one line! If you were creating another fill-in for another letter, you would press Page End (do not do it now) and go through the same steps for the next fill-in as you did for the one you just finished.

CREATING THE DOCUMENT SHELL

The Document Assembly Shell serves two purposes. It sets the format for the finished product, and it serves as the link between constant text and variables in the documents. Now you will create a document shell to join your fill-in and the paragraphs you choose to use.

EXERCISE 109

PROCEDURES	COMMENTS
1. Create and name a document b:docshell.	
2. Change the margins of the document to 12 and 73.	These are the margins for the final product.
3. Go to the typing area.	
4. In the typing area, turn on the Display codes.	
5. Press the Instr key and choose Variable.	
6. Type join and Enter.	This is a unique variable name that must not be the same as any in the paragraph library document. It is the link between the fill-in and the paragraph library.
7. Press the End Task key.	
	This is all there is to creating a Document Assembly Shell.

MERGING IN DOCUMENT ASSEMBLY

When you have finished all of the component parts, it is time to start producing finished products! So far, you have created the following:

1. The Document Assembly Paragraph Library.

2. The Document Assembly Fill-In Document.

3. The Document Assembly Shell.

This is all you need to start merging using Document Assembly.

EXERCISE 110

PROCEDURES	COMMENTS
1. In the Text Task Selection Menu, choose Merge Documents Tasks.	
2. In the Merge Documents Tasks Menu, select Merge with Named Variables.	
3. In the Merge with Named Variables Setup Menu, choose Shell Document Name and type b:docshell.	You want to tell the system the name of the document that serves as your shell document.
4. Now choose Fill-In Document Name and type b:choices.	This lets the system know that you want to use the paragraphs and variables you chose in that document.

There are three options regarding merging with Document Assembly.

1. You may print the merged documents and store them on your diskette. (You will be doing this.)

2. You may print them only.

3. You may store the merged documents on your diskette and print them at a later time.

If you had wanted to store the merged documents only and not print them, you would have named the document and set Print Merged Documents to "No" in the Merge with Named Variable Setup Menu.

If you needed to print the merged documents but not store them, you would not have given the merged document a name ("d" on the Merge with Named Variables Setup Menu). You would have just entered to begin merging and printing.

EXERCISE 111

PROCEDURES	COMMENTS
1. In the Merge with Named Variables Setup Menu, select Merged Document Name and Enter.	

Continued

Chapter 22 Document Assembly

PROCEDURES (Continued)	COMMENTS (Continued)
2. Type b:docassem.fin and Enter.	This is the finished product of Document Assembly.
3. Hand in the printed copies.	If you have done something wrong and want to cancel the operation while it is merging, press Ctrl--Break. Your documents will be added automatically to the print queue.
4. Check the directory to see that b:docassem.fin has been listed.	In case you have forgotten how to do this, press F3. At the prompt, type b:\ and Enter.

EXERCISE 112

Now you will prepare letters to handle the following two situations. Use paragraphs from your library and insert the variables. Date each of the letters July 25, 19--. Both letters will be signed by Dr. Inacker.

Letter #1: This letter goes to a student who wants to try out for cheerleading, is interested in the study tour, and would like to apply for financial aid. The present cheerleaders are Nancy Billett and Wanda Stitt. The person in charge of the study tour is Dr. Zimmer. The maximum amount that can be borrowed through financial aid is $2,000. (Do not forget that the variable name "Aid" was changed to "Money.") The name and address of the student is Paul Hulsman, 2842 El Dorado, Placentia, CA 92670-2883.

Letter #2: This letter goes to Kaye Kessler, 810 Acacia, Fullerton, CA 92634-4312. She should be told about the availability of football tickets, the play, and the marching band tryouts. The tickets will be available August 26 and the opening game is September 10. The play will be Don Juan Tenorio and the solos will be performed by Laura Pannier, Marc Chronister, and Helen Metzler respectively. Tryouts will be September 2.

Print the merged copies.

CHAPTER SUMMARY

A. Document Assembly is done with paragraphs from a paragraph library.

B. The paragraphs in the library may contain variables or simply straight text.

C. You may revise the variables in the paragraphs.

D. The variable information for your documents is placed in the fill-in document.

E. The Document Assembly Shell serves two purposes: to set the format for the finished product and to link the fill-in with the paragraphs from the library.

F. You may print the merged documents without storing them.

G. The merged documents may be stored and printed later.

H. You may store and print the merged documents in one process.

Chapter 23

MERGING WITH FILES

When you complete this chapter, you will be able to:

1. Create a shell document with variables.

2. Merge a shell document with a file created in another program.

3. Restart the merging operation.

4. Set math format for numeric variables.

5. Give instructions for the inclusion of conditional text.

6. Give math instructions.

7. Give skip-to-line instructions.

8. Create and revise file descriptions to use with BASIC files.

INTRODUCTION TO MERGING WITH FILES

You know how to merge constant text with variables created in DisplayWrite 3. However, what happens when your variable information is contained in a file generated by another software program? You can merge text typed in DisplayWrite 3 with information from certain other programs to produce repetitive letters that do not require rekeying of data. The programs that can be used are listed in your User's Guide, Volume 2, that came with the DisplayWrite 3 program. Data files are composed of fields and records.

A field is a category of information containing numbers or letters that are entered into the computer's memory as a unit of data. There are two types of fields used with DisplayWrite 3. They are numeric fields and character fields.

Numeric fields can only contain numbers, a decimal point, or the symbols for plus or minus. Numeric fields may be from 1 to 17 characters in length.

Character fields may be from 1 to 500 characters in length and contain alphabetic characters.

The field names serve as variable names that you can use when merging. Since the variable names you use must match the field names exactly, you should know that field names must be unique names. They should also be descriptive of the kind of material they contain. They may contain numbers, underscores, or letters but may not contain more than 16 characters, including the underscore. Field names are case sensitive (they know an uppercase character from a lowercase character) and may not contain marks of punctuation. Character fields must start with a letter.

The first example of a data file is a spreadsheet created in the Lotus 1-2-3^{TM}* program. The column headings serve as field names. Each intersection of a row and a column is called a cell. Each column of cells is a field. Each row of cells is a record.

A record is composed of a cell in each field in the file. Notice how the information in each cell relates to the other cells in that record. Each row or record contains information about one person.

In the case of a customer list, all of the information, including the name, street address, city, state, ZIP Code, and accounting data for one person comprise a record.

In short, the rows serve as records and the columns as fields. Each cell is in an individual field of a particular record. For example, in the data file named b:Customer.dif, the name Bonnie is in a cell. It is in the field called First (for first name) in a record for Bonnie Short. Title, First, MI, Last, Street, City, St, Zip, Balance, and Overdue are field names. An appropriate name for this data file might be "Customers."

---

*Lotus is a trademark of Lotus Development Corporation.

Chapter 23 Merging with Files

CREATING A SHELL DOCUMENT

You may think of a data file as taking the place of the fill-in document that you learned about in the chapter on merging with named variables. Instead of using a fill-in document in DisplayWrite 3, you will use information from a data file created in another program. For the following exercise, you will use the Lotus 1-2-3* file named b:Customer.dif shown in Figure 23.1.

Title	First	MI	Last	Street	City	St	Zip	Balance	Overdue
Ms.	Bonnie	A.	Short	P. O. Box 203	Long Beach	CA	90806	$110.00	$20.00
Miss	Denise		Fugita	35 Elmcroft	Fullerton	CA	92633	$ 75.00	
Mrs.	Sheila	L.	Ard	88 Oak Street	Burbank	CA	90555		
Ms.	Kim	I.	Carberry	949 Estellita	Rancho Mirage	CA	92884	$ 34.00	
Mrs.	Cassie	W.	Toomey	17 Bristol	Santa Ana	CA	92645		
Dr.	Maria	V.	Hernandez	53 Alicante	Irvine	CA	92673		

Figure 23.1   Lotus File

Only the information contained in the fields that are named as variables will be used. The rest of the information will be ignored.

The letter you will merge with the information in the file is named b:Fashion.txt.

EXERCISE 113

PROCEDURES	COMMENTS
1. Create a document named b:Fashion.txt.	This document contains the variables.
2. Set your margins at 10 and 75.	
3. Go to the typing area and turn on the Display codes.	
4. In the typing area, type the letter shown at the end of this exercise, placing named variables in the appropriate places. Be sure that the variable names are typed in your document exactly as they are typed in the letter.	If you need to brush up on named variables, you may wish to review Chapter 21. If you type the wrong variable name and wish to correct it, revisions of named variables are handled no differently when merging with a file than they were when you merged with named variables.

Continued

*Lotus is a trademark of Lotus Development Corporation.

PROCEDURES (Continued)	COMMENTS (Continued)
5. Insert Volume 3. In the Text Task Selection Menu, select Merge with File Task and Enter.	The File Specification Menu will appear on the screen.
6. In the File Specification Menu, choose Data File Name and Enter.	
7. At the prompt, type b:Customer.dif and Enter.	
8. Choose Data File Format and Enter.	
9. Type 3 and Enter. Enter again.	You are choosing the "DIF" format.
10. In the Merge with File Setup Menu, the name of the data file will appear on the upper status line and the name of the shell document will already appear for choice "a." Since you wish to save the merged document on your disk, choose Merged Document Name and Enter. At the prompt, type b:Success.txt and Enter.	
11. Press Enter.	You will not change the rest of the menu since the default choices are the ones you want. A Merge with File Status screen will appear. The word "Merging" will appear in the upper left portion of the screen. The prompt "(B:SUCCESS.TXT) added to the print queue" will appear across the bottom of the screen.

Continued

Chapter 23 Merging with Files

PROCEDURES (Continued)	COMMENTS (Continued)
	If your computer is attached to a printer, the printer will start printing your job. There will be a slight pause between the printing of each page.

March 25, 19--

!Title! !First! !Last!
!Street!
!City!, !St! !Zip!

Dear !Title! !Last!:

As one of our valued customers, you are invited to a seminar and fashion show given by our in-house business attire consultant, Martha Fender. Ms. Fender's impressive credentials are enhanced by her professional experience serving as advisor to many Fortune 1000 firms across the nation.

She will address the following subjects:

       Style and color in a basic business wardrobe
       Geographic difference in taste
       Dressing for rain
       How to dress for travel
       Business dressing on a budget
       Conservatism and fads

The event will begin at 1:00 p.m. on Thursday, April 2. Enclosed is your ticket for the gift certificate drawing. We hope that your schedule will allow you to attend.

Sincerely,

Hilda Roberts
Vice President

Enclosure

MATH FORMAT FOR NUMERIC VARIABLES

For the sake of clarity, numbers can be expressed in a variety of ways. For instance, money amounts are preceded by a "$." This makes it much easier to distinguish between currency and other figures in text. In DisplayWrite 3, the form of expression is called a format. This program has four active formats for math. The four active formats are as follows:

Format Number	Example	Explanation
1	0.00	two places to the right of the decimal point, no dollar sign
2	$0.00	currency format with a dollar sign and two places to the right of the decimal showing on the screen
3	0	just for whole numbers
4	0.0	one place to the left of the decimal point and one place to the right

If you do not choose a math format, the system will show the information exactly the same as it is typed in your file. This format is considered to be Format Number 0. Figure 23.2 is b:Refunds.dif, the data file you will be using for the next exercise.

```
        Last              First            Due
     Thompson            Danny            21.84
     Hergersheimer       Donald            8.47
     Anderson            Merle            19.55
     Anthonisen          Danielle         17.08
     Blankenship         Harold            1.19
     Stoltz              Jan              15.07
     Sangerfroiden       Hans             17.69
```

Figure 23.2   Data File

Notice that the amount of the credit balance is not in a currency format with a dollar sign and two decimal places (Format Number 2). In the next exercise, you will work with the math format in the shell document by telling the system that you want the numeric variable to be printed in a math format that reflects money.

EXERCISE 114

PROCEDURES	COMMENTS
1. Create a document and name it b:Mathform.txt.	Make sure that Volume 2 is in drive B. A copy of b:Mathform.txt is found at the end of this exercise.
2. Turn the Display codes on, and type the document.	
3. When you have finished typing the document, return to the variable named !Due! and press Continue. Select Output Format and type the number "2." You are telling the system that you wish the printout (output) to be in the second math format. This format is for money.	
4. Enter to leave this menu.	
5. Since Display codes is on, you can see that the variable now says !Due,2!. The 2 indicates the math format being used. End this document and print a reference copy.	
6. Using your knowledge of merging text with files, merge the document "b:Mathform.txt" with the file "b:Refunds.dif."	Do not forget to choose "DIF."

Nofification of Credit Balance

Name of Customer: !First! !Last!

You now have a credit balance of !Due! that can be applied to a purchase or refunded. If you have not applied the credit toward a purchase within 90 days, we will issue you a check in the amount of the credit balance.

CONDITIONAL TEXT

Fields do not always contain information. Sometimes they are empty, as is occasionally the case with fields for middle initials, because not all people have middle names. You can instruct the system to do a variety of tasks depending upon a condition. Often that condition is whether or not the field is empty or contains information. When merging with conditional text, the system can do the following:

1. Ignore a field when it is empty.
2. Include the contents of the field if the field contains information.
3. Print text if the field is empty.
4. Print text if the field is not empty (contains information).

Examples are as follows:

1. Skipping a field if the field does not contain information.
2. Printing the information contained in the field if the field does have information in it.
3. Printing text such as NMI (no middle initial) if the field does not contain information.
4. Printing text other than what is in the field if the field contains information.

Conditional text is text that can be printed depending upon whether a field is empty or contains information. For instance, if there is a field in your data file called "Balance," and an amount appears in it, the conditional text may read something like this: "Our records show that your account is currently past due."

The conditional text is called into play when you use a conditional text statement. In order to use this type of statement, you must type one of three kinds of conditional text instructions. These instructions must be used in pairs.

Following samples of conditional text instructions with the text to be printed in the merged document between them.

/If Not Empty, Field name/conditional text/End If/

/If Empty, Field name/conditional text/End If/

Those two lines are examples of conditional text statements. The conditional text may be the following:

        field contents of the data file
     text and any needed additional spaces
          field contents and text

In the following exercise, you will be merging a document with the data file called b:Customer.dif.

EXERCISE 115

PROCEDURES	COMMENTS
1. Create a document and name it b:Conditio.nal.	This is the shell document. Make sure that you have Volume 2 in the machine in order to type a document.
2. Type the document which appears on the next page to the point of the first conditional text.	
3. Strike the Instr key and choose Merge_file/text from the prompt line.	
4. In the Merge File/Text Instructions Menu, choose Conditional Text: Field or Variable Empty and Enter.	This is the choice when the field does not contain information.
5. In response to the prompt, type Balance.	
6. Enter.	
7. In the typing area, type the first conditional text.	
8. At the end of the conditional text, press return two times to begin a new paragraph. Press Instr and choose Merge_file/text.	
9. Choose End of Conditional Text and Enter to leave the menu.	
10. Press Instr and choose Merge_file/text.	
11. In the Merge File/Text Instructions Menu, choose Conditional Text: Field or Variable Not Empty and Enter.	

Continued

November 8, 19--

!Title! !First! !Last!
!Street!
!City!, !St!   !Zip!

Dear !Title! !Last!:

Our annual fashion sale is underway this month. The store hours have been extended to 10:00 p.m. every night except Sunday.

/If Empty, Balance/Our records show that you have not used your charge card recently. Why not take advantage of your credit privileges now?

/End If//If Not Empty, Balance/Why not take advantage of your credit privileges to purchase a new suit or dress?

/End If/Thank you for your business in the past, and we look forward to serving you in the future.

Sincerely,

Elizabeth Chaney
Vice President, Marketing

xxx

PROCEDURES (Continued)   COMMENTS (Continued)

12. In response to the
    prompt, type the varia-
    ble name Balance and
    Enter.

13. In the typing area, type
    the second variable
    text.

14. At the end of the condi-
    tional text, press re-
    turn two times to begin
    a new paragraph. Press
    Instr and choose
    Merge_file/text.

                                    Continued

Chapter 23 Merging with Files   353

PROCEDURES (Continued)	COMMENTS (Continued)
15. In the Merge File/Text Instructions Menu, choose End of Conditional Text and Enter to leave the menu. 16. Finish typing the document and print a reference copy. 17. Merge the document b:Conditio.nal with the data file b:Customer.dif.	

MATH INSTRUCTIONS

Instructions may be given to the system to perform certain math operations during the merge. This operation requires two numbers. They can be as follows:

1. A number that you have typed into the math instruction, such as an interest rate or service charge.

2. The result of a calculation that has already taken place.

3. A number from a numeric field in the file with which you are working.

The four basic math functions that may be used are addition, subtraction, multiplication, and division.

Math instructions are very handy when you would like tax, a service charge, or a discount figured and the result inserted in the merged letter. Since the math instruction will not print, it is very easily typed on the first typing line of the shell document where it will stand out from the rest of the text on the screen but will not appear in the printed version of the merged letter. It will only print on a reference copy of the shell (not merged). The answer variable will print in the document that is being merged. The answer variable is the result of the calculation. It will print where you indicate you wish it to appear. You may indicate where you want the answer variable by placing a variable bearing the same name as the variable answer. If your correspondence requires multiple calculations, place the math instructions in the order in which they will be performed and before the text in the letter. At the end of a math instruction, the system inserts a zero index return. This means that, although you can see the math instruction taking up a line by itself on the screen, it will not take up a line in your document.

Chapter 23   Merging with Files

EXERCISE 116

PROCEDURES	COMMENTS
1. Create a document and name it b:Interest.txt.	You can find the document named b:Interest.txt at the end of this exercise.
2. On the first line in the typing area, press Instr and choose Merge_file/text.	
3. In the Merge File/Text Instructions Menu, choose Math and Enter.	
4. Choose Variable Name for Answer, and type Total.	
5. Choose First Number and type Price and Enter.	
6. Choose Calculation and type 3.	This stands for multiplication.
7. Choose Second Number and type 1.05 (be sure to use the number "1" and not the letter "L") and Enter.	
8. Enter to leave the menu.	
9. Return four times and type the document.	
10. When you finish, go back to the variable and change the active math format to "2."	
11. Print a reference copy of this document.	
12. Merge this document with the data file named b:order.dif.	The field name in b:order.dif is price and the information in the field is 90.

Chapter 23 Merging with Files

/total = Price * 1.05/

November 8, 19--

Ms. Shirley Oliver
365 Oakhurst Street
Fountain Valley, CA 92678-5110

Dear Ms. Oliver:

Thank you for your inquiry relative to our antique vases. Yes, we can deliver the one you want. Since you live within 25 miles of our store, we will deliver to your home free of charge.

The total for the vase is !Total!. This includes tax. If we can serve you in any other way, please let us know.

Sincerely,

Kenneth Knight

SKIP-TO-LINE INSTRUCTIONS

You can tell the system to place text on certain lines in DisplayWrite 3. You may need this feature when working with forms. Sometimes company format for various types of reports requires that text fall on a specific line. In the next exercise, you will place information at the bottom of the page using a skip-to-line instruction. Figure 23.3 is b:jobs.dif, the data file.

Last	First	Street	City	St	Zip	Phone	Position	Interviewer	Salary
Kelder	Sue	11110 Alondra	Yorba Linda	CA	92647-4634	714-697-9354	Accounting Clerk	Chris Simkanin	1,200.00
Vielma	Virginia	2985 Ventura	Anaheim	CA	92805-3656	714-539-0987	Marketing Director	James Sanchez	2,400.00
Amaral	Diana	2209 Valley	Arcadia	CA	90765-8076	213-555-9812	Systems Analyst	Leonor Duran	2,300.00
Fusco	Robert	3980 Rodeo Drive	Beverly Hills	CA	91876-3421	213-949-9607	Programmer	Teri Lepe	2,000.00

Figure 23.3   Data File

Following is b:Skipline.txt, your shell document.

Applicant's Name: !Last!, !First!
Address: !Street!
!City!, !St! !Zip!
Telephone: !Phone!

Position: !Position!

Interviewed by: !Interviewer!

Salary: !Salary!

Place interview notes below.
/Skip to Line,59/
_____

Information entered by: !Interviewer!

EXERCISE 117

PROCEDURES	COMMENTS
1. In the typing area, type the document as it appears until you reach the skip-to-line instruction.	This is where you will tell the system to start moving down the page until it reaches a certain line.
2. At that point, press Instr and choose Merge_file/text.	
3. In the Merge File/Text Instructions Menu, choose Skip to Line.	
4. In response to the prompt, type 59 and Enter.	You want the system to skip to line number 59.
5. Enter to leave the menu.	
6. In the typing area, finish typing the document.	
7. Print a reference copy of the document.	
8. Merge b:Skipline.txt with the data file b:jobs.dif.	

Chapter 23 Merging with Files

FILE DESCRIPTIONS

If you are using BASIC fixed length or BASIC sequential data format files, you must describe the fields in those files before you can merge them with text. This involves telling the system the field name, type (numerical or character), and the length of the field.

BASIC fixed length and sequential files require that the field description be identical to the type of field you are using. If you are using fixed length files, the field length must match the field length in the file description. When working with sequential files, the field length you define in the file description must be at least as long as or longer than the longest item in the field.

In your file descriptions, you must describe the fields in the same order in which they appear in the data file. For example, if the first field contains titles, you would specify the first field name as Title. The variable name in the shell must match exactly the file description field name. The file description needs to be on the same diskette as the data file. Every field in the data file must be described in the file description.

The data file you will be describing, shown in Figure 23.4, is named b:mailing.dat. The extension "dat" stands for data.

```
Ms. Beth A. Smith     5319 Hamlin Ave.   Baltimore     MD  21215-3265
Mr. Carl S. Brown     1305 Pratt St.     Cedar Rapids  LA  52212-6512
Mr. Rick B. Garfield  876 Oak St.        Washington    DC  20006-2908
```

Figure 23.4   Data File

Notice that there are no field names. You will supply these names when you describe the fields so that the system will be able to use this file when merging.

Look at the information carefully. The first field will be named "Title." It is composed of characters, and the field length is "4." You are using a field length of four characters because the longest title you will encounter is Miss, which is four characters.

The second field will be named "First" because it contains the first names. It is made up of characters, and the field length is ten because it is possible that some first names will take up to ten characters.

The third field you will name is "MI" for middle initial. It is a character field, and the field length is two. One character is allowed for the initial itself and one for the period.

The fourth field will be named "Last" for the last name. It is a character field. The field length is 15 to allow for very long last names.

The fifth field is for the street addresses and will be called "Street." It will be described as a character field and not numeric because the numbers in this field will not be used in any mathematical calculations. They will be treated as characters. The field length is 20.

The sixth field is for the city and will be named "City." It is a character field and the length is 15 characters.

The seventh field will be named "State" because the two-letter state abbreviations go here. It is a character field, and the field length is two.

The eighth field will be named "Zip." It is a character field. This is because the numbers will be treated as characters here. The field length is 10.

In the next exercise, using the information you have just read, you will create a file description for the data file.

EXERCISE 118

PROCEDURES	COMMENTS
1. In the Text Task Selection Menu, choose Create File Description.	
2. In response to the prompt "Type file description name; Press ENTER.," type b:Mailing.des and Enter.	If you had not typed "des" as the extension, the system would have assigned it to the file description name.
3. In the Create or Revise File Description Menu, choose Create Field Descriptions.	
4. In the Field Description Menu, choose Field Name and Enter.	
5. Type Title and Enter. Do not type anything for field type since the system default is character and the Title field is a character field.	You can see "Create Field Descr" on the status line. You are now describing the first field by naming it "Title."

Continued

Chapter 23 Merging with Files

PROCEDURES (Continued)

6. Select Length, type **4**, and Enter.

7. Enter again to bring up a new screen.

8. Using the information you just read about the fields, continue describing the fields in order until you have finished with the last one (Zip). Remember that these field names must match the named variables exactly.

9. When you have finished the last description (Zip), Enter until you are back in the Text Task Selection Menu.

COMMENTS (Continued)

The system default for character is 200, and the maximum is 500 characters. You are choosing "4" because the longest item in a title field could be "Miss."

The message "Field added to File Description" appears each time you have finished adding a field description. Fields containing numbers that will not act as quantities are placed in character fields instead of numeric fields. Examples of these numbers are those that appear in address, phone number, and social security number fields.

The system default for numeric fields is 10 characters, and the maximum is 17 characters. This takes into account 15 numeric characters, one for the decimal point (optional), and one character for the + or − (optional) which would go before the number.

REVISING FILE DESCRIPTIONS

You can revise the file descriptions in case those you have already described contain errors. In the next exercise, you will look at your descriptions to double-check them for accuracy. If they do not contain information that is absolutely accurate, your merge will not work, and you will need to revise the descriptions. If your descriptions match the information you read about the fields in b:Mailing.dat, you need not do any revising. They will match the names of the variables in the document named b:Mailing.txt which follows.

M E M O R A N D U M

Date: August 25, 19--

To: Personnel Department

From: Debbie Dwight, Data Processing

Subject: Changes to our Mailing Label List

This is to notify you of a mailing address change that was made in our data file today. Please revise your records to reflect it.

!Title! !First! !MI! !last!
!Street!
!City!, !State!   !Zip!

EXERCISE 119

PROCEDURES	COMMENTS
1. If Volume 3 is not in drive A, put it there now. In the Text Task Selection Menu, select Revise File Description and Enter.	
2. At the prompt, type b:Mailing.des to indicate that you want to revise the file description named Mailing.des that is located on a disk in drive B.	The file description b:Mailing.des may appear on the prompt line if you have just finished working on it. If it does, you will not have to type it.
3. In the Create or Revise File Description Menu, choose Revise or Display Field Descriptions and Enter.	
	Continued

Chapter 23 Merging with Files

PROCEDURES (Continued)

COMMENTS (Continued)

4. In the Revise Field Description Menu, you will see the field names displayed for you to examine. Make sure that each of them starts with a capital letter. None of them should be typed in solid capitals. You should have eight fields listed (a through h) on the screen. The information on your screen should look like Figure 23.5.

5. If any of the field names do not match, you will need to revise them.

6. To revise a field name, choose the ID of the field name that needs to be changed and Enter. You will see the Field Description Menu on the screen. At that point, just change the choices you wish to revise and Enter. When you have made all of the changes, Enter enough times to return to the Text Task Selection Menu.

```
ID    FIELD NAME
      START OF FIELD NAMES
 a    Title
 b    First
 c    MI
 d    Last
 e    Street
 f    City
 g    State
 h    Zip
```

Figure 23.5 Field Names

Now that you have completed the file description, you are ready to merge the file with the document. In the next exercise, you will do just that. The procedures are very much similar to those used in merging with a data file that is not written in BASIC. The major differences are that you will choose the BASIC sequential file format and the system will ask you for the name of the file description.

EXERCISE 120

PROCEDURES

COMMENTS

1. In the Text Task Selection Menu, choose Merge with File Task and Enter.

   Be sure that you have Volume 3 in drive A and that it is NOT write protected. The system will create a temporary file on Volume 3 and then delete it.

2. In the File Specification Menu, choose Data File Name and Enter.

3. At the prompt, type b:Mailing.dat and Enter.

4. Select Data File Format and Enter.

5. Type "2" and Enter.

   The "2" designates a sequential file format.

6. Enter again.

7. At the prompt, type .des and Enter.

   You will not have to type in all of the file description name because the system has already typed b:Mailing for you. You just need to add the extension.

8. In the Merge with File Setup Menu, choose Merged Document Name and Enter.

9. Check to make sure that Shell Document Name is b:Mailing.txt. If it is not, you must change it to b:Mailing.txt.

   The extension .Mer tells you that this document is the product of a merging process.

10. At the prompt, type b:Mailing.mer.

11. Do not change any of the other items on this menu.

    Because you named the merged document, it will be saved on your disk.

Continued

Chapter 23   Merging with Files   363

PROCEDURES (Continued)	COMMENTS (Continued)
12. Enter to begin the merging process. 13. When the merged documents have printed, press Continue to return to the Text Task Selection Menu.	

As in merging with named variables, you could have performed the following:

1. Only printed the merged documents without saving them on the disk.

2. Only saved the merged documents on the disk without printing them.

3. Printed and saved the merged documents on the disk.

CHAPTER SUMMARY

1. You may use DisplayWrite 3 to create documents with named variables to merge with data files from other sources.

2. The named variables in the DisplayWrite 3 documents must match either the field names in the files or the field names in the file descriptions exactly.

3. Math formats can be used to cause the numbers in the merged document to be expressed in terms of money and not other ways.

4. Conditional text can be inserted in a document depending upon whether or not a certain field does or does not contain information.

5. Math instructions in a document can cause the result of a mathematical computation to be placed in the document.

6. You can print on a certain line by using the Skip-to-Line instruction.

7. You must first describe fields that will be used when merging with BASIC fixed length and BASIC sequential files.

8. As in merging with named variables, the merged document may be printed only, saved on a disk only, or saved and printed.

APPENDIX

LINE AND MID-LINE FORMATS

To Change line formats within the Document or Alternate Format, choose the Change Line Format option in the Document or Alternate Format Menu. The Line Format Menu displays and provides options to change:

--Line Spacing (Single, Double, Triple, One-half, One and one-half)

--Line Alignment (Left, Justify, 1/2 Justify)

--Typestyle Number (Pitch, style and design identification)

--Lines/cm or in. (The number of typing lines per vertical inch)

--Adjust Line Endings (Yes or No)

--Zone Width (Area before right margin used for hyphenation decisions)

MERGE DOCUMENTS

Before using the Merge Documents task, you must create a shell and a fill-in document. Display_codes (F6) should be on when typing a shell or fill-in document so that variable names display.

In the shell document: Type constant text to the point where a variable should occur. Choose Variable from the Instruction (F8) prompt line choices, and type the variable name in response to the prompt.

In the fill-in document: For each variable, choose Variable from Instruction (F8) prompt line choices. Type the variable name exactly as it appears in the shell document and press Enter. Type the variable text for that name as it should appear in the final document. End with a carrier return. If the variable text contains multiple lines, press carrier return after each line. Press Page End (Ctrl-End) after the last variable text entry for each merged document. DO NOT paginate the fill-in document.

Merging the shell with the fill-in document produces a merged document for each page of the fill-in document.

SCREEN FORMAT INFORMATION

The following format items are found on every screen:

Status Lines - The first two lines are dedicated to system status information. A brief description of the various fields begins on the next panel.

Prompt Line - All interaction with menus and prompt line choices takes place on the prompt line.

Message Line - The last line is reserved for system messages. Informational messages are removed upon the next keystroke. Action messages are removed by pressing Message (Ctrl--F10).

KEYS

Alt	Alternate	Allows typing with keyboard extensions and the use of programmable function keys.
Shift	Shift	Allows change from base to shifted key function and the use of programmable function keys.
Ins	Insert	Switches between Insert and Replace modes. Characters are inserted or replaced at the cursor location.
Del	Delete	Deletes the character at the cursor location.
Home	Home	Moves the cursor to the beginning of the current page.
Ctrl-Home	Find	Begins the Find function.
End	End	Moves the cursor to the end of the current page.
Ctrl-End	Go To	Moves the cursor to the beginning of a specific page.

Index

A

Adding:
  columns, 254-255
  columns to numeric table,
    222-225
  job to queue (background
    print), 72
  job to queue (foreground
    print), 70
  keystrokes to keystroke
    program, 297
  rows, 254-256
  text, 31
Adjust line endings:
  defined, 56, 83, 141
  illustrated, 57, 82
Aligned lines, 56-57
Aligned paragraphs, 205
Alternate format:
  creating, 130-132
  defined, 113, 130
  using, 132
Auto carrier return:
  defined, 12-13
  off, 109
Automatic:
  dictionary hyphenation, 85
  outline feature, 284-285
  pagination, 81-84
  search, 49
  spell checking, 190
Averages, 258-259

B

Background print:
  adding jobs to queue, 72
  canceling print jobs, 72-73
  defined, 67
  displaying print queue,
    72-73
  display queue or cancel
    print job menu, 73
  managing queue, 72-73
Begin:
  bold code, 149
  keep code, 143-144
  overstrike code, 43-44
  spelling check code, 191

Block delete, 26, 28
Blocks of text:
  recalling, 178
  saving, 177-178
Body text, 266
Bold text, 149

C

Calculating averages, 258-259
Canceling print jobs:
  background print, 72-73
  foreground print, 69-70
Capture function, 296
Capturing keystroke programs,
  296
Carrier return:
  auto, 12-13, 109
  required, 109-110
Cell, 345
Center key:
  defined, 14
  illustrated, 14
Center tab, 216
Change:
  draw character, 289-290
  indented paragraphs, 152
  line format, 117-119
  margins, 62
  page format, 60-61
  playback mode, 297-298
  print job order (foreground
    print), 69-71
  text column format, 211-212
Character delete, 26-27
Character field, 345
Characters:
  DOS global, 101-102
  leading, 285
  replaced-with, 49-51
  searched-for, 49-51
  trailing, 285
Character strings, 49-51
Check document, 113
Clear tab:
  defined, 62
  illustrated, 62
Code:
  bold, 149
  delete, 27

display, 21
footnote, 267
format change, 134-136
indented paragraphs, 150, 152
keep, 143
overstrike, 43-44
page end, 77-78
required page end, 92-99
required space, 145
revising format change, 134
spelling check, 191
stop, 315
word underscore, 23
Column layout, 200
Columns:
adding, 254-255
copying in numeric table, 228-230
creating text, 213-214
deleting from, 221-222
moving in numeric table, 226-227
isolating, 219-220
revising format in numeric tables, 230-234
revising text, 209-211, 219-221
setting up text, 200-201
Command:
DOS task, 113-114
get, 309
Compressing documents, 106-107
Conditional text:
defined, 351
instructions, 351
statement, 351
Constant:
defined, 261
establishing, 261
using, 261-262
Conversion printing step, 67
Copy:
columns in numeric table, 228-230
documents, 103-104
text, 39-40
to a different disk, 104
Copy function, 39-40
Creating:
document, 10
envelope with letter, 178-179
footnoted document, 267-268
numeric tables, 216-218
table using reference areas, 238-243

Cursor, 12
Cursor draw, 288-289
Cursor movement keys, 19

D

Date prompt, 2
Decimal aligned tab, 216
Decimal system page numbers, 79
Defaults, 8. *See* also system defaults
Delete:
block, 26, 28
character, 26-27
codes, 27
keystrokes, 297
Delete key:
defined, 27
illustrated, 27
Deleting:
column from numeric table, 225-226
document, 104-105
footnote, 269-270
from column, 221-222
required page end code, 93
text, 26
text inside a box, 290
subscripts, 158
superscripts, 158
Descriptions of file, 357-358
Dictionary hyphenation:
automatic, 85
decision procedures, 88
defined, 83
illustrated, 82
prompted, 85-91
Dictionary program:
revising supplement, 196-198
supplement, 192
Directory:
defined, 102
illustrated, 102
selecting from, 103
Disk:
formatting, 3-5
inserting, 2
Disk operating system, 2
Display codes:
defined, 21
illustrated, 22
Displaying print queue:
background print, 72-73
foreground print, 69-70

Display queue or cancel print job menu:
  background print, 73
  foreground print, 70
DisplayWrite 3 background printing. See background print queue
Document:
  check, 113
  comment, 10
  compressing, 106-107
  copying, 103-104
  create fill-in, 324-326
  creating, 10
  creating a footnoted, 267-268
  creating paragraph library, 330-331
  creating set-up, 203-204
  creating shell, 340
  deleting, 104-105
  ending, 14
  fill-in, 321
  merged, 321, 327-328
  naming, 9-10
  printing, 15
  producing personalized, 316
  recalling, 19
  recovering, 107-108
  renaming, 105-106
  revisions, 19-32
  shell, 321
  storing paragraph library, 330
  utilities, 101
Document assembly:
  creating fill-in, 336-339
  defined, 330
  merging, 340
Document extension, 9-10
Document format:
  defined, 55, 113
  returning to, 132
Document or alternate format menu:
  illustrated, 58
  revising formats, 134-136
DOS. See disk operating system
DOS command task, 113-114
DOS global characters, 101-102
DOS prompt, 3, 4
Draw:
  changing characters, 289-290
  cursor, 288-289
Drawing figure, 289

E

End key, 19
End task, 14
Envelope or paper size:
  defined, 59
  illustrated, 60
Envelopes:
  creating, 175
  creating with letter, 178-179
Erasing figure, 289
Esc key, 8
Exact character match, 49-50
Exiting playback, 298
Extension. See document extension

F

Field:
  character, 345
  defined, 345
  numeric, 345
File descriptions:
  defined, 358
  examples, 346
  revising, 360
Fill-in document:
  create, 324-326
  defined, 321
Find key, 19
First typing line, first page:
  defined, 59
  illustrated, 60
First typing line, following pages:
  defined, 59
  illustrated, 60
Flush left tab, 216
Flush right tab, 216
Footers:
  alternating page numbers, 165, 167
  creating, 160-162
  creating alternating, 165, 167
  page numbers in, 161-162
  revising, 163
  revising alternating, 167-168
Footnote codes, 267
Footnoted document, 267-268
Footnote library, 279
Footnote menu, 278

Footnote reference, 266
Footnotes:
   adding, 269
   changing format, 278
   deleting, 269
   illustrated, 266
   resetting number, 276
   revising in library, 281
   storing, 278-280
   using in library, 280-281
Footnote text:
   defined, 266-267
   revising, 268-269
Foreground print:
   adding jobs to queue, 70
   canceling print job, 69-70
   changing print job order, 69-71
   defined, 67
   display queue or cancel print job menu, 70
   procedures, 67-68
Foreground print queue:
   displaying, 69-70
   managing, 69-71
Format:
   alternate, 113, 130-132
   changing text column, 211-212
   choices, 56
   command, 4
   document, 55, 113
   math, 113
   paginate, 113
   prompt, 4-5
   returning to document, 132
   revising change codes, 134
Function:
   capture, 296
   copy, 39-40
   keys, 7
   math, 254
   move, 36, 39
   overstrike, 43-44
   pause, 300
   search/replace, 48-49

G

Get command, 309
Go to key, 19

H

Headers:
   alternating page numbers, 165, 167
   creating, 160-162
   creating alternating, 165, 167
   page numbers in, 161-162
   revising, 163
   revising alternating 167-168
Help key, 8-9
Help panels. See help key
Home key, 19
Hyphenation. See dictionary hyphenation
Hyphenation choices, 142
Hyphens, 109-110

I

IBM logo, 5-6
Indented paragraphs:
   changing, 152
   code, 150, 152
   illustrated, 151
Insert:
   keep codes, 143
   page end code, 77-78
   required page end code, 93
   text, 31
Inserting required space:
   defined, 145
   illustrated, 145
Insert key, 32
Insert mode, 31
Instructions:
   math, 354
   skip-to-line, 356
Isolating columns, 219-220

J

Justified, 139

K

Key:
  center, 14
  delete, 27
  end, 19
  Esc, 8
  find, 19
  go to, 19
  help, 8-9
  home, 19
  insert, 32
  line adjust, 110, 141,
    212-213
  tab, 14
Keyboard template:
  defined, 7-8
  illustrated, 8
Keys:
  cursor movement, 19
  programmable function,
    303-304
  screen movement, 19, 248-250
Keystroke programming, 296
Keystroke programs:
  add keystrokes, 297
  capturing, 296
  illustrated, 304
  playing back, 296
  playing back containing
    pauses, 301
  recalling, 306
  saving, 305-306
Keystrokes:
  delete, 297
  playing back, 296-297

L

Last typing line:
  defined, 59
  illustrated, 60
Leading characters, 285
Left alignment, 139
Left temporary margin, 150
Libraries:
  construct a document using
    paragraph, 314
  paragraph, 312
Line adjust, 212-213
Line adjust key, 110, 141
    212-213

Line alignment:
  choices, 139
  defined, 56-57
  illustrated, 57
Line endings, 141
Line format:
  changing, 117-119
  return to starting, 119
Line format change menu, 118
Line format menu:
  choices, 56-57
  illustrated, 57, 139
Lines/cm. or in.:
  defined, 56
  illustrated, 57
Line spacing:
  defined, 56
  illustrated, 57
List device prompt, 5
Loading DisplayWrite 3, 5-6

M

Manual pagination procedures,
    77-79
Margins, 62
Margins and tabs changes,
    62-63
Margins and tabs menu, 62
Math format, 113, 349
Math functions:
  defined, 254
  using, 257-258
Math instructions, 354
Menu:
  defined, 6
  display queue or cancel
    print job (background
    print), 73
  display queue or cancel
    print job (foreground
    print), 70
  document or alternate
    format, 134-136
  footnote, 278
  ID letter, 6
  item description, 6
  line format, 57, 139
  line format change, 118
  line format choices, 56-57
  margins and tabs, 62
  page format change, 123
  page format choices, 59-60
  paginate document, 82
  print document, 67

printer description, 67
search/replace, 49-51
text task selection, 7
Menu-driven software system, 55
Merged document, 321
Merging:
document assembly, 340
documents 327-328
text with named variables, 321
Message:
defined, 6
illustrated, 7
Move:
function, 36, 39
tabs, 62
Moving:
column in numeric table, 226-227
entire screen width to the left, 251
entire screen width to the right, 251
length of screen, 251-252
text, 36

N

Names variable, 345
Naming a document, 9-10
Numbering pages, 163
Numeric field, 345
Numeric table:
adding column to, 222-225
copying column in, 228-230
creating, 216-218
deleting column from, 225-226
moving column in, 226-227
revising column format in, 230-234

O

Outline:
automatic feature, 284-285
illustration, 284
levels, 284-285
resetting characters, 288
revising, 286-287
Overstrike:
codes, 43-44
function, 43-44
text, 43-44

P

Page end code:
illustrated, 92
insert, 77-78
Page format:
changes, 60-61, 121-124
return to starting, 124
Page format change menu, 123
Page format menu:
choices, 59-60
illustrated, 60
Page numbers:
on alternating footers, 165, 167
on alternating headers, 165, 167
decimal system, 79
in footers, 161-162
in headers, 161-162
system, 79
Pages numbering, 163
Paginate document menu, 82
Paginate format, 113
Paginate from page:
defined, 82
illustrated, 82
Paginate on exact line count:
defined, 82-83
illustrated, 82
Pagination:
automatic, 81-84
defined, 77
manual procedures, 77-79
system defaults, 77
Paper or envelope size:
defined, 59
illustrated, 60
Paragraph library:
construct a document, 314
printing reference copy, 335
Paragraph library document:
creating, 330-331
storing, 330
Paragraphs aligned, 205
Pause:
function, 300
using, 300
using while capturing keystrokes, 301
Personalized document, 316
Playback:
change mode, 297-298
exiting, 298

Playing back:
  keystroke programs, 296
  keystroke programs
    containing pauses, 301
  keystrokes, 296-297
Print:
  document, 15
  background, 67
  foreground, 67
Print document menu, 67
Printer description menu, 67
Printing paper source:
  defined, 59
  illustrated, 60
Printing process, 67
Print queue:
  background, 72-73
  foreground, 69-71
Profile USER.UPR, 112
Programmable function keys:
  defined, 303-304
  illustrated, 304
Programming:
  defined keystrokes, 296
  illustrated keystrokes, 304
Prompt:
  date, 2
  defined, 6
  DOS, 3-4
  format, 4-5
  insert diskette, 4
  list device, 5
  time, 2
Prompted dictionary hyphenation, 85
Prompted search, 49
Prompt line choices, 7

R

Recalling:
  blocks of text, 178
  document, 19
  keystroke programs, 306
Record, 345
Recovering documents, 107-108
Reference. See footnote reference
Reference area:
  creating table using, 238-243
  defined, 237
  revising in, 245-248
  setting up top, 243, 245
  side, 237
  top, 237

Renaming document, 105-106
Replace. See search/replace
Replace-with characters, 49-51
Replacing text, 31-32
Required carrier return, 109-110
Required hyphens, 109-110
Required page end code:
  defined, 92
  deleting, 93
  illustrated, 93
  inserting, 93
Required space code:
  illustrated, 145
  inserting, 145-148
Resetting:
  footnote number, 276
  outline characters, 288
Revising:
  alternating footers, 167-168
  alternating headers, 167-168
  column format in numeric tables, 230-234
  columns, 220-221
  columns of text, 209-211
  document, 19-32
  file descriptions, 360
  footers, 163
  footnotes in library, 281
  footnote text, 268-269
  format change codes, 134-136
  formats in document or alternate format menu, 134-136
  headers, 163
  outline, 286-287
  reference areas, 245-248
  supplement dictionary program, 196-198
  text inside a box, 290
  variable names, 334-335
Rows addition, 255-256

S

Saving:
  blocks of text, 177-178
  keystroke programs, 305-306
Scale line:
  defined, 12
  illustrated, 13
Screen:
  movement keys, 19, 248-250
  moving length of, 251-252

Search:
  automatic, 49
  prompted, 49
Searched-for characters, 49-51
Search/replace:
  command, 50
  function, 48-49
  menu, 49
Separator line, 266
Set tab:
  defined, 62
  illustrated, 62
Set-up document, 203-204
Shell document, 321, 346
Side reference area, 237
Skip-to-line instructions, 356
Spacing line, 56-57
Spell:
  automatic checking, 190
  checking, 185
  page, 185-186
  word, 185-186
Status line:
  defined, 12
  illustrated, 13
Stop codes, 315
Storing:
  footnotes, 278-280
  footnotes in a footnote library, 280
Subscripts:
  creating, 157-158
  defined, 157
  deleting, 158
  illustrated, 157
Superscripts:
  creating, 157
  defined, 157
  deleting, 158
  illustrated, 157
Supplement dictionary program:
  defined, 192
  revising, 196-198
Suspend capture. See pause
Syllable hyphens. See hyphens
System:
  disk operating, 2
  page numbers, 79
  starting up, 2-3
System defaults:
  defined, 55
  illustrated, 55
  pagination, 77
  See also USER.UPR profile

System page numbers:
  in footers, 161
  in headers, 161

T

Tab:
  center, 216
  clear, 62
  decimal aligned, 216
  flush left, 216
  flush right, 216
  levels, 151
  move, 62
  set, 62
Tab key:
  defined, 14
  illustrated, 14
Table:
  creating numeric, 216-218
  creating using reference areas, 238-243
Tabs and margins changes, 62-63
Template. See keyboard template
Temporary left margin, 150
Text:
  adding, 31
  body, 266
  bold, 149
  conditional, 351
  conditional instructions, 351
  conditional statement, 351
  copying, 39-40
  creating columns, 213-214
  deleting inside a box, 290
  footnote, 266-267
  inserting, 31
  merging with named variables, 321
  moving, 36
  overstriking, 43-44
  typing inside a box, 290
  recalling blocks of, 178
  replacing, 31-32
  revising columns of, 209-211
  revising footnotes, 268-269
  revising inside a box, 290
Text columns:
  changing format, 211-212
  setting up, 200-201
  typing in, 201-203

Text task selection menu, 7
Time prompt, 2
Top reference area:
  defined, 237
  setting up, 243, 245
Typematic, 141
Typestyle:
  changing, 126-128
  return to starting, 128
Typestyle number:
  defined, 56
  illustrated, 57
Typing:
  text columns, 201-203
  test inside a box, 290

U

Underscore:
  broken, 23
  continuous, 23
Undo delete, 30
USER.UPR profile, 112
Utilities, 101

V

Variable:
  merging text, 321
  names, 345
  revising names, 334-335

W

Word match, 49-50
Word underscore code, 23

Z

Zone width:
  defined, 56, 141
  illustrated, 57

ILLUSTRATION REFERENCES
International Business Machines

Chapter 1:   Page 3, Figure 1.3; page 4, Figures 1.4 - 1.7; page 5, Figures 1.8 - 1.10; page 6, Figures 1.11 and 1.12; page 7, Figures 1.13 - 1.15; page 8, Figure 1.16; page 9, Figure 1.17; page 13, Figure 1.18; and page 14, Figure 1.20.

Chapter 2:   Page 22, Figure 2.1; page 23, Figure 2.2; page 24, Figure 2.3; page 27, Figures 2.4 and 2.5; page 28, Figure 26; and page 32, Figure 2.7.

Chapter 3:   Page 36, Figure 3.1; page 40, Figure 3.3; page 45, Figures 3.5 and 3.6; page 46, Figure 3.7; page 49, Figure 3.9; and page 50, Figures 3.10 and 3.11.

Chapter 4:   Page 55, Figure 4.1; page 56, Figure 4.2; page 57, Figures 4.3 and 4.4; page 58, Figures 4.5 - 4.7; page 60, Figure 4.8; and page 62, Figure 4.9.

Chapter 5:   Page 68, Figures 5.1 and 5.2; page 70, Figures 5.3 - 5.5.

Chapter 6:   Page 77, Figure 6.1; page 78, Figures 6.2 and 6.3; page 79, Figure 6.4; page 82, Figures 6.5 - 6.7; page 83, Figures 6.8 - 6.10; page 84, Figures 6.11 and 6.12; page 87, Figure 6.15; page 88, Figure 6.16; page 92, Figures 6.18 and 6.19; page 92, Figures 6.18 and 6.19; and page 93, Figure 6.20.

Chapter 7:   Page 101, Figure 7.1; page 104, Figure 7.3; page 109, Figures 7.4 - 7.6; and page 110, Figure 7.7.

Chapter 8:   Page 118, Figure 8.2; page 119, Figures 8.3 - 8.5; page 123, Figure 8.7; page 124, Figures 8.8 and 8.9; and page 125, Figure 8.10.

Chapter 9:   Page 139, Figures 9.1 and 9.2; page 142, Figure 9.3; page 144, Figure 9.6; page 151, Figures 9.7 and 9.8; and page 152, Figure 9.9.

Chapter 10: Page 157, Figures 10.1 and 10.2; page 160, Figure 10.3; page 161, Figure 10.4; page 162, Figure 10.5; page 163, Figure 10.6; and page 165, Figure 10.7.

Chapter 16: Page 255, Figures 16.1 and 16.2.

Chapter 17: Page 266, Figure 17.1; page 267, Figure 17.2; page 268, Figures 17.3 and 17.4; page 269, Figure 17.5; page 270, Figure 17.6; page 279, Figures 17.11 and 17.12; and page 280, Figure 17.13.

Chapter 19: Page 300, Figure 19.1; and page 304, Figure 19.2.

Chapter 21: Page 322, Figure 21.1.

Chapter 22: Page 331, Figure 22.1.